Turning Adversity into Success

Turning Adversity into Success

by

Mark Malmin

Turning Adversity Into Success
Copyright © 2009 by Mark B. Malmin
All Rights Reserved
All inquiries should be directed to:
Bethany Press International
6820 West 115th Street
Bloomington, MN 55438
www.bethanypress.com
(800) 341-7400

Cover and interior design by Bethany Press International.
Printed by Bethany Press International.

ISBN: 978-0-578-02996-2

PREFACE

If you want more out of life and you wish that your spiritual life could be richer, more meaningful, more exciting and joyful than it has been, then this book is written just for you. If you don't have a spiritual life, then this book may help change that for you.

The premise of this book is intended to be a challenge to each of us to examine specific ways in which we can overcome adversity and become committed followers of Jesus. By constructively examining attitudes and behaviors we live by which diminish our effectiveness as Christians, and rob us of an abundant life that Christ intended us to have, we can stop shooting ourselves in the foot and learn to become more than conquerors in our walk with the Lord.

If you are willing to examine your own heart and pay the price of spiritual obedience, discipline and walk in faith, then nothing shall be impossible to you in Christ. To the extent that sometimes we find our spiritual lives dissatisfying, the desire to understand our failure and change becomes a motivating, positive exercise. Remember the words of Christ when you ask him for help: *If you then, being evil, know how to give good gifts to your children, how much more shall your heavenly Father give the Holy Spirit to them that ask him? (Luke 11:13)*. My prayer for each of you is that reflective analysis will prompt you to examine your own heart and develop a desire to want more out of life. Asking God to help us accomplish this is the genesis of achieving full potential.

The Bible is full of tremendously valuable <u>principles</u> designed to help us overcome adversity and live successfully. The biblical facts that present themselves become <u>principles</u> because they are not limited only to the individuals and their circumstances when they were given, hundreds or thousands of years ago, but like the law of gravity, they apply to all of us, even today. One of the wonderful biblical principles given to us is from Jesus, our Lord, who said: *Seek and ye shall find; knock, and it shall be opened unto you.* In the Old Testament the prophet Jeremiah speaks for the Lord to the children of Israel with these words: *If you search for me, you will find me, when you search for me with all your heart (Jeremiah 29:13)*. This verse is as true today as it was two thousand years ago. If you seek the Lord with all your heart you will find him! Jesus not only offers forgiveness of sin, but he offers an abundant life and he wants to partner with us, bless us, and help us overcome adversity.

TABLE OF CONTENTS

ACKNOWLEDGMENTS

This book is dedicated to the memory of my father, Reverend Edward J. Malmin, an apostle and mighty man of God. I was very blessed in this life to have had such a wonderful father. My father's ministry and faith helped inspired much of this book.

I also want to thank my good friend, Sue Passailaigue, for the many hours of editing that she provided for this book, and her thoughtfulness and encouragement to me as I worked on the manuscript.

FOREWORD

I write this book based on my imperfect Christian life experiences and failures, and also from perspectives I derived from my career in police work. I had an unbelievably exciting law enforcement career! I can't believe that they paid me to do this, because I would have done it for free! I got to live out real life adventures, the kind of which movies are often made about. Our spiritual lives represent a journey that bring us face to face with real battles of life, death and of giants we encounter along the way. Your spiritual life can be every bit as exciting as police work.

My background and training allow me to examine spiritual laws and principles and explore truth with you in much the same way as I would carefully examine the legal requirements and benefits of state law. It's wonderful when the law is on your side! It can offer you great protection and recourse. Having an appreciation for how earthly laws work will give you an even greater appreciation for heavenly spiritual laws that change not with changing times. Observing spiritual laws and principles can open heavenly doors for you that produce great blessings.

My analysis to overcoming adversity is a little like that of a good, tenacious physical trainer or coach who pushes you and who won't accept hollow excuses. As a tough street cop won't accept phony excuses for speeding, my spiritual mind-set is simply intended to promote constructive, critical self-analysis, accountability, and encourage honest thinking from the heart. There is some tongue and cheek laughter along the way. I believe life should be rich and rewarding and that it is a crime to not have fun along the way.

If you are not truly interested in self-improvement, failure analysis, honesty, hard work, character development and spiritual growth, then you should put this book down and have a piece of chocolate cake instead.

My personality is a little bit like that of Jonah (from the story of Jonah and the whale) because I find that sometimes I am just baptized in pickle juice! I am learning, as God sends me to charm school, that this is not how life has to be. I want to become more charming and compassionate. I obviously haven't quite mastered this principle yet because the last time I was asked whether other people should be shown compassion or forgiveness I thought, as Jonah did, absolutely not! It's not that hard to see the sour pickle juice in such thinking or why I should be in charm school but eventually I hope to get it right!

I hope you enjoy this book, but more importantly I hope it encourages you to reach to the stars for your heavenly Father.

CHAPTER 1

CAREFUL, THERE'S A COP RIGHT BEHIND YOU!

A personal career perspective

When I was about four years old I had an occasion to be in the car with my mother as she was driving us back to our residence in Chicago. Along the way she decided to make a couple of pit stops. One of those turned out to be the Cook County Courthouse, where she intended on paying a fine for a speeding ticket she had received. I find it amusing in some ways because my family was so engaged in sharing everything with each other that this would have certainly been one of those things that would have been talked about at the dinner table. I also know that our sense of humor would have been keenly displayed with this little incident, if we had known about it.

My father was a wonderful, loving, kind, compassionate and forgiving man. If he had a weakness it was that he was too nice. I assure you, I have more than made up for that weakness in our family. In any event, I find it strange that my mother never mentioned that little indiscretion to the rest of the family. My mother said something to the effect that, I'll just tell Daddy this check I'm writing today was for a "pullover" that I got, and he'll just think it was a sweater. Liar! Liar! Pants on fire! I remember that she giggled and laughed when she told me this, but I was too young to really appreciate the whole thing. What a lost opportunity! If the rest of the family had only known what had really happened, we would have teased my mother relentlessly.

After walking up the steps of the courthouse, my mother and I entered the building. Inside this cement building on the ground floor was an office with a clerk and a bank-like teller window at the end of the hallway. As my mother stood in line to pay her ticket, I observed a uniformed deputy sheriff walk by us. He stopped to talk with someone who wanted to ask him a question. I watched intently from just a few feet away. He was very polite and well mannered. I so vividly remember staring at him. I was fascinated with his neatly pressed uniform, his badge, his gun, the distinctively thick gun belt he wore, and his military-like polished shoes. I was stunned with how cool this guy looked. This was the neatest thing I had ever seen! It wasn't the man as much as it was the uniform, but the whole incident was surreal and bigger than life and it just made me weak at the knees. If the officer had invited me to go out on patrol with him, I would have gone right then and there, and probably would not have even said good-bye to my mother. You know how boys are! My mother undoubtedly must have smelled the testosterone emanating within the car on our way home. I don't think I said a word to my mother about it, but in my heart I thought, whatever it is that this guy does, *that's what I want to do!* Of course, I had absolutely no idea what that was, but all it took was just one look!

Little did I know at this young age that I too would be wearing that uniform later in my life. From time to time, over my twenty-eight year career, I had to pinch myself a couple of times to make sure all of this wasn't just a great dream. I can't believe they paid me to do this because I would have done it for free! There is nothing more wonderful than being able to realize your passion and do what you absolutely love. In my case, it wasn't reading to the blind, as wonderful and worthy as that might be. I wanted to chase armed and dangerous bad guys over fences and backyards and down freeways at speeds in excess of a hundred miles per hour. Every day I woke up with this incredible enthusiasm, knowing that I got to go to work. As David faced Goliath, my dream was to face evil and prevail. My motto was simple: Glory to God, somebody is going to jail today!

To commemorate the many cherished memories I accumulated over the years as I transitioned into retirement, I had a professional portrait taken of myself in uniform. Even though I put on some extra weight and lost some hair along the way, the honor of serving made me feel wonderful. The photo itself is not that great, or perhaps I should say, I don't look that great, certainly not handsome, but deep inside my gut all of this made me feel like a mighty warrior. I felt a tremendous gratitude toward God that I had been given this opportunity to have served him in this very unique capacity.

Some of this is hard to even put into words and not have it perhaps sound arrogant. I hope it does not come across that way. The sense of accomplishment one derives from this career is the knowledge that not everyone can do this job. Making the correct legal and moral decisions that affect the rights and liberties of others, and doing so under tremendous pressure and emotional stress and getting it correct is the goal. It is the satisfaction of knowing that by and large, we got it right. Knowing your efforts could result in the ultimate, irrevocable sacrifice adds a unique dimension to this line of work. The sacrifice of one's life comes suddenly, on demand and without the luxury of being able to decide beforehand if it was necessary, prudent or worthwhile. This devotion to duty and level of service is what cops call the *thin blue line*, the difference between law and order or disorder and chaos. Remember, when all hell breaks loose, who are you going to call, a sociologist or a politician?

This bond, which I am attempting to describe, cannot be entirely put into words because it goes deeper than words, but it reflects, in part, the knowledge and feeling that officers share among themselves: a commitment, a brotherhood, a trust in each other and a commitment to cover each other, no matter how ugly it gets, even unto death itself. Face it, most husbands and wives don't even share that kind of a bond. This rare commitment makes for an incredible bond and profound sense of trust among officers. That is why in large urban areas you will see a funeral service attended by three thousand or more officers when one of its brothers is killed in the line of duty. Officers will come to attend these funerals from every corner of the state, and some from out of state. It is pretty special, to say the least! This feeling of being a member of the *thin blue line* also embodies the sense of satisfaction in knowing that while evil clearly exists, you personally make a difference to those around you and your presence and commitment precludes evil from reigning unabated in your community. In California, law enforcement officers are generically defined by law as "peace officers." What a great title and how wonderful it is to think that Jesus said, "Blessed are the peace-makers." Finally, for me, this deep satisfaction represents the honor and joy of service, including the many memories of all the bad guys I chased and caught, and all the fun I had along the way; something that will last forever. People write books and make movies about this stuff and pay Hollywood actors big bucks to portray these men and women.

I was talking about this subject with another officer I was working with in Redwood City, California. He was reminiscing with me about his own view of the job and how exciting it can be. He pointed out that while all others in the courtroom talk about what someone else did, usually based on police reports and witnesses, he is able to speak directly and first hand about his own action and contribution to each case in which someone is brought to justice. His point was that chasing the crook and catching him is far more rewarding than talking about someone else who did it.

While some actors like John Wayne got to say lines on the silver screen like, "You've got till dawn to get out of Dodge," I got to actually do this job. I still look at that photo sometimes when I walk by it and feel a sense of tremendous pride, honor and accomplishment in having worn the uniform and served in that capacity. Most of you can sleep safely tonight because these folks are on point, ready to give their lives to protect you and take care of business.

There is something truly wonderful about being able to pursue one's true passions in life. Having an opportunity to do that turns ordinary work or duty into an extraordinary adventure, which is deeply meaningful and, at times, a lot of fun. Why can't more people have such a rewarding, exciting life? I think you can and I hope these next few chapters will entice you into possibility thinking, which will motivate you to dream bigger, aim higher, and begin identifying your dreams and passions in your spiritual journey.

As I look back in retrospect at my career, I can tell you unequivocally and without hesitation that, everyday I hit the street I was committed to my duty and prepared to give my life to accomplish that day's mission. The rush was at times intense and awesome. Living on the edge makes you feel alive and appreciate life itself. It also has a way of teaching you to take one day at a time. I'm still trying to learn that concept.

This bond that officers build which each other, the camaraderie, and trust in each other in life and death situations is something very special and profoundly deep. It's not something that you can have or share with just anyone. In fact, sometimes not even family completely understands this phenomenon.

More than anything I want to have this same burning passion, commitment, enthusiasm, trust and profound emotional connection with my Lord as I enter my post career season. I also want to be able to share this with people and move into the next higher dimension of my life. I don't want to stop experiencing exhilarating life or great things. My sense is that the best is yet to come.

This unabashed enthusiasm for life is very childlike on my part, I suppose, but I never want to lose this feeling that life should be rich and enjoyable. There is such a beauty and purity in childlike innocence, faith, laughter and joy. Aside from the fact that metaphorically we are all God's children, it is no accident that Jesus spoke on this subject or used parables that spoke of children. Jesus said that except you be converted and become as little children you will not enter into the Kingdom of heaven (Matthew 18:3).

Children also lack guile and sophistication. For some it takes years of training and grooming to become treacherous, nefarious and malevolent. One of the wonderful qualities that children have, which I suspect is one of the reasons why Jesus used this parable about children, is that they tend to be completely accepting and full of faith. If you tell them that God loves them and that he hears each one of their prayers, they accept that at face value, as well they should. If you tell them that there is nothing too difficult for God, they accept that at face value and don't question it like a lawyer. If you tell them to be good and follow Jesus they just accept it and they don't ask you to define "good" or ask you put it in writing. If you tell them that Santa Claus knows who's been naughty or nice and he'll only come down the chimney if they are good, they pretty much figure out that you're a liar.

Observing our own children or the children of our family and friends can help us put our own needs and weaknesses into perspective. This simple comparison can help us better understand our heavenly Father and ourselves.

How about just a warning this time, Officer?

All of us want grace, preferably without consequences. Sometimes we want another chance without any discipline or accountability. With very small children the grace approach, which demonstrates love and forgiveness, can be very powerful and constructive for growth and development. If you seldom received grace you were cheated! Grace is the kind of thing that is always wonderful if you are receiving it.

Notwithstanding how serendipitous grace feels instead of consequences, it would be non sequitur to think this approach is effective all the time in our character development. Accountability sometimes requires consequences. Consequences serve as an effective tool for developing behavior modification. When you get stopped by the police for speeding or some other infraction, the first thing that usually comes from the heart and gets sent to the brain for processing and marketing is some convincing statement to get you out of this tenuous situation. The sales pitch comes out something like this: *I'm so sorry Officer; can you just give me a warning, this time?* You don't want consequences; you want grace. Perhaps you wouldn't say, could I have a warning "this" time because you are well aware that there have been "other times." Sometimes women, not altogether unattractive, become flirtatious, hoping that will get them out of a citation. Christians always tell you who they are and that they are on their way to church or some other holy event, or that they know Billy Graham.

People know intuitively that the police officer has the power to grant their request and give them grace rather than consequences. There is no harm in asking. Sometimes I think that way myself. I suppose there is no harm in asking God. After all, he knows that last year I contributed fifty dollars to the Katrina Disaster Relief Fund, or was it the year before? I can't remember. That's gotta be worth something, right? He owes me!

As a police officer, it always brings a warm, fuzzy feeling to see the joy, love and appreciation that beam on peoples' faces when they get a warning. It is also kind of intriguing because, while the appreciation is real enough, the deceitfulness about how they are never going to commit that violation again is so phony, that it's funny. It's like telling God you're never going to sin again.

I always wanted to have a divine word of discernment and knowledge so that I could stop some poor guy and walk up to him and say, "Sir, you rolled through that stop sign, and you're driving too fast, but more importantly, you haven't been tithing and God knows all about it! Now, get out of here before I change my mind and start tithing." Can you imagine how that might turn out, if you said it to the right guy? I haven't had that opportunity yet, however, the day is still young. I've seen just about everything else you could possibly see in police work and I've heard just about every lame excuse the mind can think of.

The following incident is a real life story of a fallen believer that I arrested for being under the influence of drugs after he caved into adversity.

This man had been "speed balling," which in California we describe as the practice of using heroin, a "downer" (depressant) while at the same time shooting up with an "upper" (stimulant) like cocaine or methamphetamine. It is a way of slamming yourself with high and low at the same time, creating a specific euphoric effect on the body. If you consider your life to be a little on the dull side because the only hot and cold you have ever experienced at the same time has been hot fudge syrup over vanilla ice cream, that's not necessarily a bad thing.

What was interesting about this character was his reply when I asked him how he got so entangled with drugs.

He said, "Well, Officer, you'll never believe this but I used to be the pastor of a church."

"Really," I replied, "tell me more!"

The suspect then explained to me that he had previously walked with the Lord for many years. At one point after he injured his back and could not get rid of the pain, out of desperation, he tried street drugs and got instantly hooked, just like that! He went on to explain how his life went to hell in a hand basket from there and how he lost his family and his relationship with the Lord. He told me that he didn't expect me to understand any of this.

I said, "Well, you're not going to believe what I have to say either, but I'm going to tell you anyway."

I proceeded to tell this guy that of all the officers he could have run into that night, the Lord sent me to arrest him and this was no coincidence.

Later in our conversation I told him, "When you get to the jail, don't waste your breath telling the deputies how sorry you are; they won't care about that. What you need to do is fall on your knees, right there in the jail, and repent. Ask God to forgive you and then change your ways and walk justly before him."

That was quite a conversation we had that evening. There are times that people need tenderness, encouragement and hope, and there are other times that people need a kick in the butt with a dose of reality. He got the latter. I hope our little encounter was a life defining moment for him. In some respects it was for me, because I felt anointed while speaking to him. I said what I felt I was supposed to say. It will be interesting for me when I get to the other side to see if this guy is there.

I think it was the providence of God that allowed me the honor to arrest this guy and witness to him about his spiritual condition from the privacy of my own patrol car. I felt like a missionary. It was wonderful. This guy was higher than a kite, just loaded on dope and he needed straight talk about repentance.

Most people think of missionary work as being something that someone else does in another country. For cops working the streets, their beat is another country, one most people only see on T.V. or in some documentary. Missionary work is not limited to Africa; it's talking to your next-door neighbor. So, the next time you leave your residence visualize in your mind a large sign posted at the end of your driveway, which reads: YOU ARE NOW ENTERING THE MISSION FIELD.

Does anyone really want a ticket?

Allow me to invite you back into my patrol car. Let's see what the day brings us. Maybe we can have a cup of coffee along the way while we talk. Half of you want to ask a cop how they decide who gets a ticket and who gets a warning. Some of you wonder if driving a red car draws the attention of the police and makes you more likely to get a speeding ticket. Do cops have quotas? It is wonderful to be able to find a cop when you need one, don't you think? I'm available just for you, today!

It has always been a little annoying that at a party or social event I almost always run into someone who is compelled to talk to me about traffic enforcement the minute they find out about my career. Even since retirement this happens. Most people won't ask you about the homicide rate or the last rape case you solved or the bank robber you arrested. No, they want to talk about a traffic ticket that some other cop issued them, and they want you to comfort them and maybe tell them the other cop was wrong.

This conversation invariably suggests that they were singled out (unjustly) for a citation. If I read between the lines correctly, the person is usually trying to tell me that they really did not deserve the ticket. They offer an endless litany of reasons, the most common of which boils down to the argument that they are a pretty "good" person, far better than many others, and as such, they could have been given just a warning. The fact that they did not get a warning is a travesty of justice, in their mind.

We all want mercy rather than punishment and, of course, I am no different than you in that regard, but that sometimes begs the question. The question that no one wants to answer at the party is whether they were actually driving over the speed limit or not. Did you roll through the stop sign or not? If you want to dispute the facts of the case, that is your absolute right to do so, and I would be the first one to defend your right to do so. In all fairness to everyone involved, if we are going to retry the case it needs to be done with the issuing officer present, and you should have an impartial judge that will be fair not only to you, but to the members of the public and the county and state in which you live.

When all is said and done we will either come to the conclusion that we need to take responsibility for our mistakes, and our sins, or we will come up with some other lame excuse short of repentance. Will you argue about your speeding or parking ticket on the other side? Probably not, since there will be much greater issues to consider.

I, too, am like the guy at the party, in some ways. I really am not, deep down in my heart, unwilling to acknowledge my indiscretion, as much as I want mercy and forgiveness for my indiscretion. When you get to the other side, it won't be your parking ticket, but your sin that will be the issue; sin that only Christ can forgive. Understanding our need for a savior who can forgive our sins is probably the most wonderful thing that could ever happen to any of us, because it leaves us with a choice, and all we have to do is sincerely ask for forgiveness.

You just never know who is going to need to be rescued or saved from disaster or when. It might be *you* today!

Sometimes cops are wanted in the worst way because of a crisis. Other times we are taken for granted, and, at other times, we are not wanted at all. This may reflect how we view the Lord. Sometimes we need God because of a crisis in our lives, but other times we would be uncomfortable having him around at all. Be available to help me if there is a life-threatening crisis, but don't be too close...it might make me uncomfortable.

I once explained to this lady who was very upset about receiving a speeding citation, that traffic enforcement was not the only duty that I performed, but I just happened to be assigned to the Traffic Division Unit and it was my exclusive duty to seek out traffic violators and enforce the law. This conversation began, in part, with a sarcastic question she threw in my face, "Don't you have anything more important to do beside stop people like me for some minor thing?"

I pointed out that traffic enforcement was an important issue and that the public in general, including residents of the city, complained to City Council regularly about this issue. Citizens wanted traffic enforcement to be a priority. As such, the police department was responding to the needs of its own residents and the requests made by the public for us to do our jobs. I sincerely pointed out to this lady that I understood no one wants to get a ticket, but I asked her to look beyond that as the only thing I did. I explained to her that if she dialed 911 because an intruder had broken into her home, I would risk my life to get to her home as quickly as possible and protect her. My job entailed a whole lot more than simply writing people speeding tickets. I wanted this woman to know that she should be glad to have me out on the street because I was prepared to give my life in service to overcome horrible crimes that are committed against people every day, and I was willing to do that for <u>her</u> as well, if it boiled down to it.

This woman saw in my eyes and heard the sincerity of my voice that I meant every word I had just told her. This wasn't something I was taught to say; it was something that came from my heart. She intuitively knew it. The conversation changed everything. She realized with appreciation after we talked awhile that the next medical emergency call I received might have nothing to do with redundant crime, but it could be a call to her house if her baby stopped breathing and I might be the one to first administer CPR to her baby. She apologized to me for being initially unfair to me and thanked me for my service to the community. A very negative contact ended on a very positive note.

Just like people driving down the highway over the speed limit don't want to be stopped or held accountable, most of us probably view the accountability of our own sin the same way. My sin is nothing like that of a bank robber or rapist. My sin shouldn't even be called "sin."

Do you catch yourself thinking this way? Sometimes we are disinclined to call our behavior for what it really is, sin. Unkindness might be described as just being a little impatient or grumpy. The fact is, when you are speeding down the highway you really don't want to see a cop around you just then, and certainly not behind you! Most of us would not want even the Lord sitting right next to us in the car either, unless maybe you thought he could get you out of the ticket by explaining to the officer what a wonderful person you are. This phenomenon of trying to avoid consequences is very representative of people in general and no less so of our spiritual lives. This is partly what this book is all about, being honest with ourselves. We often just don't want to take responsibility for our behavior and so we point out to God, or the traffic cop as the case might be, that we are pretty "good" people. The insinuation is that we don't need to be punished or held accountable or, perhaps more accurately, that we *should be* forgiven because we are good. That is quite different than saying, please, forgive me, I'm guilty! No one is "good" except God and Jesus had to point that fact out to us (Matthew 19:17).

Would you want the Lord riding with you in your car as you drove to work? It would be stressful, don't you think? You might be talking like a sailor even though you try to be careful and control yourself. It just seems to slip out at the most inopportune moments. Perhaps you have a very high degree of self-control and you discipline yourself so that you do not swear. I do that when I am around the general public or in church, but when I am in the car all by myself, I never cease to amaze myself, if you know what I mean.

The problem with people that don't swear is that sometimes their thoughts are as bad as someone else's swear words. *I don't drink and I don't smoke, and I don't chew, and I don't associate with those who do.* I am sure that somewhere along the line you are going to get an extra piece of cheesecake for your good works. When you are walking in the Spirit, the fact that you don't swear is good, and it reflects self-discipline and control, but trust me, you can walk out of the realm of the Spirit and into the flesh faster than you can blink your eyes. You may not swear but sometimes our thoughts are just as bad as our words. Our thoughts are often disguised with guile and we don't see our own subtle motives, sin or ugliness.

Sometimes I almost wonder if it might be better to swear because it reveals exactly where we are, even if it's pretty ugly. It's easier to catch yourself and realize how foul your attitude is and repent right on the spot. Lord, that was pretty ugly of me and it doesn't reflect you at all; I'm sorry. Lord, help me to want to do a better job of representing you especially under adversity. Forgive me Lord, because sometimes I don't even want to do the right thing. Give me a heart for righteousness.

I submit to you that this prayer recognizes my human weakness and sinful nature and, if the prayer is sincere, it reflects humility of spirit and a desire to change my character. We don't always know how our character is doing or just how pure, or impure, it is, because we rarely ask the Lord: How am I doing? Give me a report card. Are all my ways pleasing in your sight, Lord?

Nevertheless, when you are under pressure, part of the *real you* shows. If you are made of gold, the fruits of the Spirit come out of you. If you are not in the flow of the Spirit, but are in the flesh, lemon juice will come out of you, or other impurities. Jesus said the following about this: *O generation of vipers, how can you, being evil, speak good things? for out of the abundance of the heart the mouth speaketh* (Matthew 12:34). There is that word "good" again.

Somebody cuts you off in traffic and an ugly word just slips out of your mouth and I can almost assure you that it won't be, "Oh, pooh-pooh!" If the Lord was riding with you in your car he might use just the right touch of humor to ask you if your mother knows you talk this way. That would probably break the ice and make you laugh a little. As you continue driving down the road, the Lord would ask you if you saw that last lane change. That guy nearly ran you off the road, just so he could cut in front of you, the Lord might say.

With the express purpose of both teasing you and compelling you to think about what just happened, the Lord might then ask you whether this rude driver should be punished or be forgiven. You are taken completely off guard because you didn't say a word to begin with. He just seemed to read your thoughts. Before you can even formulate a proper, politically correct response, the Lord reminds you that this was the very reason he gave his life as a ransom for our sin. By this time the picture becomes crystal clear. You start to remember all that stuff you learned in Sunday school. Your heart softens and your eyes begin to fill with tears. In the same way that the disciples tried to come up with something intelligent to say after they witnessed the Transfiguration of Jesus, you inform the Lord that you love these bad drivers and you ask the Lord to give *them* one more chance. Even when our hearts begin to soften the first thing we may be inclined to think is that God needs to change somebody else. The thought of asking God to help us change our own thinking and behavior does not even occur to us. Our first prayer might be Lord, help the cops to catch this guy, but not because we really care that much about him. We just want him to get caught and be punished.

Why are some people easier than others to forgive?

How is it that we could so easily shoot some people or feed them to the sharks out at sea and yet there are others that we can seem to forgive or at least feel compassion for? How does that all work?

I was working in the detective bureau and we were looking for a dangerous bank robber who had robbed a half a dozen banks in the Bay Area. We didn't know the guy's name yet because he had not been fully identified so we nicknamed him the "Bug Eyed Bandit" because his eyes popped out like ping pong balls during the bank robberies and this was captured on bank surveillance photographs.

When we spotted him in a trailer park in East Palo Alto my partner and I were in an undercover police car dressed in plain clothes. We had seconds to grab him or he was gone. It happened so fast! We saw a subject appear out of nowhere and begin walking into the roadway at the trailer park. We slowly drove toward him. As we approached we got close enough to recognize him as our suspect. I almost drove past the guy! I abruptly stopped the car, threw the gearshift into Park, which caused the car to rock forward awkwardly. I jumped out of the driver's seat and confronted the suspect at gunpoint, ordering him to the ground. My partner covered me with his gun drawn and pointed at the suspect. We had him boxed in! He had nowhere to go. The suspect was taken completely by surprise. The suspect got down on the ground on his belly with his arms extended and we handcuffed him without incident. All of this happened very fast within twenty seconds or so. It went down beautifully and no one got hurt. The element of surprise had more importance than we realized. Just another day at the office baby! I can't believe they paid me!

While interviewing the suspect and filling out a booking sheet, I asked the suspect certain routine questions that were required for the booking sheet. When I asked him what his occupation was he replied, "Well, I'm a chemist by trade." I was very surprised by his answer because bank robbers are never chemists or professionally schooled people. Why would a highly skilled professional, capable of making a salary in excess of a hundred thousand dollars a year, rob banks, one would naturally wonder. I asked him. The guy told me that several years prior he began dating an attorney who turned him on to heroin. He then became hopelessly addicted to this drug over a several year period of time. He robbed banks to support his heroin addiction. He told me he knew he would eventually get caught and that he understood that he would end up going to prison for a very long time and that he had no intention of going to prison. His plan was that he was going to point an empty, unloaded gun at the cops when they came to arrest him, knowing that the police would shoot him. This unfortunate but common practice is called "suicide by cop."

I felt a sense of compassion for this guy. He had screwed his whole life up and thrown a wonderful career away and part of his life as well. He wanted the police to kill him so that he would not have to go to prison or face life. Needless to say, this guy was not proud or happy with his accomplishments. He wanted to die. Fortunately for me, I was not forced to kill him. Having a sense of compassion for someone like this is not hard. The guy was remorseful.

There were two thieves being crucified on either side of Jesus. Just that fact alone is representative of all humanity because we are all on one side or the other of Jesus. One thief talked trash to the Lord and disrespectfully railed to Jesus: "If you are the Christ, then save yourself and us." The second thief rebuked the first one by telling him that they both deserved the just punishment they were receiving for their deeds. The second thief then defended Jesus by saying the Lord had done nothing wrong. The remorseful thief asked that the Lord would remember him when Jesus entered his Kingdom. Jesus answered him: *Today thou will be with me in paradise* (Luke 23:39-43). It is all about attitude, humility and repentance! Christ forgives those who ask for it. If your heart is calloused and you don't see your need for a savior, it's pretty safe to say you probably won't be asking for forgiveness. You have to want Jesus to come into your heart and make you whole and clean. We need to recognize our sin and be remorseful and repentant about sin. Feeling bad about it is not enough. We need to specifically ask Jesus for the precious gift of his forgiveness.

Words make a difference. We use them to pronounce life or death. Judges in courtrooms use words to sentence people to death in capital cases. We use words to convey love or hate to each other and we use words (even if only in our thoughts) to ask God to forgive us. Words can stir up passion and anger or express sorrow and repentance. Jesus said, *For by thy words thou shalt be justified and by thy words thou shalt be condemned* (Matt 12:37).

I was driving somewhere in the city of San Jose, California, a town of 975,000 people. My mind was elsewhere and I wasn't paying attention to my driving. I made an unsafe, dangerous lane change right in front of some poor guy who had to slam on his brakes and veer to his right to avoid hitting me. The man was justifiably angered at my bad driving. He pulled up alongside of me with his window rolled down and just screamed at me. If looks could have killed, I would have been dead right then and there. I rolled my right passenger window down and leaned over toward him making eye contact, and in a loud voice I said, "I screwed up really bad; I'm very sorry!" His reaction was the most beautiful thing you ever saw. A picture is worth a thousand words. His face instantly turned from anger to softness and he was stunned, delighted, and speechless all at the same time. The only response he could come up with on such short notice was, "Well, all right then!" My words, my expression of remorse and the sincerity in my face changed everything for this gentleman. The result produced instant forgiveness toward me. We both used words to express what was in our hearts. We both drove away feeling better.

The games we play when we drive down the road don't usually end this way. The one guy that you unleash your anger on may be the one who shoots you. This is the very reason why you never want to display only one finger of appreciation at anyone. It's O.K. to politely wave hello with all five fingers, but not just one.

We don't usually make eye contact with other rude drivers. We just cut them off or prevent them from getting in front of us, but we never actually face them or look directly at them. It's so much easier to be this cold and un-kind if you don't have to look into their eyes and it provides a ridiculous illu-sion that you don't even see each other. Oh, I didn't realize you were trying to cut in front of me or I would have shot you sooner! In the case of the guy that I cut in front of who I just described, he probably never had anyone look him straight in the eyes, let alone apologize. The whole thing was resolved in an instant with repentance and with kind, civil words. He probably went home to his wife or girlfriend that evening and said the most amazing thing hap-pened to me today. A rude driver apologized to me! It was just as wonderful for me because I felt badly that I had cut this guy off and I wanted to make it right. In fact, I wanted to apologize for every bad driving maneuver I had ever made, but never had the class to apologize for.

Some people are easy to forgive. Others are not. Imagine if I had said something rude and nasty in the preceding example.

When I was working for the San Mateo County Sheriff's Office our county jail housed the infamous Scott Peterson in Redwood City, California. Peterson was accused of murdering Laci Peterson, his wife, and her unborn child. The Sheriff's transportation unit would escort Peterson to and from the jail and courtroom during the jury trial. This trial, you may recall, drew national attention. The case involved a beautiful woman who was murdered and dumped into the bay. Peterson denied killing his wife and baby. The case was entirely based on circumstantial evidence. (Much the same as our alleged Christian faith; for better or for worse, it's all circumstantial; does the evidence tend to reflect the image of Christ inside of you like a mirror or is the jury still undecided about you?)

What was remarkable to me about Scott Peterson was how quickly he seemed to learn some of the inmates' behaviorisms in the jail. Peterson had no known prior criminal record. He had never served jail time for anything. I found it amazing to see how quickly he picked up the arrogant strut and swagger, which he displayed as we walked him down the back hallways to the courtroom each day. Peterson's demeanor was very cocky and arrogant and while he always spoke respectfully to the deputies, his body language said it all. He almost had a little dance or jiggle in his walk. If the whole thing had not been so serious I might have joked with him and said something stupid like: Hey, Scott! I see you coming, dude! Shake it baby, shake it! Show us your moves, Scott. He tilted his head backward and leaned it from side to side as he strut down the hallway. It is hard to describe this because you had to actually be there to see it, but the overall appearance provided a very confident, defiantly arrogant look. It was reminiscent to me of fashion models who ostentatiously flaunt themselves while walking down the runway, except models are paid to jiggle in expensive clothes and they are not on trial for murder. I also have to say it wasn't just my perception. All the deputies noticed Scott Peterson's arrogant strut, and we talked about it in the transportation unit.

The whole body language thing when he walked to the courtroom was disgusting and very pronounced and exaggerated. The Peterson "walk" was a form of flaunting arrogance and mockery that said you will never be able to prove it and I'm going to walk right out of here when it's all over. I've seen quite a few murder suspects go to trial and not display the level of arrogance that I witnessed with Scott Peterson. Even hardened criminals that are really bad actors usually have enough street sense and savvy to know life is unpredictable and full of unexpected turns. You don't celebrate in the end zone until the game is over. The scripture that most fits what I saw with Scott

Peterson is: *Pride goeth before destruction and a haughty spirit before a fall* (Proverbs 16:18).

The day Peterson was found guilty on all counts, the deputies escorted him out of the courtroom and they walked him right past me in the back hallway where I was stationed for extra security. I will never forget the dejected, forlorn look on Scott Peterson's face. His head was hanging downward and all the dance and pompous strut was gone from his walk. He appeared totally stunned by the verdict, at least for those few minutes. I wanted so badly to say something mean like: Scott, you don't look so good today! Is everything O.K.?

As a Christian, promoting within these pages the riches of Christ, servanthood and discipleship, I regret to tell you that I had those thoughts in my mind because they were spiteful and malicious on my part and it was wrong for me to entertain those thoughts, but I did. I wanted to rub it in Scott's face and punish him. Vengeance is mine, saith the Lord (Romans 12:19). The job of law enforcement is never to punish, but to bring the nefarious of this world to the courts of justice. In my mind I disregarded that even though I knew better. I refrained from saying anything at all to Scott because I wanted to be professional and I certainly did not want to do anything to jeopardize the trial or bring attention to myself or get in trouble. Nevertheless, aside from my deplorable, hypocritical thoughts I find it pretty hard to not think of what some of these guys are going to face when they stand before the throne of God Almighty in the next life. I suppose it is exactly the stakes of that kind of eternal judgment that should make us more compassionate right now.

It is quite easy to not have compassion for some people. For me, Scott Peterson, was one of those people. What characteristically tips the scale for me or makes it hard for me to have compassion? Typically, two basic ingredients: I need an abiding, unwavering opinion that the person is guilty, based on the totality of the evidence, and I need to perceive that the person manifests a total absence of remorse or repentance. Some of these degenerates gloat over their evil deeds and handiwork, and, at times, mock the entire criminal justice system of man and God. Those are times where I want to see David reappear in the name of the Lord. No more hearings, no more lawyers, no more talking. It is hard to not want immediate justice. Let our faith rest in the Lord. This great psalmist wrote:

> *Commit thy way unto the Lord; trust also in him; and he shall bring it to pass. And he shall bring forth thy righteousness as the light, and thy judgment as the noonday. Rest in the Lord, and wait patiently for him: fret not thyself because of him who prospereth in his way, because of the man who bringeth wicked devices to pass. Cease from anger, and forsake wrath: fret not thyself in any wise to do evil (Psalms 36:5-8).*

Not everyone is called to be a soldier or a police officer, but thank God we have people that do these jobs.

I also believe there is such a thing, at certain times in life, as holy, righteous indignation. You may recall from scripture that, when David slew Goliath, he did not render CPR or first aid. David did not engage in foolishness by trying to change Goliath's theological outlook and he didn't try to rehabilitate him or bring him to the peace table. This was the enemy and Goliath represented the personification of evil, the hand of Satan extended toward Israel with sword and spear, threatening God's people. This was for David, and is for us now, the time and place for battle. David, empowered by the Spirit of God, took Goliath's sword and cut his head off (I Samuel 17:45-51). My superiors would have been upset with me if I had done that. Administrators can be so politically correct sometimes.

In God's perfect timing there can be a time, place and season for everything in life including justice. The hard part is letting God bring about the circumstances that lead to justice. Human weakness, being what it is, makes us want to witness the distribution of punishment, or even worse, be the agent who carries out the judgment of God. The Lord is not looking for executioners, but rather for servants.

Another perspective on road rage

What makes the guy who cuts you off in traffic so easy to hate? Often, it is the wanton disregard for safety and the total selfishness of the act in most cases. I use the word *hate* loosely because it's not the guy that you necessarily hate, it's his behavior. I also have to say there is a big difference between someone who accidentally screws up by not paying attention, or maybe because they just aren't a very good driver, compared to someone who is knowingly taking great risk and putting others in great peril because they are in a hurry and they are simply selfish.

Intentionally reckless people are bold sometimes because they pretty much think that they will get away with it and they rationalize there is nothing that you can do about it. If these selfish, cowardly people were not in the safety of their own cars they would never do what they do. For instance, a jerk would never walk up to the front of a long line of people and push some football player out of the way and cut in front of everybody because he would get his butt kicked, plain and simple. This typically does not happen, however, because these people are cowards to begin with and they commit their selfish acts on others who are in an unlikely position to effectually respond.

Why though, you may ask, does it make us so collectively angry? I know there is some pious person out there who is not angered by any of this. You are more mature than the rest of us. Most of us do get annoyed or upset by this, especially when the stakes are high and the conduct is outrageous. So, why do most of us get angry? Well, no one likes a selfish cheater who doesn't play by the rules. Additionally, there is the frustration of not being able to do much, if anything, about it. There is an injustice that occurs and the violator simply gets away with it. We are a nation of laws. Everything about God's universe and creation is based on order. People put others in harm's way on the roadway because they perceive there are no law enforcement officers around to stop them. It's not O.K. to break into my house and harm my family. I would never tolerate that. What makes you think that you can almost run me off the road and not elicit a reaction? It's not wrong to feel angry.

Again, I think it's important to ascertain whether the behavior is deliberate and malicious or just incompetence or stupidity. One's state of mind is important. It would be a whole lot easier to forgive someone who accidentally killed one of your children in an auto accident because they inadvertently ran a red light and they felt terrible about the incident. Circumstances change dramatically if the death of your child was the result of drunk driving, or, worse yet, some cold blooded murder. Toss into this mix a lack of remorse and your blood will boil. It is the state of mind and intent of the person that becomes so important in these circumstances. Even a dog or cat knows the difference between accidentally bumping into them and deliberately going after them in violence.

Knowing all of the facts is pretty important, wouldn't you say? That's why Jack Web used to say in that television series about Los Angeles cops, "Just the facts, Mam." Over the course of my police career I worked half of it at night and arrested well over a thousand drunk drivers. Things are frequently not what they appear to be. Sometimes they are. Knowing the difference requires additional information. I became quite good at detecting impaired drivers but, as I said, things are sometimes not as they appear to be. Many a time I saw a driver weaving very badly to the point where some of them bumped into the curbline of the raised center divider. When you see something like that the first thing that naturally enters your mind is, there is a drunk driver if I ever saw one! Of course, some of those drivers were as sober as a judge and the reason for the severe weaving or erratic driving was varied. If you dropped a lighted cigarette between your legs and it rolled down into your crotch you would probably be weaving, too.

When you see two people fighting and exchanging words it's hard to know at a glance who the aggressor is or who started the whole thing, and perhaps more importantly, what the background and history is leading up to the event. All of these things require further investigation and more factual information. Do you see where I'm going with this? None of these things are at your immediate disposal when you see some apparent jerk driving down the road cutting people off while changing lanes. In all fairness as to whether they should burn in hell for their egregious driving, you need more information. In all likelihood you probably aren't going to get it.

Allow me to proffer this mitigating factor. During the years that I worked as a traffic cop, I became a radar instructor and I issued thousands of speeding tickets, more than ten thousand of which were radar assisted. That's a lot of citizen contacts under lots of different circumstances. You have no idea how badly someone's day is going unless you are in the position to investigate and talk with people. There are people out there hurting so badly and wounded by the words of others that they are ready to kill someone or maybe themselves. You would not know this unless you talked to them. So, the next time you see Johnny B. Goode cutting you off in traffic, try not to flip him off with your favorite finger. He may have just lost his job, his wife and his peace of mind. Do you really want to kick him in the teeth right now?

Step back and think about this for a minute. Should you feel guilty for feeling anger when you are exposed to some guy that nearly ran you off the roadway? Not at all, but just understand that things are not what they always appear to be, and you don't know what the facts are which led up to this person's day, or their state of mind.

I share this outlook with you to provide perspective and so that you do not feel a sense of guilt for wanting others to follow the rules of the road. God loves righteousness and justice. God wants us to have a tenacious, unrelenting spirit of justice for the widow and orphan, but not for our own interests. Put that energy to the defense of others, not yourself. The scriptures tell us, *Say not I will recompense evil but wait on the Lord and he shall save thee* (Proverbs 20:22).

Having said all of this, I acknowledge there are, nevertheless, Philistines around us in need of a dosage of righteousness and they are sure to encounter it! Your problem is you want to see them get caught and punished, and you will most likely revel in their punishment. The Lord, in his love for you, does not want you to see it or rejoice in their day of judgment. Proverbs says, in part, *Rejoice not when thine enemy falleth, and let not thine heart be glad when he stumbleth, lest the Lord see it, and it displease him* (Proverbs 24:17-18). The Bible says that a man reaps what he sows. The world says, "What goes around, comes around." It's all the same. He who lives by the sword dies by the sword.

The intentionally malevolent driver, who delights in putting others in real danger, day in and day out, will eventually do so to the wrong person, who has no restraint, and immediate judgment will be executed right then and there on the spot. *The Lord hath made all things for himself: yea, even the wicked for the day of evil* (Proverbs 16:4). Our problem is not that justice will not prevail ultimately, but that the Lord is longsuffering and full of mercy and goodness, and slow to anger. It is the very reason that Jonah did not want to go to Nineveh because, as Jonah put it, *I knew that thou art a gracious God, and merciful, slow to anger, and of great kindness…*(Jonah 4:2). Don't you wish people would accuse you of this! Jonah was angry, of course, because Nineveh repented and because of that God changed his mind and withheld destruction of the city.

The story of Jonah is absolutely fascinating. This angry, unhappy, miserable prophet wanted Nineveh to burn! When I think about how Jesus gave us a new commandment, to love one another, even as he loved us and gave his life for us, it bewilders me to think how God could have such an unhappy camper as Jonah on the payroll. Jonah was the antithesis of Mother Theresa. I've concluded that what makes the Jonahs of the world qualified to be on God's payroll is their love for and pursuit of justice. Jonah could have been a cop. His people skills sucked but that is where we can learn from his mistakes. It makes me think maybe there is hope for me! The love for justice is only part of what we should practice or learn to develop.

My problem is that I am too much like Jonah. I want total accountability and justice. I want evil people to be caught and punished. I want rule breakers to be caught and punished. Oh, and did I mention, I am thy humble and willing servant who is ready to enforce the judgment of God upon Nineveh? The truth, unfortunately, is not that I lack a heart for justice, but that I lack compassion for the lost and dying. My problem, like Jonah, is that sometimes I don't have an ounce of compassion in me. And, if I don't have some quiet time with Jesus, I am willing for unsafe lane changers on the freeway to spend time in state prison.

What happens if we are not careful is that we will start looking too hard for failure in others. In fact, we search for it and we focus on it to the exclusion of our own sin and failure. In reality we are all guilty of sin of one kind or another, and so in the final analysis we are all deserving of God's punishment for our sin. We forget that we are all fallen and in need of a savior and that in our own flesh *there is none righteous, no not one* (Romans 3:10). To put it in other words, if we start looking or focusing on what we deserve, we are all in trouble because we deserve to pay for our own sin and the wages of sin is eternal death. You could never pay the wages, cost or ransom that was paid through the cross for your sin. As disciples of Christ we need to focus on the grace of God, which he provided to us through his blood on the cross.

Forget about your rights; this isn't about you. Change your mind-set so that you are willing to give yourself completely to Christ in service, whether it be in life or in death. Lay all your rights down at the foot of the cross and give them to Jesus. He is deserving of our all in all. If you are a born-again believer, you are not your own. You belong to our Savior. You were bought with a price...the precious blood of Jesus! We need to follow him and act like we mean it.

The New Testament standard by which we are to live is summed up pretty well by the great apostle Paul, who wrote, *Let all bitterness and wrath and anger and clamor and evil speaking be put away from you, with all malice: and be ye kind one to another, tenderhearted, forgiving one another, even as God for Christ's sake hath forgiven you* (Ephesians 4:31-32). Let this be your mission statement and standard of conduct when you get behind the wheel of your vehicle. To this end we have to die to our own flesh because that's what it takes to truly follow Jesus. I want to punish people and Jesus wants to save them. Even when I intellectually grasp the concept, my flesh doesn't really want to surrender or go to the cross, but that is exactly what Jesus invited us to do (Mark 8:34).

In order to actually love one another and forgive one another, we need to die on our own metaphorical cross if we want to be like Jesus. That's where the expression comes from, that we all have our own cross to bear. When it gets right down to where the rubber meets the road, dying to our own selfish interests is not easy. It takes Christ's help to accomplish this. We need to not be delusional in thinking that it just appears out of the thin blue air. This kind of profound change of our character is the phenomenon of "being born again" and developing a new heart. We have to seek it and pray for it and develop this sense of mercy and forgiveness toward one another. This is a process of growth and development in Jesus. For me this is the hardest part of walking with the Lord. I'm not predisposed to forgiving anyone. I have to work really hard at being compassionate. I look at people and focus on their failures. Oh, you broke the law, you filthy animal. I want to punish them. Jesus looks at people and focuses on their potential and offers them help. I'd like to shoot half of them and Jesus wants to save and forgive them! Lord, can't I at least shoot some of them, maybe in the leg and just wound a few of them? You can see the Lord needs to send me to charm school!

So, when you are driving on the freeway or highway and E. Coli appears, like you know it will, it's O.K. to have an honest feeling of frustration or even anger. Your feelings are real and God never told us we could not experience emotion. It's a matter of how far are you going to go with it and how long and how deep are you going to let it affect you and ruin your disposition. Don't be baptized in pickle juice like Jonah! The other thing is that you can minimize your frustration a little bit by simply reminding yourself that you are absolutely guaranteed to encounter one or two or three of these situations every single time you get into your vehicle to go anywhere. That being the case, don't be surprised that there are idiots on the road. Expect them and you won't be disappointed. In the off chance that you don't encounter one, when you arrive at your destination you should get out of your vehicle and lie prostrate on the ground and praise God that you were spared testing and temptation, unlike what the rest of us ordinary folk have to go through.

I have deliberately tried to be a little tongue and cheek about some of this, but I am also drop dead serious as a heart attack. It is a mistake to let the driving and behavioral patterns of others rob you of the peace and joy that you should have with Christ if you are a born-again believer and disciple. We are to overcome the world, but not as executioners. When the disciples asked Jesus if they could call down fire from heaven and destroy the towns and cities that did not want to hear the Lord's message, the Lord rebuked them and reminded them that he came to save the world, not destroy it. That is our daily focus. Be patient and longsuffering, and loving towards others.

The next time you drive anywhere remember that. Ask the Lord to ride shotgun with you. Ask the Lord to give you some of his compassion for the lost and hurting world around you. Ask the Lord to give you a servant's heart and remember your mission. Some of you don't even remember what the mission is anymore! We are to love one another even as he loved us! Talk to the Lord and ask him to give you a new heart and to remind you that it's not all about you; it's about the Kingdom (of heaven) business. Ask the Lord to accomplish his will in your life today as you drive down the road. Pray that God's plan and purpose for your life will produce fruit for the Kingdom of God. Practice the fruits of the Spirit. You may not recall what they all are (Galatians 5:22). Look them up and read about them and ask God to help you develop them in your life.

If you become completely devoted to servanthood and feeding the Lord's lost sheep, you will feel less victimized by the casual events of life. And when someone speaks evil of you or treats you badly, you will find the strength to forgive them because you invited Jesus to walk with you this day.

You cannot overcome your own carnal, sinful, human nature just by wishing to be a better person. We need the power of Christ in our lives to change our character and give us new hearts. If you invite the Lord into your heart, he will come in and make you a new creature. It is a pretty wonderful thing. I recently celebrated my fifty-third spiritual birthday of walking with the Lord and I can tell you that it gets sweeter and deeper as the days go by. We need to be empowered by the Holy Spirit. Ask the Lord to lead and guide you and ride shotgun with you. Though all others fail you, or turn against you, the Lord of Host will remain faithful to his promises for he hath said, *Lo, I am with you always, even unto the end of the world* (Matthew 28:20).

Autobiographical sketch of God's leading hand in my life

I would like to share with you my story of how I got into that uniform and patrol car I've been talking about. This is my testimony of how the Lord opened up law enforcement as a career for me. It's almost not possible to explain how important and personal this is to me, because of how deep my emotions run with the events I am about to share with you.

Before I can make any biographical sense of my life or career, however, I need to be conceived and born, and those events, by all earthly standards, should have never happened, but for the unbelievable love and grace of God shown to my father.

My father was born Edward John Malmin in Chicago in December of 1915. Those early days of adversity occurred during the Prohibition Days. Those were tough times back then. My dad grew up in the streets of Chicago when gangsters, working for Al Capone, were peddling the illegal sale of alcohol throughout the city.

One night in Chicago, around 2 A.M. my dad, a youngster of tender age, was in the back room of a bar where men were drinking and gambling. The police raided the joint and kicked the door down and came running in. Tables were overturned and poker chips went flying in the air. Men frantically ran out side doors and into the arms of waiting cops. My father hid on the floor under an overturned table afraid for his own safety and worried that there was going to be gunshots. I think the Lord was looking out for Dad, even then. A uniformed cop pushed the table aside and saw a mere kid looking up toward him. The cop tossed my father a poker chip and said to him, "Go on kid; get out of here!" Dad walked away unharmed.

My father, while still at a young age, lost his mother to a hit and run driver. My father's dad was an alcoholic, so it shouldn't come as any surprise to you that my father became an alcoholic also, at a very early age, I might add. By the time he was a teenager my father had earned the nickname "Half Pint" from the cops. Dad said he used to go fishing in the city parks and the Chicago police would end up chasing him on foot through the parks for city ordinance violations. Every time he got arrested, which was often, Dad had a half pint of whiskey in his back pocket; ergo, the nickname "Half Pint."

My dad spent most of his time drinking and "hoboing" around the country. I asked Dad what he meant by the word "hobo." He explained it to me as being a bum or a vagabond, and that it accurately depicted him during those drinking days of his life.

Dad said he and some of his friends, one of whom was named Bill Kerns, used to travel all around the country as hobos, usually to warmer states like California, jumping onto passing trains riding from one city and state to another.

Dad told me that they would wait till a train came along and then run as fast as they could trying to get close enough to the side of the train to grab one of the footrails that were located on the sides of each boxcar. On one such occasion dad was jumping boxcars with another hobo friend and his friend was running alongside the moving train attempting to grab one of the footrails when his hand slipped off the rail and he fell under the wheels of the train. Dad told me he saw it happen and turned his head away to avoid seeing his friend's body being severed in half. Dad climbed up to the top of the boxcar and lay there quite shaken. A minute later his friend crawled up to the top of the boxcar from the back of the train and joined my father. Dad asked him in amazement what happened, exclaiming that he saw him fall. The man replied, "I know; an angel pulled me out." You might be inclined, as the good scientist that you are, to write this off as simply the folklore of two drunks and conclude there was no angel involved with this incident, unless his name was Jack Daniel's. It's O.K. if you choose to view it that way. I also find it hard to ascribe much credibility to drunkards because my own tendency at times is to just write them off as being completely unreliable. I have learned from experience that my bias has often times been ill founded and that it depends on the individual as to whether they are truthful or not. Substance abuse alone does not preclude people from being truthful. Moreover, it's not the stature of the drunkard that is really at issue, but rather the stature of God and our willingness to understand that he has all power, including that over life and death. For me personally, the greater miracle is not that God saved someone else's life while falling under a train, as wonderful as that may be, but that his power in my life has changed my own selfish nature and softened my stony heart. I consider this change in my own heart to be a miracle work of God.

The hobo adventure and lifestyle my father lived for several years might sound exciting to a 20-year-old kid who is looking for a short, but exciting summer in California, and when you don't have money for airfare, then trains work just fine. The truth is it's cold living under bridges, not having a warm and safe place to sleep or call home. Not eating regularly is not that great. Drinking yourself into unconsciousness is not as much fun as you may think either. Depression sets in and one's self-respect goes down the toilet. After this you lose hope and stop seeing your options and alternatives, and life gets pretty dark and meaningless.

Dad was in such a state. He was walking toward a bridge in Chicago so that he could jump off it and commit suicide. As he walked toward the bridge, a Christian man named Stemmy, who pastored a church in Chicago, was on his way to a board meeting at his church. Stemmy later related the following wonderful story. Stemmy said he noticed Dad walking on the shoulder of the roadway as he drove past him, but didn't think anything of it until he felt the Lord quietly speaking to him and instructing him to turn around and go back and pick this man up and "talk" to him.

The human condition is both amusing and amazing at times. Stemmy was just flesh and blood like the rest of us and with all the same cares of life that weigh us down and preoccupy our thoughts. After all, Stemmy had a church meeting he needed to attend. Even when we have a heart for God, we struggle with hearing the voice of the Lord, and we struggle with surrendering our own agendas, in order to align ourselves with "thy Kingdom come, thy will be done." Even with a heart for God we want to do things our way, on our terms, on our time schedule. What I find to be so amazing is how preoccupied we get with our own schedules even when we are completely devoted to serving the Lord. We usually don't like interruptions or detours and if they come along, we complain and ask ourselves, why me? What we are really asking is why can't things go smoothly, my way?

Stemmy said his first thought was, I don't have time for this. I have a business meeting to go to. Stemmy might have also unconsciously thought: Can't you see I'm busy? I'm already doing the Lord's work, don't bother me right now. I offer that not because I know Stemmy had those thoughts or words in his mind, but it's the way I think half the time, and my own fallen nature makes it hard for me to hear the voice of the Lord. Even if I'm pretty sure it's the Lord, then I want to argue about it anyway, or worse yet, talk to the Lord contentiously like I do when I am talking down to my wife. Our diminished thoughts, our habitual ways, our predictable irrationalities, *but that's how I always do it,* all seem quite pathetically amazing! Stemmy said the Lord spoke to him three times, before he obeyed. Each time the Lord said the same thing and offered no explanation.

I find all of this so interesting because it so reflects the human condition in all of us. It also demonstrates how the Lord doesn't always share the entire mission plan he has for us. He simply asks us to trust him and obey. His plans are higher than our plans. We want our car headlights to shine around corners even though we can't see that section of roadway yet. If we saw what was ahead of us, most of us wouldn't even go there, yet we seem to want to know what we are getting into. If we are not inclined by our own will to follow the plan, then we typically try arguing with the Lord about the plan. Moses did that when the Lord told him to go and speak to Pharaoh (Exodus 3:10-15/ Exodus 4:1-16).

If we only knew how great God's plans are we would trust him more and stop asking questions and just obey the Spirit's leading. The heavenly Father saw a man walking toward death and saw a man's soul and the potential of his life and future. The Lord looked even beyond that and saw my future. Stemmy saw the clock and thought, I don't have time for this; nevertheless, he obeyed God. Thank you, Lord, that your faithful servant, Stemmy, listened and obeyed.

Stemmy turned his car around and drove back to where my father was walking and pulled up alongside of him and said, "Say there, can I offer you a ride?" Dad had not been actually thumbing for a ride. He was just walking down the road, but since Stemmy pulled up alongside him and offered to give him a lift, he got in the car. The two began talking. Stemmy told my dad how much God loved him and that God sent his only son to the cross to save us from our sin. The Holy Spirit anointed Stemmy's words and these words touched my father's heart. My dad wanted Christ to come into his heart, and so the two men prayed and Stemmy led my father to the Lord right there in the car. Stemmy was late for his church board meeting.

My father had been a classic, "hopeless" alcoholic. But with God nothing is hopeless and all things are possible. Most alcoholics have to go through a tough journey of recovery and rehab. If you have ever dealt with alcoholics you would know that they are enough to make you want to scream. Their denial is astounding. They will lie, steal and cheat and take advantage of everyone they can if they can just get one more drink. They are on the wagon and off the wagon until you lose all your faith, hope and strength to cope, and they make you want to give up the ghost and just die yourself rather than deal with them sometimes. They not only destroy themselves, they hurt everyone they come into contact with. It's a profoundly terrible disease. Many a family has been devastated or completely destroyed by an alcoholic.

When my father stopped drinking it was all at once, with complete and total delivery by the undeserving grace of God. No withdrawals, no physical symptoms, nothing. His coworkers thought he had completely lost his mind because he stopped drinking all together and they considered that to be a horrible thing in itself. His drinking buddies could not imagine why anyone would want to stop drinking, but if that was not bad enough, Dad couldn't stop talking about Jesus!

Allow me to introduce my mother to you. This woman was very special in many ways. She was handpicked as the most promising bachelorette my father would find in an exhaustive global search, and the neat thing about it was, my father didn't have to waste his time with 24 other contestants, who probably weren't filled with the Holy Ghost. My mother was full of love, grace, compassion, tenderness, mercy, commitment, faith and joy. She told me that as a young adolescent, before she committed her life completely to the Lord, she loved to dance. She once said that she would rather dance than eat. I consider that to be a wonderful trait that will be put to good use in heaven, as there will be dancing and joy, the likes of which we have never known!

My father was planning on going to Bible school and was committed to serving the Lord the rest of the days of his life. Praise God! As he planned to do these things he worked for a season with the United States Postal Service as a mail carrier. Thus, he became Malmin, the mailman.

One day in Chicago while on his mail route, after finishing lunch he saw a church across the street so he decided to go inside and have a few minutes of quiet prayer. As he opened the door and stepped inside he saw a woman kneeling at the altar praying. Her back was facing my father and her head was bowed forward so that you could not see her face. The Lord spoke to my father through the Holy Spirit and told him, *That woman will be your wife.*

That would scare most of us to death because inner beauty at that point would be inconsequential...well, unless you are really spiritually mature. As it turned out, she was quite beautiful in every way. My mother's name is Judy and she was the most wonderful partner my dad could have ever had. The Lord sure did a wonderful work in selecting a mate for my father and a wonderful woman who would later be my mother.

My parents went into full-time ministry and my father became an ordained minister with the Assemblies of God; you know, those people who sometimes speak in tongues. While I was only a lad of seven my family sold everything they possessed and went to the country of Brazil to preach the gospel, with signs and wonders following.

My sister Bonnie, who is six years older than I, almost died in the jungles of Brazil from appendicitis. Gangrene was setting in and the doctor told us the appendix was about to rupture. In times of crisis, especially life and death, it is pretty common for us to ask the proverbial question, God where are you? Hello, is anybody there, Lord? I hate to bother you just now, but this is Brother Malmin speaking, and I am in a real bad spot right now, just in case you didn't notice. Well, the Lord does notice, even when the sparrow falls. In this particular case, the Lord was speaking to a dishwasher in Chicago who had the habit of worshiping God by praying and singing in "tongues" all the time.

My sister was getting worse by the minute. My dad, who prayed for people all the time and expected each one of them to be healed, did not get results when he prayed for my sister. I don't know how all of this works, but I saw him pray for demon possessed people who were miraculously delivered right in front of a host of witnesses, but his prayer for my sister did not produce any apparent results.

So, we stuffed my sister in a small jeep and drove over 100 kilometers on a bumpy, dirt jungle road to get to a hospital. She screamed in horrible pain every time we went over bumps in the road. I still remember how terrible her screams sounded. This was probably the first time in my life, but not to be the last, that I felt helpless, hearing someone scream, but being able to do nothing about it. Finally, we reached this hospital. Well, that's what some people called it. Let me just say it wasn't Stanford Hospital in California. There were chickens walking down the hallway of the hospital. I'm talking about a hallway that had patient rooms on either side. This was in the jungle and no one thought that much about it. Some communist doctor who, of course, did not believe in God, and who might have been happy to teach us a lesson, if he had been so inclined, cut Bonnie open and removed the appendix and put it into a jar, which he then handed to my mother. When the doctor handed her the jar, I thought about cracking a joke and asking for a couple of eggs over easy to go with it, but I took one look at my mother's face and realized that she was not in the mood for joking around, so I didn't say anything.

Now, the Lord was working behind the scenes and I suspect was trying to show my father that there was more than one way that God could provide for our needs. I have no doubt that God didn't unexpectedly lose his power to heal and that he could have healed my sister if that had been his plan, but it wasn't his plan. He had another plan. I know my father was not the least bit shaken because of it.

The hospital and doctor bill came to a total of exactly $110, after the conversion rate was calculated. Understand that this happened many, many years ago in the jungles of Brazil, and while that would not pay for even the sutures today, back then it was a lot of money, and when you have none, a hundred and ten dollar hospital bill might as well have been a million and ten dollars.

Money in this instance was a bigger test of faith and trust in God than faith for healing. My parents were in the jungle living purely by faith that God would provide for them. There was no corporation or religious organization that was funding this spiritual mission. There was no guaranteed paycheck from any religious institution, no IRA or pension plan, no stock options and no Kaiser health plan.

The dental plan was a pair of pliers we had purchased from Sears before we left home. The only *plan* my folks had was to preach the good news of Jesus to a dying world in the jungle. Having no money to pay the doctor and the hospital was a pretty big thing. Such a financial failure would not lift the name of the Lord up high to all those around us, if the missionaries who preached about Jesus didn't pay their medical bills. I don't think that would have really brought honor and glory to our heavenly Father.

In Chicago there was an unattractive, bald headed man who immigrated to the United States from Poland who spoke with a heavy accent. He washed dishes for over thirty years, working at the same restaurant in Chicago. He had no education, no social life and no family. He rented a small room in a dump of a hotel. His name was Hammerwall. The Lord spoke to Hammerwall and told him to send $110 to the Malmins in the jungle of Brazil. Hammerwall used to pray and worship the Lord from his room with the window open because of the scorching heat and lack of air conditioning. He would sing unto the Lord, loudly at times and sometimes speak in tongues. My father told me that people used to laugh at him and mock him. Hammerwall put exactly $110 (eleven ten-dollar bills) in an envelope and mailed it to my father. Hammerwall's obedience to the voice of God was an answer to prayer and a priceless gift.

Stuff like this makes you fall to your knees and weep because you know this money is not coming from someone with means, but from someone who can't afford to buy a car. It was like getting a check for a million dollars from a widow who went without for ninety-eight years then sent you all the money she had saved over a lifetime.

The fact that Hammerwall sent the money without knowing anything about my sister's condition was a miracle in itself. The fact that my folks ever saw the money was a second miracle, perhaps greater than the first one. The locals in this town used to steal all the mail and magazines that were sent to us from the United States. That had been an ongoing problem for a long time. Once a month we would drive into this town from the bush and purchase food and supplies, and usually treat ourselves to a bottle of Coca-Cola. It's amazing how capitalism and marketing exists everywhere, maybe even all the way to the gates of hell. I'm sure they will have ice-cold Coca-Cola in hell. Nobody will be able to drink it, but it will be there in plain view to torture the thirsty.

My father once went to one of the local newsstands in this town and saw a magazine on the shelf that had a mailing address label on it with our name on it. My father boldly protested to the proprietor, "That's my magazine; give it to me!" The man declined to argue the assertion and meekly handed my father the magazine. "If it's yours, here, take it," he said. Letters that were sent to the post office would be slit open and any money or checks inside would be gone, especially any cash. The fact that Hammerwall sent an envelope with eleven ten-dollar bills loosely placed in it, and we received it, was nothing short of another miracle.

My sister's appendicitis was not the only adventure we experienced while living in the jungle. I was only 8 years old, riding my bicycle on one of those jungle roads, returning home after putting some salt out on the ground where we found deer tracks near the edge of a coffee field and dense jungle. I wasn't far from home, maybe three or four miles. An adult laborer who worked in the coffee fields was going to take me deer hunting. The deer loved to lick the salt and it ensured the deer would keep coming back to the same spot if you put the salt on the ground for them.

While returning home I was peddling uphill in soft dirt and moving slowly. I saw a bright colored object out of the corner of my eye coming toward me from the side of the roadway, falling from an overhanging tree branch. I saw the snake dropping from the branch and realized it would probably land right on top of me unless I did something immediately. I jumped off the bike in one fluid, leg-rolling movement, landing to the left of my bike in the soft dirt. A Coral snake landed right on top of my bicycle! The snake was not attacking me per se; it simply dropped off the branch it was hanging onto and then onto my bicycle. That was what I originally thought, but if the snake had landed directly on top of me and I had grabbed it with my hand to get it off me, the snake probably would have bitten me.

If you read all the things that occurred to Job, a righteous man, Satan was allowed to test Job beyond anything man has ever known. I could see how the devil would have been very happy to allow such a snake to kill me, or bring me close to death, hoping that might end my parents' ministry in these jungles. If any of the danger I encountered that day had anything to do with the world of spiritual warfare in which Satan tried to destroy my life and touch our family, then God surely said no, I have other plans for the Malmin family. Glory to God, I'm still hanging around, kicking and fighting, thank you very much!

What I understood to be true back then was that the Coral snake was one of a half-dozen or so snakes on the planet considered to be deadly. Back at that time in 1959, there was no cure for its bite. Perhaps modern medicine has a cure for the Coral snake bite today, I don't know, but back then I could not have even called for help. Cell phones did not exist at that time. I was *all alone* [not!] in the middle of the jungle. Even if someone had found me or wanted to help me, there weren't any ambulances just driving around in the jungle waiting to transport me to some rickety old hospital where chickens patrolled the hallways. As the inmates in the jail like to say, do you *feel* me? I was not all alone!

I killed the snake with a long tree branch. I knew the snake was deadly because I had been warned about them beforehand and I knew what they looked like. The incident frightened me. I particularly remember that this snake did not die easily. The fact that it was a small snake didn't seem to matter. When I smashed the snake with a long tree branch it severed the snake in half. The half of the snake with the head crawled toward me, opening its mouth as if it wanted to bite me. This amazed me that the snake could do this and it scared me even more. I didn't want to get too close to the snake since it was still crawling. It was hard to hit the snake precisely because the snake was moving and the branch was awkwardly big and hard to handle. I hit the snake at least two more times with the branch. This slowed the snake down but it still wasn't dead. Only after I crushed its head did the snake stop crawling altogether. I went home thinking that God had just helped me survive a life-threatening event. Regardless of whether this was an incident of chance or something more ominous, I'm not sure if it made any difference. If I had been bitten, I would have never made it home. God's hand of protection was there for me, that much I am sure.

That was not the only time I was protected by the hand of God. While living with my parents in these same jungles, I found a large, dark brown colored scorpion crawling on the ground. I was fascinated with its movement and how it had this long thin tail, which it could bend forward past its head. The tip of its tail was like something that could stick you, so I reasoned, like the bee that stung me when I was three years old. I decided to be careful. I grabbed a small stick from the ground, about the size of one that you find in an ice cream bar. I then picked the scorpion up at one end of the stick and watched it, as it crawled back and forth on the stick, bending its tail backward and forward as it came closer to the opposite end of the stick and my fingers.

As I was standing outside the old wooden church building that my father would preach in that night, another American gentleman and his wife came walking toward me. They were on their way to the church service. I exclaimed to the couple, "Look at this neat little bug!"

The man gasped and became flustered.

"Drop that thing, Mark! Drop it to the ground, right now!" he commanded.

"Do as I say! Don't let it touch you!" he shouted.

"Why?" I asked.

I remember the man telling me that it was poisonous, like a rattlesnake. I understood that, so I immediately dropped it, feeling fear that I had been in such danger without knowing it. My father was already inside the church doing Kingdom business and had no idea anyone else was outside of the church also doing Kingdom business, looking out for my welfare. I am not, of course, speaking only of the American gentleman.

My father was a mighty man of God and a mighty warrior of the faith. I grew up knowing God's hand of grace and protection was upon my life. I felt blessed to have had such a rich heritage and such wonderful parents. I thought of my father not only as a fearless warrior, but also as a spiritual giant or mighty prophet of God, like maybe Elijah or some other great biblical hero. His faith seemed to be contagious. My father's great faith somehow increased my faith because I knew that when he prayed, look out, anything could happen.

Just before our family went to Brazil I was involved in a very serious car accident. I was even years old. I was riding my bicycle down the middle of a street when I was hit by a car approaching me from behind. I remember seeing the car and thinking that I had plenty of time to cross in front of the vehicle, but I was wrong. The car had defective brakes. I was dragged completely under the car for forty feet. I was covered with blood and fading in and out of consciousness. I remember lying on the ground, then sitting up briefly before losing consciousness. I saw that my torso was soaked in blood, and I realized this was crunch time: the time in which to either abandon ship and abdicate, or call out to God and ask for help. My heavenly Father knew there were still lots of people out there that needed to go to jail at my hands, and I was only seven years old, so I had a long way to go. God wasn't done with me yet! So many bad people, so little time! Lord, I'm not giving up! I told the paramedics that I wanted my father to pray for me. I knew that if my dad prayed for me, God could raise me from the dead. My faith dares me to trust God, and be bold and courageous and expectant like Joshua or Caleb. Much of my father's faith has rubbed off on me.

Rest assured, these are not the only times God has looked out for me and protected me, either in the fields and jungles of Brazil, or on the streets of our cities which I patrolled every night. On several occasions I could have been shot by armed and dangerous suspects I encountered and arrested. These personal incidents are only a few of the things that reflect God's protecting hand on my life, and for these, I am very grateful. There are more but I wanted you to have some flavor for what my family upbringing looked like. If my father, on any given day, had ever said that we were going on a rescue mission to the gates of hell to get somebody out of harm's way, my mother would have agreed and simply said fine, I'll pack us a lunch.

What a great partner my mother was for my dad. There are some partners in life that wouldn't follow you to the corner store if the circumstances weren't just right, or if the weather was overcast or chilly. My mother was ready to bake cookies and follow us all the way to the gates of hell because she knew how the mission worked, she was a part of our *unit*, and she knew how to operate that Ham radio channel of prayer that goes straight to the gates of heaven, if things got ugly. She knew how to call down reinforcements from heaven. My mother was also a prayer warrior. We should have gotten her a DELTA Force tattoo. Get out of our way Satan or I'll call down an air strike from heaven! Both of my parents could have been on the SWAT team today. How much time do we have before we roll? Just enough time to put war paint on our face!

Seeking God's will for my life and career

When it came time for me to figure out what I was supposed to do career wise with my own life, I experienced a fair amount of consternation over that issue. Although I had not felt called to a conventional style of full time ministry like my father, I did have a very deep personal faith and respect for God and a desire to do right in his eyes. It was more than that. It was a desire to serve the Lord with all my heart, but I was terrified that I might have to become a preacher too, and that the Lord might tell me that my wife was at the altar praying also, and I was worried that she might look like a lame duck. When you are 19 years old it's hard to have much wisdom.

As I earnestly prayed about all of this I tried to be honest with myself and with God. I knew that running away from Nineveh and from God did not get Jonah a room with a view, but more importantly I believed that in the long run, obeying God would enrich one's life far more than anything we could do for ourselves in our own human power or efforts...at least that was the politically correct answer in my mind. Part of me actually believed it and part of me wanted to live like James Bond. The idea of reading to the blind made be want to puke.

On the other hand, I intellectualized that when you really got down to it, the only thing in life that really mattered was to prepare yourself and others for eternal life. The time which we are allotted on this earth is relatively short and it should be wisely used for growth and development and service to others, something far more eternal and lasting than simply satisfying our own personal earthly desires. What could possibly be more honorable than telling others the good news of Christ, like Stemmy did with my father, and, as my father did with so many others himself?

I was all of twenty years or so in age, but I prayed the most sincere and heartfelt prayer I could have ever prayed at that time. It was an offering of myself to God that was analogous to making a contract, and it was a lifelong deal. I told God that my own personal first choice was not to be a preacher or minister, but that I wanted to serve him and give him my first fruits and my best efforts. I opened my heart and prayed to God that if he wanted me to be a minister I would yield, obey and follow him. Not only that, but I would put all my heart, soul and energy into it, and I would learn to love it with all my heart.

As things developed and progressed I went into the Army for a few years and ultimately went back to college to finish my education when I got out of the Army. I enrolled in San Jose State University and, after much soul searching, prayer and several years of hard work, I obtained a B.S. degree in Criminal Justice Administration. I became deeply drawn toward police work and I reached a point where several police agencies were all trying to hire me at the same time and I had to pick one. It was sort of like you can't be engaged to marry more than one woman and do the marriage justice.

What happened next stunned me. The medical examination that a prospective employer requires is one of the last things you go through in a long hiring process. It's expensive so they don't do this unless they are very interested in hiring you. My medical exam revealed a possible abnormality with my lower back. I did not know this at the time, of course, but back and knee problems are an anathema to police agencies. You might as well have leprosy or AIDS. Knees and backs are the leading two causes of disabilities and medical retirements that cities shell out millions of dollars for each year.

The problem over a period of many years became so pervasive and problematic that cities all across California were essentially getting burned or taken to the cleaners by officers retiring at the onset of their careers with lifelong medical pensions that the cities were forced to pay. To avoid this real problem they simply cracked down on whom they would hire. If you had problems with your back or knees, police agencies looked very hard at each applicant and each medical condition. The agency took additional X-rays of my back, but ultimately I was refused employment.

In California all police standards, requirements and training are governed by a state run agency called PORAC (Peace Officers Research Association of California). While PORAC can't legally prohibit a city from hiring a particular applicant, they do have authority to establish and adopt uniform standards for all law enforcement agencies in the State of California. This includes hiring criteria as well as disqualifying criteria. The uniformity is a good thing because it sets standards that everyone can agree on and you don't have cities or towns doing whatever they feel like. It mandates training requirements so that everybody in the state gets the same consistent standard of training for every police academy throughout California. No matter where you work, all recruits will receive the same legal training and have to pass the same vigorous tests in order to do this job. The standards are high and they are good ones. In my case, the disqualifying criteria went against me. The significance of that meant that, for all practical purposes, once you got disqualified for a medical condition, it would be unlikely that any agency would risk hiring you against the good advice of PORAC.

This meant that it wouldn't do any good to apply to other agencies throughout the 58 counties in California because of the aforementioned issues. No one would take you. My medical disqualification was like a career death sentence for me.

I was literally in a state of emotional and mental shock for several reasons. I had spent several years preparing myself for this with school and other training. I had played sports throughout high school, college and the Army and never had a problem with my back or anything else for that matter. My health had been excellent and now someone was telling me they found an abnormality that would eliminate me from police work.

Wow! I had taken some aptitude tests while preparing for this career. Those tests asked scores of questions to measure interest and suitability for various fields of work. Some of the questions would make me laugh, after sitting at the table for four hours answering them, probably because of fatigue. Would you rather fly an F-16 fighter jet at Mach 3 or read a story to a blind child? Would you rather read a Bible story to small children or chase armed and dangerous bank robbers over fences and down alleys? If someone asked me another question about blind people I was going to kill them. You can pretty much guess how I answered these questions. The results of the aptitude test revealed that out of six hundred different occupational possibilities the top two careers for which I was most suited were that of a police officer and a soldier. And don't even think about asking me to read stories to anyone. I'll choke you right there where you sit and render you unconscious!

On a serious note, I was emotionally devastated. What was of paramount importance to me and what deeply bothered me more than anything else, including whether or not I even got into police work, was the greater issue that I had sought God's will for my life on this, with all the honesty and integrity that I could possibly have, and with sincere and earnest supplication, over a very long period of time. Had I deluded myself into thinking that God had given me a green light to pursue this, but I was mistaken, because God never did so? Had I just talked myself into all of this because it was what I wanted? Did I miss the boat this badly? Could I ever trust my own mind or emotions again with anything spiritual? If I did not get this right, how could I have faith for anything else? I thought to myself, God might tell me to go to Africa and read to the blind, but I would think, yes, but didn't you give me a green light to go into police work too? Which one is it? Which one am I not hearing correctly?

As you can surmise from what I have shared thus far, I had a strong belief in God, his goodness and his ability do perform present day miracles. The problems of life as I saw them were not questions or doubts about God's power, authority or ability; they were more about tactical matters and strategic planning, or more simply, about his divine will and plan in our daily lives. The problem is never God; we are the weak link. I was not horrified that perhaps God had failed me as much as I was worried that maybe I screwed up and failed myself, by hearing only what I wanted to hear.

It is always easier to see these things in someone else's life rather than your own. My sister was an example of that. I could know with confidence that God had the power to heal my sister out in that jungle because I had already developed a faith in which I knew miracles occurred. My father, Hammerwall and my sister were all walking miracles. When miracles did not occur it was not because God took the day off or because he stopped being God, it was because of his choosing not to perform them as part of his divine, greater plan. Back then in the jungle I was only eight years old. I was not old enough to have any anxiety over the money issue that my parents faced in that situation. From my empirical childhood experiences I was learning that God takes care of those who put their faith in him.

When you are the one going through the fire, is it interesting how all these things seemingly change and become so much more complicated. Perception is sometimes reality for us. That is the reason we need to get our focus off our problems and focus on God's power and provisional ability. If you focus on your problems they become overwhelming and that is exactly what I did.

I can appreciate that not all of us share the same life experiences. I was fortunate to have experienced a rich spiritual environment where supernatural things not only could occur but they did occur. If you have never had a prayer answered, or better yet, a result that you could describe as scientifically verifiable and miraculous, then it becomes understandable that you could have skepticism that anyone else has experienced answered prayer. Add to this all the guile and deceitfulness of the flesh and mental illness that is around us wherein psychotic people hear voices which they believe are from God, telling them to murder someone, and I can really appreciate why some professional people don't believe in anything that can't be measured in a test tube.

It was just such a well educated, critical thinker as Jack Deere who authored a wonderful book I recently read entitled, <u>SURPRISED BY THE POWER OF THE SPIRIT: Discovering How God Speaks and heals Today</u>, published by Zondervan (1996). If you, like many others, have theological issues or skepticism about whether God actually performs miracles today, this is a wonderful book to read. I so appreciated this author's humility and honest investigative work and critical analysis in researching this important theological subject.

I knew deep in my heart that God can and does heal people and that healing is not just an apostolic occurrence of past biblical times. I knew God could heal me if he wanted to. Healing wasn't the central issue for me. It wasn't a matter that I could not embrace healing, or that I did not believe God *could* heal me, it was more complicated than that in my mind. There were other issues here in addition to healing.

The Bible lays out a foundation and explanation of God's spiritual, supernatural gifts. They are often referred to as the "gifts of the Spirit" not to be confused with the "fruit of the Spirit." Sometimes the latter is referred to using the plural, as the fruits of the Spirit. The fruits of the Spirit are: *love, joy, peace, long-suffering, gentleness, goodness, faith, meekness, and temperance* (Galatians 5:22). These are the fruits, which should emanate out of born-again disciples who reflect the character of Christ and who walk in discipline, self-control and humility.

The Biblical authority and context for the "gifts of the Spirit" are found in I Corinthians Chapter 12 and outlined by the great apostle Paul; they are described as such: *the word of wisdom, the word of knowledge, the gift of faith, gifts of healing, the working of miracles, the gift of prophecy, the discerning of spirits, divers kinds of tongues, and the interpretation of tongues*, all of which Paul describes as gifts from the Holy Spirit (I Corinthians 12:4-10).

I wanted to meet with, talk to and pray with a servant of God who possessed at least one of these gifts. I had seen the manifestation of some of these gifts in my parents' ministry and I knew that they were real, and that God could clarify the direction I needed to take regarding this important issue I faced. I wanted to figure out if I had made a huge mistake pursing police work or if there was something else I needed to do. Regardless of what it was, I did not understand what was happening in my life. I had offered God my life to be a full-time minister if that was what he desired of me, but everything seemed to lead me down the road into police work until the door got slammed shut in my face. I had to know if I had missed the boat and simply talked myself into this whole mess.

While in school at San Jose State University, an interesting internship became available to me, working as a trainee with the United States Customs Service, under the Treasury Department. I worked in uniform, armed as a federal officer, while receiving law enforcement training with U.S. Customs officers. It was good training for me. It was while I was in this internship that I got medically disqualified from police work. This distressed me so much emotionally, by being disqualified from police work, that my mental state of mind began affecting my physiological health, and I started actually developing lower back pain for the first time in my life. You can imagine how this weighed on me.

The physical condition, which was detected in my lower back, turned out to be visible on X-rays. The condition was called *spondylolisthesis*. It was not that severe but enough to disqualify me from police work by California's high standards. All of this seemed overwhelming to me. I was like in a state of quiet hysteria. This was no small thing to me, as if someone were to ask, would you rather be a plumber or an electrician. It was the most important thing in my life at this time. I felt as though I had not only sought but also followed God's leading and now all of that seemed to be in question. This whole thing felt analogous to a medical student who had completed four years of medical school only to be now told that he could not take his state board exams to become a doctor for some crazy, technical reason. I felt like I was facing my own Red Sea. I think the worst part of it was that I felt no sense of faith or courage.

Struggling with Pentecostal theology and humility

I was brought up and raised in various Pentecostal churches of the Assemblies of God from early childhood. Most of these denominational folk believe in the "fullness of the Spirit" which is to say God, through his Holy Spirit, is still in the business of not only saving people, but healing them also and performing miracles. The Assemblies of God, as an organization, don't just believe in some miracles; they believe in all of the miracles and gifts of the Spirit. The miracles of yesteryear are still being accomplished today through dedicated prophets and servants who obey the leading of the Spirit. The Assemblies of God, as an organization, is comprised of many wonderful people. Pastor Stemmy, who led my father to the Lord, was an Assembly of God minister. My father was an Assembly of God minister and missionary. I never felt anything except pride and respect for the work my father did. My father had human weaknesses, to be sure, but I considered his faith in God to be profound and deeply anchored in Christ. My dad's love for Jesus and his desire to feed the Lord's sheep was staggering. It reflected to me the essence of what Jesus commanded us to do: love one another. Dad's sole mission was to minister to the lost and dying world around him.

Unfortunately, I am also saddened to say that, as all human endeavors go, all religious denominations and organizations suffer from various forms of weakness and human shortcomings. I have come to realize that there is no family on earth that doesn't struggle with something. Even the most wonderful and seemingly perfect families have issues. Most families have at least one or more members who are just plain difficult to live with. Spirit filled, Pentecostal brethren, as well as non-Pentecostal brethren, in this respect, are no different than the rest of humankind. If you look hard enough you will find human flesh and weakness everywhere. It's the very reason we all need Jesus. Sometimes we just have to look beyond human limitations and focus on the goodness of God and then practice the art of forgiving one another, even as Jesus forgave us.

A lot of Christian brethren from other denominations have been alienated from the gifts of the Spirit because of Spirit filled believers working in the flesh, with a holier than thou attitude. Ideological views and differences in doctrine and interpretation of scripture, regarding miracles and the speaking in tongues, account for some of these differences, but I believe attitude and arrogance about the gifts have been more common reasons for why many believers shy away from our Spirit filled brethren. Many non-Pentecostal believers perceive this offensive attitude to be pervasive. Consequently, as Jack Deere and others point out, some denominational difference in theology may be less a matter of believers rejecting either the Holy Spirit or, the gifts of the Spirit, and more an issue of revulsion to vessels who lack wisdom and sensitivity in their use of the gifts. Let me offer an example of this.

Some Pentecostal believers maintain a simple notion that if you don't speak in tongues as they do, you are not as good, nor as spiritual as "they" are. What follows is a perception that God can't use you as much as he uses me because I'm filled with the Spirit and I speak in tongues, so I can hear God's voice and leading, more astutely than you. This reminds me of the second grade. I'm bigger and smarter than you are! Well, of course you are! My church knows more about Jesus than your church! This kind of staggering arrogance and attitude is a turn off and such behavior does not reflect Jesus or the fruit of the Spirit. You could fool me, if I didn't know better, into thinking that speaking in tongues was either the only gift that existed, or that it was the most important one of all. It's no surprise this kind of arrogance does not bring the body of Christ any closer together.

The first pressing question many Pentecostal folk will ask another believer is whether they are "filled with the Spirit." The question itself, though not intrinsically wrong, is inappropriately posed to falsely measure spirituality and

35

superiority, and the question is cloaked and disguised in such innocence that it does not reflect what is truly being asked, but it's the first thing they want to know. Even if another believer should answer, "Yes," their simple and truthful answer probably wouldn't be good enough and an immediate follow-up question will come forth. Well, do you speak in tongues? Not everyone who asks this question has an impure motive, yet, often, without realizing it, this all-important question is designed to size you up and measure how good you are and how deeply spiritual you might be.

A lot more sensitivity needs to be applied when asking questions that lead in this direction. Most of the time the truth will surface and manifest itself and we won't need to ask anyone how deep or mature they are. We will find out quickly enough by either the presence or absence of the fruit of the Spirit in their life. Besides that, there are many non-Pentecostal pastors and lay people that are filled with the Spirit and walk in the Spirit, but they don't speak in tongues. The "gift" of tongues is different than the indwelling of the Holy Spirit in your being. One could be filled with the Spirit because you have invited the Holy Spirit to occupy your heart, mind and spirit, but not necessarily speak in tongues, or have the "gift" of tongues.

Being too eager to judge someone's spirituality is a mistake in itself, but using the standard of tongues as the yardstick for judging them compounds this blunder, and it represents a lack of discretion and good judgment. We wouldn't think of asking fellow brothers and sister in the Lord how much money they make a year, so we could size them up to determine whether they fit into a blue collar or white collar box. We don't need to be making this kind of judgment in the first place; moreover, such a question regarding tongues applies the wrong measuring stick, for assessing how deep or spiritual you are.

This singular, somewhat vacuous, question reveals nothing of your character, any fruits of the Spirit that might be present in your life, nor does it say anything about your dedication or commitment to follow Jesus and serve him no matter what the cost. There are other questions I could think of which might tell me something about your faith, but speaking in tongues is the last one on my list.

Why don't other questions ever get asked about the gifts? Do you have the gift of healing or miracles? Do you have the word of knowledge, or, the gift of discernment? Certainly, you must have the gift of prophecy? How strong is your faith bother; do you throw mountains into the sea? Oh, yeah! My friends all call me, "Mt. Thrower," for short. At a party I could introduce you guys to each other. Brother Fuller, meet Brother Thrower!

This criticism may sound a little overly harsh, like it's coming from a non-believer or outsider. The fact is I am a respectful believer and an insider and this is my family. I _am_ Pentecostal and I believe in the gifts, all of them, and I am grateful for them, all of them! If not for the work of the Holy Spirit in my life, I would still be drifting at sea, like a ship without a sail, lost in utter darkness to my own sin. The gifts of the Spirit are wonderful. I have seen the gifts manifested with awesome results. God doesn't make bad gifts. Nevertheless, I would love to see us mature in our walk and in how we practice the gifts, using more humility and sensitivity to the Holy Spirit.

We need to be bonded in our love and commitment to Jesus and not be divided by whether we throw mountains into the sea, least of all, whether or not we speak in tongues, perhaps the least important measuring stick of all our godly attributes or gifts. One of the first questions Pentecostal folk should be asking another believer is, how can I minister to you or bless you in some way? Can I pray for you about anything? There needs to be no qualification as to whether I speak in tongues or not, before you inquire as to whether you can minister to me or pray for me. Please show your fellow brothers and sisters in Christ more deference. Allow them to ask you if you have any understanding as to how the gifts work, or personal experience with the gifts of the Holy Spirit. That door, when opened with the right spirit and attitude, to someone who is seeking, may produce fruit of its own.

I don't personally care whether you speak in tongues or not when you pray secretly in your private closet. Do you have the "gift" of tongues in corporate worship and interpretation of tongues, or is speaking in tongues simply the manifestation of your baptism in the Holy Spirit? Does your gift edify the body of Christ, or just you? Do you practice self-control at home or at the office? Do you love people unconditionally in spite of their flaws? Are you filled with humility? Will you give your life in service to Christ and let others ridicule you and mock you, and still love and forgive them? You show me how deep your love is and then we will talk about your gifts. Show me your gifts and I will show you my sword (God's Word). I'm more interested in the fruits of the Spirit. Show me your humility and sensitivity and I will almost certainly be more interested in your gifts.

The seventy who were commissioned to go into all the world and preach the gospel returned with joy saying: *Lord, even the devils are subject unto us through thy name.* Jesus said unto them: *Behold I give unto you power to tread on serpents and scorpions, and over all the power of the enemy, and nothing shall by any means hurt you. Nevertheless, rejoice not, that the [evil] spirits are subject unto you, but rather rejoice because your names are written in heaven* (Luke 10:17-20). [The Lord sure protected me in the jungle from the scorpion and the serpent!]

I love this verse. Jesus is reminding us of what is truly important, and it's not whether you drive a Lexus or whether you speak in tongues. The reason Jesus came into the world was to save us from our sins (Matthew 1:21). Having our names written in the book of life is what we need to shout about, not whether we speak in tongues or have the faith to throw mountains into the sea or cast out devils. All of these are good things, to be sure, but Jesus reminded us to rejoice because *he forgives us of our sins.* That is job number one!

For those who see and smell nothing but the manifestation of human flesh and weakness in Pentecostal movements, I would respectfully urge you to not focus only on the vessel, or, the vessel's at-times-obvious human deficiencies, nor throw the so-called proverbial baby out with the dirty bath water, because the gifts themselves are not bad. It is the misuse of the gifts along with ignorance and arrogance by the vessel that are issues here, and not the gifts themselves. Don't throw healing out the window just because you choose to not identify with speaking in tongues. God might want to heal you of your cancer by using someone else to pray for you who may speak French, or perhaps some other heavenly language or tongue. Remember Job's comforters who falsely accused Job of secret sin? Did not God tell these men to have Job pray for them to seek forgiveness on their behalf, because God said that he would listen to Job's prayers? Will it make any difference to you if Job prays for you in Pentecostal tongues if you get healed of your cancer? Don't limit what God could do for you because you don't understand the gifts or how they work, or because the servant possessing the gift turns you off. Look beyond that! Some vessels leave a lot to be desired. Look at Jonah. Look at me! Neither one of us has an ounce of compassion. Remember, God uses imperfect people just like the twelve disciples to accomplish his work. We are all members of the body of Christ. We are all imperfect and we have all been bought with a price, the precious blood of Jesus.

Are all Assembly of God people like this? Of course not. My father never ran around asking others if they spoke in tongues, but he did himself, all the time. Are all cops good officers with integrity and character? Of course not. The same is true of doctors, lawyers, judges, and all other professionals, and of Catholics, Baptists, Presbyterians, and so on, and so on.

The most fundamental thing we forget, in our pursuit of ministry, is that we are to love one another, not fix them or overpower them with our superior theology. Jesus said love one another. Life is a journey. We are all at different stations or levels along the roadway. Some of us are still struggling with being potty trained and we're not ready to pray the prayer of faith to raise the dead, just yet. But we're working on it! The great apostle Paul emphasized this important issue regarding our mission statement:

> *Though I speak with the tongues of men and of angels, and have not charity I am become as sounding brass, or a tinkling cymbal. And though I have the gift of prophecy and understand all mysteries and all knowledge; and though I have all faith, so that I could remove mountains, and have not charity, I am nothing. And though I bestow all my goods to feed the poor, and though I give my body to be burned, and have not charity, it profiteth me nothing* (I Corinthians 13:1-3).

Paul goes on in this passage to define the character qualities of charity (love). He cautions us that whether there be prophecies, they shall fail; whether there be tongues, they shall cease; whether there be knowledge, it shall vanish away; but charity never fails.

This famous passage of scripture gets read from pulpits all across America yet it seems as though many of us don't somehow fully get it. We don't always practice what we preach.

There are many wonderful Spirit filled Christians who completely understand the necessity for humility and they practice the gifts in this manner. You would not know that they even have such wonderful anointing from the Holy Spirit because they don't go around bragging about it, nor do they run around asking others whether or not they speak in tongues. Mature servants use the gifts only to further the Kingdom of God and never to lift themselves up or draw attention to themselves. These precious few are, in my opinion, mighty current day apostles and prophets who are keenly sensitive to the Holy Spirit. Their work and success come from obedience to the leading of the Holy Spirit. These godly saints practice the gifts and miracles of the Spirit but they do so by practicing and manifesting these gifts through the fruit of the Spirit. If you don't see the fruit of the Spirit being displayed in someone's ministry, be very careful, as it may not be real or of God. If it's flashy and ostentatious, contradicts scripture or is full of the flesh, run away from it.

I have tried to make some respectful distinctions between what is real and what is showcasing and specious. The standard by which we should measure ourselves is whether our lives (or ministry) produce or yield the fruits of the Spirit, but more definitively by whether we love others or not.

Seek and ye shall find / knock and it shall be opened unto you

Now that I have proffered more theology than you probably wanted to hear, allow me to weave this into how it had direct application to the adversity and consternation I experienced back then in my life, as I entered into law enforcement. I knew I needed to touch the throne of God and get some answers regarding my pending career. I felt that I needed someone who could help me do that because I was at a point where I couldn't trust myself with figuring out any of what was happening to me regarding my efforts to enter law enforcement. All sorts of thoughts ran through my mind, all of them based on doubt and fear, rather than faith and courage.

Real prophets exist today. Many operate in the fullness of the Spirit, manifesting the *gifts* of the Spirit. One has to diligently look for the good ones. You could, but rarely do, find them in front of a T.V. camera anywhere because they are truly not seeking glory, fame, money or the recognition of men. They quietly work behind the scenes doing the work of Jesus without notoriety. They encourage people, show kindness, love, and goodness to others, and they wash feet of unlovely people and do little acts of kindness that no one pays much attention to. They are the hands and feet of Jesus inconspicuously ministering to those who are in need, but behold, when they pray their faith and the power of the Holy Spirit move mountains, and miracles occur.

I had met such a person during my early years and had received a powerful word from the Lord through this prophet when I needed a definitive answer from the Lord about a previous issue of importance in my life. I was delighted to find this wonderful servant was not only still alive, but living in the Bay Area at that time. Her name was Mabel Maciel.

I met with Mabel and told her all about my troubles. I told Mabel that I wanted to serve the Lord all the days of my life, but I explained to her that, unlike my wonderful father who was a preacher, I had felt led into police work, and that I wanted to serve God by dragging as many people as I could get my hands on to jail, strictly for the glory of God and the furtherance of his Kingdom. I explained to Mabel how I had spent several years preparing for this and that all of a sudden the door had been closed in my face because of my back, and it was appearing as though I could never get into police work.

What transpired was wonderful because it was straight from God. First of all, Mabel, being human herself and made of flesh and blood was filled with compassion for me and she accepted my story and account of things as though it was absolutely true and as though there was only one side to the story, mine. Just sensing her sympathy made me feel good because I could sense her love and her desire to see me succeed in my endeavor to walk with God.

Mabel asked me to kneel before the Lord so that we would pray. I knelt on the floor resting my hands and arms on an easy chair in the room. There was complete privacy, which enabled me to open up completely and not feel self-conscious. Mabel gently placed her hand on my lower back and started to pray for me because, after all, my lower back was the problem.

Mabel began praying in a soft voice with words that had the general context of: We just come to you now, Lord, and lift up Mark before you. That's all it took and the power of the Holy Spirit began falling on both of us. It felt like a warm, wet blanket that was seeping into my DNA. Instantly I could feel the presence of the Holy Spirit and I began weeping. Mabel's voice changed from soft to confident, unapologetic, full of authority and boldness. Through the Holy Spirit she began speaking the word of knowledge, wisdom and prophecy. The Lord spoke through Mabel to me and said: *I can see that the problem is not your back but in your head, my son. You have so agitated yourself with thoughts of defeat and magnified the issue until even your body is now responding with pain. The problem is not in your back but in your head and with your thoughts, my son.*

The Lord went on to say that he put this desire for police work in my heart from the very beginning and that he would use me in this field. The Lord said: *continue to study and show thyself worthy to walk before me and I will bless you in this field. I will lead and direct you to one who has increased knowledge and understanding who will open this door for you and with a full body you will be raised up and work in this field. Walk in faith, for I am with you, and stop searching for, entertaining and magnifying destructive doubt and negativity in your mind.*

Wow! These were powerful words that addressed every question I had in both my heart and mind. I flashed back to the time my mother took me to pay for her speeding ticket. I remembered my fascination with police work then and I realized that this desire had been placed in my heart way back then by the Lord. In this powerful message the Lord also gently rebuked me for my mental negativity which had so destructively impacted me that my thinking was producing psychosomatic lower back pain I had never experience before. I repented and I reversed my negative thinking and claimed victory in my spirit. The pain completely went away in a matter of days.

Shortly after this, the Veteran's Administration hired me as a police officer. About a year later I was hired by the Atherton Police Department. I spent three years there but wanted to work in a larger city that had a little more action. I applied to the Los Altos Police Department. The city sent me to an orthopedic surgeon who wrote a letter for me stating that the health and strength of my back was better than that of most other people who had no back problems. He opined that if I were going to have problems with my back I would have experienced them a long time ago. The surgeon wrote that it was as safe for the City to hire me as it would be for them to hire someone with no abnormality. The rest is history.

I then worked for the Palo Alto Police Department for ten years and then finished my career with the San Mateo County Sheriff's Office. I had a wonderful career with 28 years of service. I arrested bank robbers, murderers, rapists, child molesters, wife beaters, thieves of every kind, drug dealers, drug users, drunk drivers, and generally bad people who never went to Sunday School when they should have.

As my law enforcement career days were gradually coming to an end, I still had great enthusiasm. I can't believe they paid me to do this. When I would get up in the morning to get ready for work, my wife would ask me, "Honey, is anyone going to jail today?" I would laugh and always reply, "One can only hope, sweetheart! One can only hope!"

Hey, you! Pay attention; there's a cop right behind you!

CHAPTER 2

SO, WHY IS SIN SUCH A BIG DEAL?

Sin is so guilefully vague, ambiguous, theologically abstract, impervious to discernment, distinctly nonhomogeneous without structural design, that it defies definition by modern science. The average well-balanced person who has a sense of social morality could only describe behavioral signs or symptoms of sin in its most salient forms. In trying to get a better understanding of what sin looks like we should also consider what sin is not.

Sin is never cosmetic or just surface level

Sin is not a minor inconvenience, hygienically treatable like incipient tooth caries. Sin is endogenous. It gets worse! Sin emanates from the heart where we can't see it.

Sin is a fatal disease

We rarely view it as such. This deception alone will lead many down the wrong road. We greatly minimize its impact. We tend to look at sin as nothing more serious than a slightly elevated cholesterol level, nothing to worry about if you are young or in good health. In the same way that we think that young people don't die of cholesterol, we think people don't die of sin; they die of old age or some other disease. We completely miss the link that exists between sin and death. We would do well to view it far more seriously and have a better understanding of the consequences sin brings into our lives.

The consequence of sin is one of the biggest issues people struggle with. There are several reasons for this. First of all, we simply don't take God at his word. If God, through his word, tells us that sin will produce death, we deny it as though we knew more about the subject than God does. After we do sin and live another day to talk about it, we consider that proof positive that God was wrong all along. The very nature of sin itself makes us want to argue with God, and defend our own position. Even if it's only at an unconscious level, we want to be God, at least of our own lives. I see this in myself all the time. Don't tell me what to do! I know exactly what I am doing, and I know how to get where I'm going without a map. I know far more than you do, anyway! If I just had a miniscule amount of humility I'd be perfect!

There is much confusion over what the rules are and who makes them. This summarizes the human condition. The People rest, your Honor. We don't really know what the rules are but we have our own definition of what the rules should be. Moreover, we have our own floating definition of what justice should look like and we feel intellectually quite content and smug about our position. We are intuitively blessed to have some sense of fair play and justice and we know, even as small children that some things are just right or wrong. That is not an accident. As we grow and develop we become more inculcated with our social values, and this tends to reinforce our sense of justice over what we perceive to be right or wrong. There are some things that are so commonly accepted that they are universally adopted as laws or customs. Such behaviors become mores that everyone can embrace, not just religious people. For example, we all have laws designed to protect us against theft and murder, but there is nothing on the books about good judgment or common sense to protect us from sin. The reason for this, of course, is you couldn't find two politicians who could define common sense, let alone sin.

Sometimes we may become confused over the applicability of spiritual laws with earthly laws and their interchangeability because the principles are not distinctly clear to us and often they strike us as being roughly the same. Principles are extremely important because they represent fundamental, characteristic qualities, underlying assumption values related to law, doctrine or code of conduct. In my opinion, when applied correctly, principles offer valuable lessons because they also:

1. edify, supplement, clarify or corroborate truth or the issue at hand
2. reflect primary core values
3. reflect parallel application of value, as in earthly or spiritual dimensions, demonstrating the truth applies on more than one level, or to more than one group of people
4. typically have withstood the test of time and proven to be reliable and enduring

As long as we are correctly applying sound principles we remain on solid ground. Nevertheless, when it comes to making comparisons or drawing conclusions about sin, this is precisely where we begin to get into trouble. When it comes to sin we start making apples and oranges comparisons.

We would be incapable of convicting many people of crimes even if they confessed today because of "double jeopardy," a legal concept that precludes the state from trying someone twice for the same crime. O.J. Simpson would fall into this category if he confessed to killing his wife, Nicole, and Ron Goldman. In stark contrast spiritual laws require no reasonable doubt, because God will have no doubt. God will never need a jury to help him find out whether you sinned or not. Jesus said that whosoever looks on a woman to lust after her hath committed adultery with her already in his heart (Matthew

5:28). You can see that the standard for measuring guilt, when it comes to sin, is quite different than the standard of "beyond a reasonable doubt."

When rules are broken we learn to apply discipline in an appropriate way so that the punishment fits the crime. This is where we begin to draw parallelisms between earthly and spiritual values. In doing this, sometimes we mistakenly think we share the same value system that God has. The concept of measured discipline is sometimes referred to as "progressive discipline." If your two-year-old child fails to say "thank you" at the appropriate moment after receiving a glass of milk, it is inappropriate to beat the child and tell them not to forget this important custom. God treats us fairly in the same manner, sometimes requiring only a gentle reminder of his expectations. In more severe cases of defiance you might get a room without a view, like Jonah.

We want to apply justice or punishment in an equitable manner when the rules are broken, so that the punishment fits the so-called crime. In the same way that you would not beat your two-year-old child for not saying "thank you" for the milk, you decide that a loving God would not beat you or send you to hell for spilling milk. Such thinking seems pretty logical. We judge our own behavior as being pretty acceptable by social standards. By contrasting ourselves to others it becomes possible to argue, I'm a "good" guy; I didn't spill the milk. While our intentions might be good, we miss the boat with our assessment of the issues. Jesus already told us that there is none "good" but God. If only God is truly good, it's a mistake to think of yourself as good. By choice we manifest good behavior, we do good deeds, we have tremendous creativity and potential for good, but even the wicked are capable of displaying many of these virtues. Thieves and drug dealers share drugs and stolen property with each other and sometimes they murder others simply for the purpose of doing someone else a favor. It's like an act of kindness.

The standard for defining or quantifying sin should not be some social definition of what constitutes low-level sin. The sophistry of Satan leads us to think that there is such a thing as "low-level" sin, like innocuous little *white lies*. Your standard of justice is not *roughly* the same as God's. They are two completely different standards altogether, worlds apart. We tend to look only at *behavior*, like this was the only piece of the equation. It's not. Our self-righteous view, that our handful of low-level sins are undeserving of punishment, is based on misjudging ourselves in comparison to what others do, and not by how God defines sin. How you view this is a choice, but by the time we are done with our rationalizations, we decide that God would not, or should not, send anyone to hell, at least for small sins, such as ours.

These rationalizations lead us to completely misdiagnose sin. We make errors in defining what constitutes sin because many times we don't even recognize it when it's right under our nose. We then further error in our assessment of what the cost of sin will be, both in terms of what God requires as payment for sin, and by deceiving ourselves into thinking we might be able to pay for some of it, or somehow make it go away the old fashion way, with hard work and good deeds. Such catastrophic thinking continues when we conclude that sin is only about *behavior* and that "low-level" sin could somehow be overlooked. Our rationalizations lead us to conclude: I'm not so bad, if I compare myself to others. Nowhere does it say that if you want to have eternal life, just compare yourself to everybody else. Even if you have been smoking crack you should be able to get this one right. Nowhere, except from the lips of Satan, is there is such a thing as "low-level" sin. We should be more circumspect in our approach to assessing sin. Since the consequence of unmitigated sin has eternal results, it would seem prudent to not take too cavalier a view regarding any aspect of this subject.

In police work there was a well-known phrase about guns that every rookie would hopefully be familiar with. In order to preserve your life, the phrase teaches cops to think: All guns are loaded all the time! This is how we need to view sin. All sin is fatal all the time. Moreover, *your* sin will not be based on what others did.

The standard for the salvation of your soul is not based on a Bell curve relative to behavior or good works. The records in heaven will have every imaginable statistic you could think of just like the NFL does on how many passes a receiver caught, how many they dropped, and how many yards they gained after catching the ball, as well as how many minutes they played in the game. Every possible statistic you could think of will be available for viewing, but the one which will receive the least amount of attention will be how *many* sins you committed, because the only data anyone will care about, or, that will make any difference to you or anyone else, will be whether your *sins were forgiven.* If your sins aren't forgiven, none of the others stats, like how few times you blew it or sinned, will make a hoot of difference. Like gained yardage, it won't matter how many orphanages, schools, or hospitals you built, or how much money you gave to worthy causes; if your sins were never nailed to the cross where Jesus shed his blood for you, you will be in eternal trouble, and no one will care about whether you gained a lot of yardage running the ball after you caught it. It will be a moot issue. Jesus said, *Wide is the gate, and broad is the way, that leads to destruction, and many there be which go in this way; straight is the gate, and narrow is the way, that leads unto life, and few there be that find it* (Matthew 7:13-14).

If I just do *enough* good things along the way I will earn my way into heaven. After all, God is just. God is good and just but nothing could be more misleading with regard to this type of thinking, because you are using the wrong standard of measurement, based on a misdiagnosis of multiple factors. You miscalculate sin and you fail to understand how high the cost is that will be required to pay for it. God considered the cost of sin so high that only his son's sacrifice could redeem us. Your good deeds alone will never earn your way into heaven because good deeds don't deal with the issue of sin or your need for forgiveness. Simply put, neither your good deeds nor riches, can buy your way into heaven. If the opposite were true, God would not have unnecessarily sent his only son to die on the cross for us, nor would there be any efficacious provision for the poor, lowly and downtrodden. If wealth or riches could buy your way into heaven only the rich would make it into heaven. The Bible would be nothing but a book with chapters written on how to earn your way into heaven and only the rich would most likely possess such a book. Fortunately, this is not the case.

Sin is not limited to just our behavior. It's worse than that! It is present even in our thoughts, like the one who lusts after a woman in his heart. We are born with sin like babies who are born with AIDS, except sin is far worse. The toxicology of sin goes far deeper than we can humanly imagine and the consequence is eternal. This is the part that we just don't fully absorb or digest with our intellect. We hear the message from famous gospel preachers like Dr. Rev. Billy Graham and maybe we even read it ourselves right out of the Bible, but the words, describing sin and its cost, are perhaps so conceptually staggering that we can't fully face what we hear or read. Sin is an anathema to God and he hates it. We simply don't share the same value system as God. At some level we grasp that murder, rape, child molestation and the like are terrible crimes worthy of severe punishment perhaps, yet few of us could begin to comprehend receiving an eternal death penalty for our own little sins, like lying to our friends or simply having selfish thoughts. We want to deceive ourselves into thinking that inconsequential sin somehow exits, and that our sins fit into that category since we didn't murder anyone.

If we want to fully appreciate how fatal all sin is, as a class of evil which disqualifies us from eternal life with God, we would argue that, there is no "low-level" sin in God's theology. All sin represents a vile, reprehensible, class of behavior, which God considers intolerable. God will not tolerate any kind of sin in the Kingdom of heaven, no matter how small you consider it to be. All sin, from the little white lies we wink at, to flirtatious behavior we find cute, but which ultimately leads to lust, to the dark lies that depict deep betrayal and unfaithfulness, falls into a class of evil which God refers to as sin. No matter how we try to redefine, mitigate or sugarcoat it, all forms of sin become fatal. Some sins are truly worse than others, like certain forms of cancer are more aggressive than others and more likely to kill you sooner rather than later. But in the case of sin, remember all sin leads to death. We don't seem to fully appreciate that. We don't share God's values or his outrage over sin any more than we do injustice occurring to someone else on the other side of the world. If we don't see it, it's not nearly as offensive. In a few days we forget all about these terrible things. God doesn't look the other way or stop seeing evil. We simply don't appreciate how God views sin because he doesn't randomly stop detecting it nor does he randomly change the rules for sin, repentance, and forgiveness. We don't fully appreciate that all sin is deadly and that God justly hates all sin, in every form, more passionately than we are capable of hating the genocide of others.

We tolerate, by choice for ourselves, and often because we have no choice for the decisions others make, certain levels of dishonesty, injustice and infidelity and we think God tolerates small levels of sin because we do. We reflect back on the apples and oranges comparison of progressive discipline and we conclude that God wouldn't really send someone to hell for small sins. We also factor in that we should forgive others even as God forgives us. We ponder the concept of both forgiveness and reasonable discipline and we conclude hell doesn't make sense. I can appreciate how this can potentially be confusing but we need to be careful with this. That's why I said at the beginning we misdiagnose sin, what constitutes sin, and what cost is required to pay its wages. Sending anyone to hell would be overkill, right? Perhaps, but only if you looked at this through human eyes and by earthly standards and you came to the conclusion that not all sin was really bad. That would be a huge mistake, deciding that God could be wrong about any aspect of sin. If God views sin this harshly because sin requires a death penalty, why would you not want to ask for forgiveness, if Christ died in your place and offered you eternal life? What possible reason could you have for not asking for his forgiveness?

Is there such a thing as bad and really bad? Sure there is! There is murder and there is stealing a parking space. Now, we are right back at square one, thinking God knows less about this than we do. The more important issue that many people miss is, not whether deeper levels of sin exist, because they do, but rather, do we fully understand that all sin leads to eternal death? You don't have to murder anyone. Just have one sinful thought, because the thought, by spiritual standards, is as real as the deed itself. The wages for sin is death. It doesn't matter how many varieties of sin there are, each one leads to eternal death. We're born with it.

God looks at everything through his eyes with purity of thought in context to eternity. While we hold a delusional view of sin as a cute, harmless, little doggy that wants to hump your leg, God sees it, not only in its infancy, but for what it really is and what it will develop into if not put to death: a deadly infection of your soul, worse than AIDS, or the infected injection site of a heroin user. God understands and foresees what all sin will become just down the road, a week from now, a century from now. God views all sin for the death it bears, beginning with conception and each nurturing embryonic day-by-day life cycle, long before it has produced a visible presence of evil on an ultrasound monitoring screen. All sin is deadly all the time. There are no deadly scorpions or deadly Coral snakes that are not dangerous. If they are deadly to begin with, why would you wonder if they are dangerous? Of course, they are dangerous! We need to reorient our thinking when it comes to the issue of sin. There is no sin, of any kind, which is not by definition bad, or that does not produce eternal death! To think otherwise is a mistake. Such thinking goes contrary to what scripture and common sense teach us regarding sin, and it represents an abdication of critical thinking. Minimizing sin facilitates our desire to avoid taking responsibility for it.

In the book of Revelation (21:7) where it speaks of those who will burn in the lake of fire, which is the second death, one category of sinners mentioned on the list is "all liars." We are so tolerant of lying that we might be shocked these folk are on the Oscar list, or that the list isn't more discriminating. It doesn't even say "the worst of all liars" shall burn in the lake of fire. It says all liars! This is why we need to appropriate the cure. This is why we need forgiveness. Only forgiven liars will be in heaven. I lie to myself all the time because I can't seem to bear the truth about my own ugliness. This is why I ask God to circumcise my heart daily, and forgive me.

Here are just three, of many lies, which Satan incessantly markets:

1. As long as you "believe" in God you will be O.K.
2. Judge yourself in comparison to what others do.
3. You are not a "bad" guy so you have nothing to worry about, because God would never send a "good" person to hell.

Consider what the word of God says:

1. For all have sinned and fallen short of the glory of God (Romans 3:23); Jesus said there is none "good" but one, that is God (Matthew 19:17).
2. For the wages [required payment] of sin is death; but the gift of God is eternal life through Jesus Christ our Lord (Romans 6:23).
3. For whosoever shall call upon the name of the Lord shall be saved (Romans 10:13).

It wasn't your fault that you were born with sin in your DNA and thoughts, but it will be your fault if God points sin out to you, offers you the only cure and payment God is willing to accept, the sacrifice of his son, Jesus Christ, and you decline to accept his precious gift.

Consider what Satan promotes because he is the father of all lies. God promotes his only son who gave his life on the cross for you. Are you going to rely on what the enemy wants you to believe or the words of your creator?

Sin is a fatal disease.

That is not the half of it. Even if we intellectually and spiritually "get it" and understand that sin is very dangerous we don't see sin in ourselves until it becomes overt. Even then sometimes we acknowledge it only if we reach a point where we are embarrassed by our own behavior or feel some sense of guilt. My problem is I don't perceive my own ugliness and even if you point it out to me I may feel no guilt about it, and I may come to the conclusion that there is nothing I can do about it.

One day I was in the locker room at work. I was hot, tired and sweaty. I had not had two minutes to myself all day long, so as to even go to the bathroom. I felt like I had been deprived for two weeks. Another officer walked in, gasped, and said, "Malmin, you need to see a doctor!" Like bad breath or foot odor we are often oblivious to our own sin. Half the time we simply don't even see our own sin. Even when someone offers us a mint or stick of gum we sometimes just say, "No, thanks!" It never even occurs to us our sin is manifesting itself to others. Of course, I'm not speaking only of odor. The prophet Isaiah described the sinful condition of mankind this way: *But we are all as an unclean thing, and all our righteous ways are as filthy rags* (Isaiah 64:6).

We don't even think of some behaviors as being sin nor do we like to use that nasty little word to describe our behavior. After all, it's not sin; it's an alternative lifestyle. We want to think of "alternative" as being equal, just as good as, like a Chevy or a Ford, both being viable, reliable, good options. If we weigh right and wrong honestly, nothing could be farther from the truth because God hates sin and there will be no political compromise on this subject. We have other socially precocious words for "it" because we dislike even referring to the word sin. We tend to minimize these behaviors as being simply misunderstandings, deficiencies, oversights, imperfections, or the like. There are so many eloquent words from which to choose. We just hate using that word *sin*. Sometimes prostitutes are referred to as *call girls* or even *working girls*. Words can be so duplicitous.

When was the last time you heard anyone use the word fornication? I had to look it up in the dictionary to see if it even existed anymore. If you are gossiping at the water cooler, as people sometimes do, you ask: who are you sleeping with? The word fornicating is never used on the street or at the water cooler. At least part of the reason for this, I suspect, is that we intuitively know that there is a moral connection, or religious connotation to the word *fornication*. When we speak of things like this, we don't want to offend anyone or bring morality into the picture so we use other less offensive words.

If you were angry and asking the question as to whether someone was sleeping with your girlfriend, then other vile words may be used but I assure you they won't include fornicating. We dignify infidelity by asking if *so and so* are "sleeping" together. Sometimes people do sleep after passionate sex, but I assure you, the main even is not called sleeping!

We are truly deceitful about our own sin. I am the same way and no better than anyone else. I know that I only see a portion of my own ugliness, but never the whole. If I saw the entirety of my sin, it very well might be more than I could bear and I would recoil into my own little shell to protect myself and not face what I saw. This is where the Lord helps those who ask for it. He will not give you more than you can bear. His work in our lives is a long-term process of changing and refining our character, but it begins with circumcision of the heart.

What scares me because I see it in my own life, is that often I enjoy my sinful ways, the truth be told, and the last thing I truly want to do is either repent of it, or change my behavior. Mostly, we don't want to address this very awkward, uncomfortable subject of sin. We diminish sin and we dress it up and try to ascribe some dignity to it or acceptability. We justify sin as being unavoidable and regrettable, like collateral damage, and that attitude provides a warm shelter for it to live within our hearts. The outside of the castle has lovely landscape, but the wine cellar has rats in it.

If we are somehow forced to talk about our behavior we might say yes, but I never inhaled. Not to worry, sweetheart! I was sleeping with her but it's not what you think. Really? People actually say such things. We were just "sleeping" together. I assure you sleep had nothing to do with it. We were in bed together naked, of course, but nothing ever happened, which is just another deceitful way of trying to say we didn't form a deep, lasting commitment or bond of love (otherwise I would have left you). Some people have such a cavalier attitude about infidelity and sin that they have been known to say such things as: It was just sex; it didn't mean anything, honey.

Sin is like the tip of an iceberg. We don't see most of it; only the tip shows so there is no perception of what lies under the surface level of the water. It is pervasive and ubiquitous and we are born with it in our DNA. We are completely oblivious to our sin when we are sleeping because we are not even aware of our thoughts. We have little or no control over our unconscious thoughts or dreams.

I phrase it as having little or no control because we do have some influence over what stimulates some of our thoughts. For example, if you have filled your mind with concupiscent thoughts before going to sleep you may experience lascivious dreams. I think you probably see what I am getting at. By and large we tend to be unconscious of our sin much of the time, even though we may not want to be this way.

Sin is like a magnet. While God is repulsed by sin and cannot tolerate it, we are drawn to it like bees are to honey. Sin is to God like negative electrical wires are coming into contact with positive electrical wires. Conversely, we are attracted to sin like a magnet and it flows through us just fine like efficient electricity. Our sin alienates us from God and creates a separating barrier because God is repulsed by sin and we are attracted to it.

Like a fish is to water, we are attracted to sin. As a man is attracted to a beautiful woman, so is our human flesh attracted to sin. As a hungry man is attracted to food, so we are attracted to the things we crave. It does not matter to us if someone tells us, that particular food is not good for you. We have already tasted sin and our nature has found it to be desirable.

Understanding "The Fall"

To get a full picture of how we got ourselves into this mess we need to go back in time to mankind's demise. Mankind's fall from grace is the result of sin, which in religious circles, is often simply referred to as *the fall*. The word or phrase, as the case may be, is used in a biblical sense to describe the fall of man.

God created man and put him in the Garden of Eden and told him to dress it and keep it. *And the Lord God commanded the man, saying, of every tree of the garden thou mayest freely eat: but of the tree of the knowledge of good and evil, thou shall not eat of it: for in the day that thou eatest of it thou shalt surely die* (Genesis 2:15-17). Those words were first spoken to Adam.

And the Lord God said, It is not good that man should be alone; I will make him a help meet (Genesis 2:18).

God subsequently created woman as a "help meet" for Adam. God brought the female to Adam and Adam declared: *This is now bone of my bones and flesh of my flesh: she shall be called Woman because she was taken out of Man* (Genesis 2:23). The next verse alludes to her as having the role of "wife" but she is referred to all the way through Chapter Three as the woman. We don't learn her name until Chapter Four.

Scripture does not reveal certain details. For example, scripture does not tell us who told Eve about the fruit of the tree of knowledge of good and evil, as to whether it was Adam or God. What is clear is that both of them knew that the fruit was forbidden. Adam was told not to eat of the fruit. When the woman is beguiled and tempted by the serpent she speaks of not eating or touching the fruit. Both clearly knew the rules, which God had laid out, and the consequences.

Sometimes we don't know what the rules are. A lot of us in life cry foul because the rules of life, our job, or the circumstances we face, are not clear. There is nothing more frustrating that sticking your neck out on the line, trying to do the right thing under pressure, and all of a sudden your head is on the chopping block, because the grownups are not happy with what you did. They couldn't tell you in advance what you should have done because they, themselves, do not know, yet now because of public opinion, the politicians and the powers that be, moved by the force of the changing wind, are now against you. It may cost you your job. This injustice occurs all the time with the affairs of men. Life just seems unfair. Life is unfair; make no mistake about it. It didn't start that way; it became that way because of sin. As long as we are pointing out how unfair life is, we should remind ourselves that, in all fairness, we should be held accountable for our own sin. It was not fair that they nailed Jesus to the cross.

Decent people see the suffering of others all around the world manifested through poverty, disease, famine, and injustice and say: How could a loving God allow such terrible things? This may very well be the most prolific question Satan poses to all humanity and I don't know of a Christian on the planet including myself, who has not pondered this question. The question itself is misleading. It tends to be vaguely suggestive that perhaps, it is God's fault, somehow. Just as Jesus was tempted by the devil in the wilderness, so are we, on a daily basis, with arguments or questions that are really designed with the sole purpose of making us doubt the goodness of God. If Satan can accomplish just that, and nothing more, he has pulled a successful coup.

If we put the disobedience of mankind into another perspective, you might think of it like this: I show up at your house, as a police officer, in uniform, and ask you why you allowed your impetuous, pugnacious son to run out of the house in a fit of anger, drive the car too fast and crash. If you had neither promoted or encouraged this event but, in fact, had tried to prevent it by telling your son not to drive the car, the mere wording of the question would probably make you angry. Why would such a presumptuous question be directed at you with such offensive words? The question is intrinsically biased and suggestive that your son's bad behavior is your fault. Yet, this is exactly how Satan questions the goodness of God, by pointing to all the consequences sin produces around the world. How could a loving God allow such horrible crime, injustice, disease, hunger and famine? If we don't exercise some critical thinking we will forget that God is not the cause of these problems.

The devil wants you to question God's goodness when he asks you how can God allow all these terrible things? Satan would have you accept what he offers as the next logical conclusion, that such a God, who allows this stuff to happen, must not be worth loving or serving. I better just look out for myself in this world. God doesn't care about me or even know I exist. Satan just bought you if you buy into this lie.

God did not create life this way. God did not create sin. Man's disobedience and misuse of free choice produced sin. God made a way of escape and a plan to overcome sin. He provided the cure. This is what we need to remind ourselves every time we see the horrific results of sin around the world. Sin is a deadly disease, which manifests itself in a variety of forms including poverty, disease and famine. It's a sin that we allow poverty to flourish.

Do not let yourself be fooled by the arguments of men: that since terrible things happen around the world God must not really care about mankind. Don't be fooled into thinking that there is someone who loves you more than Jesus. My family knew such a man in the person of Jim Jones. Jim Jones represented himself in his very early days in Indianapolis as a minister of the gospel. His message of love, equality, social justice and his seemingly selfless example of feeding the poor and helping the downtrodden made him look like an angel of light. Jim Jones established himself as the leader of a large group of followers who called themselves People's Temple.

Jim Jones portrayed himself as a gospel preacher in his early days, having been ordained in the Christian Church/Disciples of Christ. Jones preached his own version of the gospel based on the Bible's social values of helping others, but it had nothing to do with sin, repentance or Christ, for that matter. Over a period of time Jim Jones gravitated away from Protestant Christianity toward a gospel of pure socialism and communism. Jones also preached the imminent end of the world and that this would occur in a nuclear war or holocaust. Towards the end of his own time, Jim Jones preached a message of fear and a message which said God did not exist. (http://www.religioustolerance.org/dc_jones.htm)

In People's Temple meetings, a handful of which I attended, Jones would feign himself to be a divine healer. The meetings had religious overtones, but Jim was the whole show and his doctrine could be put into one erroneous statement that socialism essentially cured everything. Jim Jones represented a type of antichrist to me. Jones was cunning and specious beyond imagination. Some of what he said bore some measure of truth in it, but just like Satan, never the whole truth. Jim Jones eventually began to mock the Bible and Christianity. Jones would argue that those who follow Christianity serve in vain a "Sky God" who was no God at all, and that traditional Christianity was nothing more than an opiate of religion, or, "fly away religion," a phrase used to deride the Rapture or second coming of Christ, when we, all the saints of God, go to heaven to be with the Lord.

Jim Jones manipulated people who were downcast and could not care for themselves, into following him to Guyana. This settlement or cult, however you may prefer to view it, was what I would conceptually describe as a private utopian community with pseudo-religious overtones. This settlement was nick named "Jonestown" after their leader Jim Jones. It was here that over 900 people from People's Temple died in a mass murder-suicide from Kool-Aid laced with cyanide. U.S. Congressman Leo Ryan was leading a fact-finding mission to this compound when he and four others were shot down and murdered at Port Kiatuma airstrip trying to leave the Jonestown settlement on November 18, 1978. (http://en.wikipedia.org/wiki/Jim_Jones)

Jesus offers forgiveness for sin. Jim Jones offered cyanide laced Kool-Aid. My sister, Bonnie, flew to Guyana with Congressman Leo Ryan and Jackie Speier and would have either returned with them to the United States or at least gone with them to the airstrip to say goodbye, but for the providence of God, she was led into a nearby town away from the compound where the mass murder-suicides began taking place and away from the airstrip where Leo Ryan and the others were gunned down and murdered.

I remember sitting in Jim Jones' living room in Ukiah talking to him before he and People's Temple members left northern California and went to Guyana. I was a young man at the time and did not fully understand what his true agenda was all about. Being in his presence made me nervous. He picked up a Time magazine from the end table and handed it to me. It depicted a young child that appeared ill and weak, perhaps also undernourished. Jim asked me if I saw what was wrong with the cover photo. The question was so broad I didn't have the foggiest idea of where he was headed with this. Jim said with a sense of outrage, "Look at this child; this child needs oxygen!" He then went into a tirade about social injustice and that most Christians offer no assistance. Jim railed even on the journalist covering the story who took the cover photo for the magazine. Jones argued the journalist should have been administering CPR instead of taking the child's photo.

In my mind this was a perfect paradigm of sophistry. It is not that we do not need to feed the world, nor a matter that we should not be caring for the needy. What Jim Jones said about Christians was not entirely untrue either. All these things are true but we also need Jesus. We could have a world where everyone owned their own oil well, Arco gas station and palace, but we would still need Jesus to make our hearts pure and forgive us of our sins. Sin is a deadly disease, but that is not the half of it. Sin is not limited to sexual infidelity, theft or murder. It shows its ugly face in poverty, disease and hunger.

Jim Jones knew how to tap into people's emotions and if he could find some element of compassion in you, he could twist it and try and make you believe that if all we did was feed people or give them medicine, that alone would suffice. The unspoken words between his lines of compassion were: we don't need Jesus to accomplish that. The downtrodden, the lowly, the lonely, and the hungry people that didn't have a home and who were shown basic humankindness followed Jim Jones. The very ones Jim Jones professed to love so much he murdered. Be careful who you listen to. More importantly, remember there are things more important than food and raiment: your soul!

With God, the injustice, inequity and adversity all around us are opportunities to change the world and he wants to invite us to be partners with him in bringing about this change. He tells his children to love one another so that the lost and dying world all around us might see their heavenly Father through the love and good works of his children. We are supposed to be a light unto the world that is in utter darkness. Our collective failure in accomplishing this job is not the result of God's failure; it is the result of our sin and our failure. We need to better understand the nature of sin and how it came about and stop blaming God for mankind's failures. Be careful who you listen to. Jesus offers Holy Communion. Jim Jones offered cyanide laced Kool-Aid.

If the suffering all around the world is bothering you, that's good! It needs to bother more of us. This is the very mind-set that God wants us to have. The Bible says if we claim that we love God but we hate our brother, we are liars. We are to love one another, and not just in words, but in our deeds as well. We need to love justice. Our love for God should motivate us to feed the hungry and prevent us from sleeping at night until the widow and the orphan are cared for. These are the things which are in the heart of God.

Man's disobedience produced sin; God did not produce it. God wants to use you and me to promote justice and equality and bring change to the world. God's plan is not to cheat people. Jesus said he came that we might have life, and have it more abundantly (John 10:10). God wants to use you as an instrument of his plan, and as a leader and force by which to help others.

God uses the circumstances of tragedy, failure and suffering around us in the world to change and turn things around and he uses people like you and me to accomplish that. God has a wonderful way of redeeming that which is lost and broken. *For we know that all things work together for good, to them who love God, to them who are the called, according to his purpose* (Romans 8:28). It doesn't say all things are good, but rather all things work together for good when we are in Christ. God has a wonderful way of helping us turn our failure and defeat into victory if we turn to him. God is trustworthy! This principle which I am speaking of applies to our every day lives, and it is representative of the story of mankind's sin and God's redemption for us.

As I read this story in Genesis, I find the language and chronology of events fascinating.

If we understand and accept the premise that Satan is a deceiver and the father of all lies, as we know him to be, Satan's approach to Eve on this subject should come as no surprise.

Satan, disguised in the form of a serpent, approaches the woman and poses the following question:

> *Hath God said, you shall not each eat of every tree in the garden? The woman said unto the serpent, we may eat of the fruit of the trees in the garden, but of the fruit of the tree which is in the midst of the garden, God hath said, Ye shall not eat of it, neither touch it, least ye die. And the serpent said unto the woman, ye shall not surely die, for God doeth know that in the day ye eat thereof, then your eyes shall be opened, and ye shall be as gods, knowing good and evil. And when the woman saw that the tree was good for food, and that it was pleasant to the eyes, and a tree to be desired to make one wise, she took the fruit thereof, and did eat, and gave also unto her husband with her, and he did eat* (Genesis 3:1-6).

The first sin was disobedience. God is not against creativity or diversity. God makes each snowflake with a different structural design and he knows the stars by their names. God is not against free-thinking people, creative thinking, critical analysis, independent thinking, or expressions of individuality, or even experimentation. God is against disobedience. If God had said these fruits are good to eat, feel free to try <u>all</u> of them, then there would be no issue here and preference or experimentation could have been freely exercised in the garden.

Here are the rationalizations which were made: the fruit of the tree was perceived as being good for food, the fruit was pleasing to the eyes, and to be desired for wisdom; none of these things seemingly wrong in and of themselves. I can't imagine, for example, God saying, make sure you don't drink milk because it will make your teeth and bones strong. If God did tell us such an unusual thing, we should trust God that he has a good reason, like maybe there was a parasite in the milk that would make us sick, and try not to assume that he is against people having strong bones and teeth. If we make even a small effort at being fair with God, then we could conclude that the forbidden fruit was more a test of obedience, than some divine plan to preclude Adam and Eve from ever having insight or wisdom regarding right and wrong, which is to say, the knowledge of good and evil.

Think about this. The fact that the forbidden fruit had attracting qualities did not make Eve or Adam disobey. Satan would have you believe it's all

God's fault. Even in our current fallen state of sin, people see good things all the time and are not automatically driven to pursue them, let alone take them. Sometimes this does happen but by and large people manifest an ability to control their thoughts, passions, desires and behaviors by virtue of making a *choice* to do the right thing. Evil is frequently entertained, but our choice to do the right thing can also prevail.

Experience shows us that a relatively small percentage (perhaps as little as three to four percent) of the population is responsible for all reported crimes. You can ask any cop with experience on the street this question and they will all agree that the same small percentage of troublemakers keeps officers running ragged. A beat cop knows a lot of these people by name. Another 911 call gets dispatched to the same familiar address. Oh yeah, that's the Jones family! Although everybody commits sin, not everyone acts out their evil thoughts or commits crimes. Sin is usually just the manifestation of choice.

In the city of San Jose, California, where I live, for example, there is a population of nearly one million people. You can be sure that there are many couples who, for whatever reasons, can't seem to have children of their own. The wife can't get pregnant and if she does, she can't maintain the pregnancy. These couples do everything they can to have their own child but without apparent success. These people do not run around the city stealing babies out of hospitals. Such an occurrence is extremely rare. Most people do not entertain such an idea and those few who perhaps do, simply resist the devil, and don't do it. The scripture says, *Resist the devil and he will flee from you* (James 4:7). Imagine that! Is this not exactly what God is trying to teach us?

Even the most vile, base offenders in society who want to commit crimes do not do so without some form of thought, premeditation, and decision making before acting out their evil fantasies and desires. If this were not the case, every bank in the country would be robbed every day of the week, and many more children would be kidnapped and sexually molested. Women would rarely leave the house or push baby strollers to parks because they would get raped every time they left their homes. Sin is a choice.

What led Adam and Eve in the direction of sin and what leads us to do the same, in most cases, is that we allow ourselves to be open to an opposing point of view, that being the sophistry of Satan. We don't resist the devil; we entertain his words to the exclusion of God's words. Remember, words are important and Jesus said, *By your words you shall be justified, and by your words you shall be condemned* (Matthew 12:37). We need to cultivate God's word in our hearts.

Satan tries to divert or distract your attention away from consequences, or he just flat out lies about the consequences. Satan will try to entice us with the so-called good side of sin. Well, of course, there is no good side to sin, but that is exactly what he wants you to think. The deception of Satan appears real and convincing, but the Bible warns us about him and instructs us not to marvel; for Satan himself is transformed into an angel of light (2 Corinthians

11:14). In other words, don't be shocked over this; just understand his trickery. Satan has the ability to appear as an angel of light, just like Jim Jones, but he has no power over you unless you give it to him.

Satan is very well read, understands philosophy and language well, and he is a cunning linguist. He read the same book on "Intro to Philosophy" that you read in college about the tree falling in the forest. If the tree in the forest falls but no one hears it, did it really fall? He incorporates some of these concepts into his own course when he teaches the art of sophistry at the prestigious University of hell. One of his Power Point presentations might be: if a woman is raped in the forest but nobody hears her scream, is she really raped? Another would be: if you enjoy this moment which you richly deserve, and no one knows about it, has any wrong really occurred?

Sin can have a powerful, magnetic, attracting quality. The easiest way to visualize this may be in terms of the beauty or pleasure of sin. In this context one of the best examples I can think of is the powerful sexual drive of men. Men are very visually stimulated. You can be a godly man and you will still be attacked with this temptation. You could be married to the most wonderful woman in the world but, if you are a man and still have blood running in your veins, that beautiful woman who walks by you or displays her charms will attract your attention like a magnet. In fact, for many men it seems almost impossible not to look. Even when your mind catches or perceives the spiritual issue at hand, men still can't seem to stop from taking that casual, quick look.

The first look often can't even be helped because you were not searching for it; circumstances just produced it right in front of you. Even so, your thoughts quietly say, Mama Mia! Check that out! That typically produces a second look and the second look leads to lust. Men in this position can know and understand exactly what is occurring, and be ultimately faithful, but for that one brief moment seem unable to control themselves from taking that look or, as the case may be, that second look. At least that is what we tell ourselves. I couldn't help myself. The devil made me do it. The best solution for this, upon seeing the body of a beautiful woman, is to remind yourself that she is not your woman, and turn your glance and eyes away. Maybe you need to whisper Lord, help me to not have the wrong thoughts or compromise my commitment to you. Jesus, help me! Then walk or run away (as in running away from hell).

Our hearts produce all sorts of phony excuses of diminished capacity, and attenuating lies of harmlessness. This is a two-way road with lots of traffic in both directions. Women dress provocatively because they want to be appreciated and found pleasing in the eyes of men, and men enjoy looking at the sensuality of these women and many love to take advantage of them from a position of power and control. We don't want to say it like it is. Men often say it's O.K. to just look at beautiful woman and appreciate beauty. Men will say it is O.K. to look as long as you don't touch. The problem is looking inclines us to want to touch and it also produces thoughts of lust. Sometimes even the woman will say to her mate that he can look as long as he doesn't touch. The woman who says this probably doesn't believe it herself, because she knows intuitively that looking produces lust, and why would she be O.K. with that? When the woman says this, she is acquiescing for a lesser standard in her mate, perhaps because she doesn't want to appear too rigid, demanding or unreasonable, and she understands that she cannot control his thoughts anyway; but it is not a matter that she should be unconcerned over. The absence of high standards can lead to broken relationships. Where does all this earthly wisdom, that looking is O.K. but touching is even better, come from? This is the sophistry of Satan.

One time I offered to my eight-year-old son the opportunity to watch a movie with me that, unbeknown to me, his mother had previously instructed him to not watch. In talking to him about why we don't do some things, his mother did an excellent job of explaining how we need to guard our eyes and protect our hearts and our integrity before God. My son said he could not watch the movie with me and that he should "let no evil come before my eyes." I was stunned by his words and that he was choosing to abide by them. I didn't think the movie was a problem but in his mind it obviously thought it contained evil. Watching the video would have been wrong for him. I was proud of him. King David wrote, *Thy word have I hid in my heart that I might not sin against thee* (Psalms 119:11). Oh, that we would listen to the words of God instead of others!

One of the things about Jesus that is wonderful is that he has no guile. Jesus' words are never specious. He is not deceitful and he does not sugarcoat his words or important issues. Jesus said that when a man looks upon a woman with lust in his heart he has already committed adultery with her (Matthew 5:28). The average guy might think well, what's so wonderful about that? The words of Jesus might make us all feel terrible. The Savior's words should make us feel *convicted of our sin* so that we modify our sinful behavior. Jesus' words are wonderful because his words and ways lead to eternal life and they teach us how to overcome. More importantly, Jesus forgives us and cleanses us from all unrighteousness. Righteousness is a choice and the Lord will help you, if that's what you want. My problem is that I don't even want to do the right thing sometimes, so I have to pray, Lord, help me to *want* to do the right thing to begin with.

Sin is a choice, but often, as it was with Adam and Eve, it begins as a process of deliberation. We ignore the words of God or what we believe to be the right thing, and we choose to do our own thing. Sin is extremely subtle but in failure analysis, it is a choice. Like choosing beauty to the exclusion of character, sin leads to a lifestyle. Satan tells us if you follow God's plan you can't have both; you will never have pleasure. Words are important. Even the words of Satan are important because we should remember that he puts spin and distortion on his words and that he is a lair and his words are not to be trusted. The truth is that in God we can have both beauty and character! The truth about God's word is that it promotes life, not death.

Sin is a fatal disease.

We don't see in advance the consequences of sin or its impact on us down the road. When Adam and Eve sinned they did not physically die right that moment, but spiritually they did, and their spiritual death eventually lead to physical death. Sin produced the genesis of both spiritual and physical death for all humankind.

There were also immediate changes and consequences. They had new feelings and emotions of fear and shame they had not known before.

> *And they heard the voice of the Lord God walking in the garden in the cool of the day: and Adam and his wife hid themselves from the presence of the Lord. And the Lord called unto Adam and said, Where art thou? Adam answered and said, I heard thy voice in the garden and I was afraid because I was naked and I hid myself* (Genesis 3:8-10). *One of the first byproducts of sin that we see is fear.*

> *God asked Adam, Who told you that you were naked; did you eat of the fruit, which I commanded you not to eat of? Adam becomes the first person to play the blame game. Adam's response to whether he ate of the fruit was not simply, Yes, but instead he tells the Lord that the woman whom thou gavest to be with me, she gave me of the tree, and I did eat* (Genesis 3:11-12).

This almost sounds like an attorney talking about diminished capacity or product liability. It's not my fault; the woman that you provided to be my wonderful companion was defective. Adam doesn't say that, of course, but his words have their own distinctive flavor of sin, disguised in a delicate sauce of guile and culpability. Adam did not talk this way yesterday, before he disobeyed. Adam's words make it almost sound as though it was entirely the woman's fault and he had no role in it. She gave it to me, so I had to eat it. The devil made me do it. Grown people actually say this because the world thinks it is kind of cute.

Satan will disguise himself as a benevolent consumer advocate and whisper in your ear that God created a defective product. That is a lie from the pit of hell. Yet, Satan whispers this to Christians all the time. Your marriage is not going to last because your spouse is defective and you should just get another one quickly, before life passes you by. Don't listen to the words of Satan! He is never going to tell you to wait patiently upon the Lord.

Satan's words will invariably sound plausible, ostensibly true, yet be factually misleading and errant and he will cause confusion for you over what God's word says. It doesn't matter if a portion of Satan's words are true; if the whole sentence is not true, then the entire statement is false. Remember that from the third or fourth grade? All of Satan's words and works ultimately produce death. That's what we need to constantly remember.

Don't let your guard down because the first taste of sin seemed to have no ill effects or because death wasn't instantaneous. Satan likes to use the slow, time-release method like some of our medications. Before you know it, you will get hooked on Satan's nefarious gourmet delicacies. It's a big mistake to think that if you are really careful you might be able to do business with this guy. All of Satan's roads lead to hell. That's why I repeatedly use the phrase sin is a *fatal disease* in this chapter to drive the point home that this is not a cosmetic thing that a little mouthwash will take care of. Sin is a terminal condition if it goes untreated.

God created both man and woman with free choice. Either Adam or Eve could have said wait a minute, the Lord told us not to eat of this fruit so we should ask him if there are any exceptions to this commandment before we start disobeying his words. God will not force you to follow his precepts nor walk in the path of his righteousness. We have to want to do so. Walking with God is a choice. Many choose not to.

Adam could have been a leader but he apparently made a decision by default. Do nothing; don't challenge it or question it; offer no alternative; and least of all, don't ask God for wisdom or clarification. Early American Colonial statesman Edmund Burke was credited with saying: All that is necessary for evil to triumph is for good men to do nothing.

As you will see, there were immediate, ugly, results because of sin and more to follow. *Unto the woman the Lord said, I will greatly multiply thy sorrow and thy conception; in sorrow thou shalt bring forth children; and thy desire shall be to thy husband, and he shall rule over thee* (Genesis 3:16).

Why are women not treated more fairly and equitably in the home and labor markets and why are they not given more respect in almost every aspect of life? Hello! Consider the collective sin of both genders and the subsequent consequences that followed both Adam and Eve for their disobedience. The consequences of sin resulting from the *fall* are often referred to as *the curse*. This inequality and duplicitous relationship men have with women resulted from the *fall of mankind* but it can be reversed because Jesus made it possible.

If we love our wives as Christ loved us and gave his life for us, we will learn to treat women justly, as collaborating partners. We should learn to put others above ourselves because we have become new creatures in Christ. We can forgive one another with Christ's help and we should not hold the judgment or punishment of our curse over anyone's head. We don't have to follow the natural consequence of sin, which the curse produced, but that involves, forgiveness, grace and sacrifice. Like other value judgments we make, this too becomes a choice.

Unto Adam the Lord said, because thou hast harkened unto the voice of thy wife, and hast eaten of the tree, of which I commanded thee, saying, thou shalt not eat of it: cursed is the ground for thy sake; in sorrow shalt thou eat of it all the days of thy life. Thorns and thistles shall it bring forth to thee; and thou shalt eat the herb of the field; in the sweat of thy face shalt thou eat bread, till thou return unto the ground; for out of it wast thou taken: for dust thou art, and unto dust shalt thou return (Genesis 3:17-19).

These are pretty grim words. The result of sin and the consequences which followed, are thus known as *the curse*. The good news of Christ is that he bore the sin of our curse on the cross and Jesus has overcome sin, death and the grave.

The first sin was the result of disobedience. All humankind is born with it and it manifests itself early in life, passed down to us through the generations of all our families. Disobedience can be seen in children at an early age. But even when we see it, we don't necessarily think of it as sin. Sometimes we think of it as being cute. We wink at it.

I was a very small child of about four or five years of age. My family lived in Chicago. We had moved recently to a new neighborhood and we lived close to a busy thoroughfare, which had a small mom and pop liquor store. I would go down to this store all by myself and buy an ice cream bar. Because of traffic concerns and safety issues my mother told me to not go to this store anymore. Having no money of my own, and not being sophisticated enough to rob a bank, I decided to steal some of my father's loose change, which he placed on top of a tall dresser. Using a chair, which I stood on, I reached up to the top of the dresser and took my father's money. I believe we still call that *stealing*. I then went down to the liquor store and bought myself a delicious ice cream bar. I was stupid enough to come walking into the house licking my chops when my mother saw me and confronted me. My heart sank into the pit of my stomach and I felt weak at the knees knowing I had not only stolen money, but also disobeyed my mother. By my count that was two crimes! She looked sternly at me and asked, "I thought I told you not to run down to that liquor store anymore?" Without batting an eyelash, or even having to think about plausible deniability, I replied, "Mommy, I didn't run, I walked!"

Our human nature is such that it doesn't take years to develop this kind of character guile or sophistication, only the number of months or less that you would take for an auto loan. By the time your kid is 48 months old your car loan will be paid off and your kid will have developed the ability to be deceitful. My mother tried not to laugh because she thought my deceitfulness was charming! I knew she was not talking about whether I had "run" down to the liquor store or walked down. I have been afraid of burning in hell ever since that day!

This is how sins works but that is not the half of it.

We think sin looks cute. The story may be cute but our sin is not. We forget that. Here I was, all of four or five years old but with the guile of a silver-tongued devil.

Sin is a deadly disease but that is not the half of it.

We like it! That ice cream was delicious. My mother knew better but she turned and looked the other way.

You don't think we learn from this? We learn to become accomplished liars! By the time most of us are ten years old we understand right and wrong well enough to teach a law course on the subject to people in hell. Duplicity comes naturally because it is in our own flesh, and we see it in our parents and in everyone we come in contact with. We quickly learn how to refine it, perfect it and replicate it. Duplicity taught me that if I have to pay for a speeding ticket I should tell my wife that it was for a pullover I purchased for her. If you run into someone who doesn't do these things, you just met Jesus!

The aftermath of sin impacts others

Sin is a deadly disease but that is not the half of it.

The road to hell gets worse further down the road but we never seem to consider that possibility because we reassure ourselves, during the deliberation process, that we won't get caught. Our decision to sin involves, at minimum, an unconscious decision to disregard the morality of whether it is right or wrong. The morality of our decision becomes secondary to the fact that our behavior reflects what we really want: that which is forbidden. Even if we struggle with the decision, knowing it's a bad one, we choose to cave in to our desire, disregard what God's laws would say about it, because it's what we want and, if we convince ourselves that no one else will find out about it, we decide, in effect, that it doesn't matter if God knows about it. We don't see our thinking mapped out for us in such a homilitical fashion, but it's nefarious.

We don't see where this road will lead but even if we are told we tend to disregard it. It did not stop Adam and Eve and it is not stopping us. The beginning never looks that bad. We have no idea how it will play out, nor how it will hurt us, or others. In the beginning, it may just look like the beautiful woman I spoke of earlier, pretty good. We read in scripture that the wages of sin is death and we ask for some fries to go with it.

Prostitution and drug use are victimless crimes. That is what some liberals advocate. Professors of higher learning, no pun intended, advocate some of these concepts and reduce these issues to nothing more than personal liberties and government intrusion. The genesis of such thinking comes from the father of all lies. It represents to me a paradigm of classical humanism and sophistry, which equates to justifying anything we want to do.

On the front page of my local newspaper I read headlines reporting the results of a federal probe that linked the governor of New York state to a prostitution ring, wherein he allegedly was caught on a wiretap arranging to meet with a high priced prostitute at a Washington hotel last month. The newspaper had a photo of the governor standing with his wife at his side during a news conference. The article and the governor's statements, which were obtained from the New York Times, stated that the governor apologized and it quoted him as saying, "I have acted in a way that violates my obligations to my family and violates my [sic] or any sense of right and wrong." (San Jose Mercury News 3/11/2008)

If a picture is said to be worth a thousand words, the media photo of the governor and his wife must have been the picture spoken of. The facial body language said it all. The governor, from my perception, looked humiliated, ashamed and disappointed with himself. He was quoted in the newspaper article as having also said, "I have disappointed and failed to live up to the standard I expected of myself..." The look on his wife's face seemed to reflect deep hurt that one can only imagine. The shame and humiliation of what they both must have felt facing national media is something few of us will ever likely face. The photo of them and the expressions on their faces made you want to cry. How many people in this family and beyond do you think were affected and hurt by this tragedy?

The next day, New York Governor Eliot Spitzer resigned under intense political pressure. Spitzer was quoted by the AP as having said, "I look at my time as governor with a sense of what might have been."

[Verena Dobnik & Michael Gormley, Associated Press March 12, 2008] (http://news.yahoo.com)

So, why is sin such a big deal?

Sin destroys what might have been. We don't ever foresee the full impact or the consequences of sin before harvest time because the beginning doesn't look problematic. We later think: *If I had only known what the outcome was going to be I would have never done this.* Well, God is trying to tell us all along that sin leads to death.

My friend is a school teacher. Her principal was recently exposed in an affair with another staff member from the same school. Staff members had been talking about their suspicions for months. Tremendous animosity arose among some of the staff because of the perception of favoritism. As this saga continued to unfold two staff members got into a verbal argument at school, over school business matters. The principal appeared to unjustly punish one of the parties over the incident.

Eventually, it came to light that the other involved party in the argument, the one who was not punished, was sleeping with the principal. Talk about a conflict of interest! Everybody in the school district gradually became aware of the affair and the malfeasance or perception thereof. The principal was transferred to another school. My friend and one of her coworkers spoke with the principal in private about this incident. The principal openly wept tears in front of both women and apologized for violating the trust of all staff members and for his lack of integrity in not disclosing the relationship to his staff. He never planned for things to happen the way they turned out.

This is exactly how sin works, not at all the way we planned it.

Both of these incidents are examples of how we deeply wound and hurt other people by our sin and how we have no idea of how our conduct will impact others until after it happens.

Luminaries who sit behind mahogany desks, live in opulent, custom designed homes, within safely guarded neighborhoods, who draw lucrative salaries, and who write articles pontificating that drug use is a victimless crime, either don't have real life experience outside of academia and sheltered environments, or perhaps they live in a theoretical utopia of strawberry fields and delusion, or use drugs themselves. Sure makes me wonder what they are smoking.

If you ride along with the officers who patrol and protect our streets you will learn quickly that nothing could be farther from the truth. The Narcotics Task Force (NTF) for San Mateo County Sheriff's Office can document crimes in which babies have been sold for crack cocaine. Please do not insult me and other professionals in the criminal justice field with vacuous statements that suggest drug use is a victimless crime. The addiction to drugs is so strong that these users, while victims themselves, rob, steal, cheat and plunder anyone they can, including their own family members, just to get their next fix. Babies, born under the influence of heroin or methamphetamine, sometimes with birth defects, are not victimless users of drugs.

If you ever get an occasion to see a heroin user with an infected injection site, you will discover that the whole appendage eventually becomes infected. In some cases the lack of medical care or hygiene will result in amputation. These people wrap their infected sores with filthy bandages or unsanitary dressings, which further contribute to the infection. When they are brought to the jail the bandages must be removed. The sight and disgusting smell of infected flesh, from which puss drips off their injection sites, are enough to make one vomit. I'm sorry, but neither sin or drug use is a victimless crime.

The California Department of Corrections (CDC) conducts interviews of felons who are housed in the state prison system. CDC supervises these felons during the term of their parole. The CDC collects statistical information on recidivism rates along with other interview data. This information shows that felons commit a staggering number of felonies in comparison to the few that they are actually sentenced for. The number of victims and family members that are impacted by each felon is probably impossible to even calculate, if one counted the broken heart of every felon's mother as well. There is no such thing as a victimless crime or sin.

So, why is sin such a big deal?

You're kidding, right?

Sin flourishes under nearly every condition, requires no fastidious maintenance, cultivation or nurturing, feeds off of itself, replicates itself and spreads aggressively, becomes cyclic, generational and self-fulfilling. Governments can't eliminate it and science does not understand it. Moreover, sin is extremely toxic and hazardous and impervious to all human or synthetic cleaning agents. Unlike Plutonium-239 with a half-life of only 24,000 years or so, sin produces eternal toxicological results. It is the most deadly substance known to mankind. The only substance known to destroy this incredibly deadly disease has proven to be the blood of Jesus!

We don't tell babies not to touch the hot stove because they don't understand words yet, nor can they understand the danger of hot stoves until they learn how to speak and communicate and learn from empirical experience. If you tell a small child not to touch the stove because they will burn themselves, the child will still have no idea of what you are talking about until they can develop some sensory perception of what that actually means. We show them that fire, or other heating elements may glow orange or red and we allow them to feel the warm air coming out of the heater. We then tell the child, as only a mother can, "Hot! Don't touch!" Good parenting and training promotes learning.

The full dosage of that teaching never completely sinks in until the child actually experiences some small level of pain from the heat. Only then does the child completely understand what you are talking about when you warn them to be careful because the stove is hot. Until the child experiences this defining moment of pain, they may, based on your training, be intellectually thinking the stove is warm.

The heat that came out of the furnace on the wall was warm, but you did not tell them that. The child does not fully understand what hot is until the child gets burned, and because you are most likely a good parent, the burn is superficial, and so the child still has not fully grasped just how bad hot can be. Neither the child nor you have adequately visualized what hell is like, or that sin really leads us there.

Satan understands this as well and since you have not experienced eternal hell and cannot fully comprehend it, he tempts you with beguiling words. Try this exotic flavored dish of gourmet sin; you'll like it! If you question it, he might reply that it's not *that* hot, it is more like what I would call warm or spicy. If he thinks you are not into hot, warm or spicy, and that you are attracted to cold, he may try and persuade you that they have ice-cold beer and Coca Cola in hell. Be careful who you listen to.

Sin is a deadly disease but that is not the half of it.

We don't teach this to our children and we don't see how it impacts family life. How can a child come to understand and appreciate eternal matters if we don't properly teach them? The Bible says, *Train up a child in the way he should go, and when he is old, he will not depart from it* (Proverbs 22:6).

Kids pretty much grow up not appreciating spiritual consequences because all that so many can seem to fathom or cope with is the present and the immediate. Children are not adequately learning about delayed gratification because their families and our social fabric and institutions are not teaching it well enough or modeling it for them. We don't do enough to promote consequences at any level so how do we expect people to fully appreciate and plan for the eternal consequence? We don't even talk to them about sin or help them understand how sin hurts us and how to avoid it. A lot of kids don't get enough love or nurturing. If basic human love and nurturing are not provided, how can we expect a child to understand higher spiritual matters?

We grow up seeing others cut corners, breaking rules and cheating and, by and large getting away with it. When we get caught we laugh at each other or wink and say you're *bad*, and that is more often than not, taken as a compliment! Earthly laws work or succeed largely because of compliance. Kids who are learning all the wrong things in life may not appreciate that the heavenly standards of accountability based on spiritual laws are very different from earthy forms of accountability.

How sin impacts parenting, children and adolescents

Words are important. Your words will make the difference between life and death. Yet, we quickly learn as children that words sometimes mean next to nothing. Failure to obey does not always produce consequence. This failure in turn diminishes our understanding of what accountability is about. We sometimes witness examples of this with poor parenting. Mothers, who are underappreciated, overworked, underpaid, and who lack resources and support of all kinds, often lack the knowledge of how to effectively parent. The state requires a driver's license for driving but nothing for parenting. Mothers and fathers both fall into these categories of being underappreciated, overworked, and underpaid, but since the mother is more often at home with the little ones, we see some of these issues occur more with the mother since she cares for the children all day. Mothers who have little or no support tell their kids: just wait until your father gets home; I am going to tell him what you did! For better or for worse, nothing happens.

We see a distraught mother in the supermarket who is at her wit's end telling a two-year-old over and over the same repeated broken song: Don't do that! I told you not to do that! Didn't mommy tell you not to do that? Mommy is going to punish you if you do that again. What did I just say? Stop it! Don't do that! How many times do I have to tell you not to do that? Mommy is going to spank you if you do that one more time!

After a few minutes of this nonsense I am ready to scream. The child may even feel the same frustration I do. In fact, if this keeps up, the child in a few years will tell his mother to shut up. That may happen sooner than you think. It actually starts with simply disobedience. Does that sound familiar?

The child will test the waters with slightly less pugnacious language to see what the reaction is, but all of this will eventually lead to contumacious behavior and insolence from the child. The child learns from the parents' behavior that there is little to no accountability, and that disobedience is usually met with only verbal protests. The child will listen to the ideas of their friends who openly and defiantly practice sinful behavior with their parents. The child may also learn from others how to deceitfully manipulate application of the law and their parents' understanding of the law so as to falsely and unjustly threaten their parents with child abuse. At this stage precocious kids can sometimes get away with almost anything. Once the minor has reached this level of perfidious behavior they will probably become bold enough to use stronger language than just "shut up," some-where right around age fifteen or so, and when that happens it will be wrong, but it will not be difficult to understand why it happened.

Many of these kids run away from home when they are around fifteen years old. Parents initially act shocked. If you talk with parents and review the family history, the parents usually agree that kids don't just wake up one morning out of the thin blue air, from a completely healthy family environment, and decide they hate their parents and don't not want anything further to do with them. When events such as this occur, they usually happen because there has been dysfunction in the family for a long time. That doesn't make it all the parents' fault either, but if there has been an absence of love or nurturing or a healthy cultivating relationship in the minor's life, the juvenile will look for it elsewhere. Attempting to fill this vacuum is why some kids get into gangs and others meet predators on the Internet.

The parent who lacks love, righteousness and justice, and who is all talk and hot air, effectually teaches their child that the parent's ranting, vociferous tirade of endless words is meaningless. This child is going to have a very difficult time grasping the concept of accountability because their home life and parenting environment do not model this for them. Accountability is completely absent. This is a destructive form of sin that gets passed from the parents down to the children, largely because of the parents' failure to lead godly lives, teach their children godly values, and hold them accountable to godly standards.

I have seen this over and over again in dysfunctional families who call the police for assistance. A distraught mother would lament, "Officer, I told Johnny that I didn't want him out past 2 A.M. drinking on school nights since he is only 15 years old, but he just told me not to worry and walked right out the door. I'm worried he might be hanging out with the wrong crowd." Go figure! I have actually seen parents tolerate this behavior because the kid, although an affiliated gang member, was actually getting quite good grades, and so the parents decided to expect nothing more. By the time some of these kids grow up they have learned a lot of bad habits.

Some of these parents are unskilled and their lives so overwhelmed by poverty, need, the absence of meaning in their own lives, and by sin, that while they may actually love their kids, they have nothing to offer them. The parents need nurturing themselves.

Some of these kids could not tell you or remember when they last sat at the table and had breakfast together as a family. For many families, the only common thread that the family shares is alcohol. Many of these kids could not tell you the last time their father spoke to them without swearing at them or the last time their father said a kind word. Many of these kids could not tell you the last time they saw their father or the last time they saw him sober. Some of these kids could not tell you who their father is.

Most of these kids grow up without experiencing healthy, well-balanced forms of accountability, love and nurturing and discipline. Everything in life that is healthy, wholesome, loving, good, nurturing, protective, enduring, and altruistic is representative of God's ways. In contrast, all sin leads to hell.

The complete dysfunction and collapse of some families is so profound that some of these people cannot maintain basic home hygiene or safety. Many homes are found to have victimized children of real sexual and physical abuse. Social Services has to step in and take the children away from the family.

Sin is a deadly disease.

As a juvenile detective I saw how confused some kids get over authority and accountability because of poor parenting and, ironically, because of the juvenile criminal justice system itself.

The philosophy of the California Juvenile Justice System is that the system is designed to be therapeutic and rehabilitative. The system is not intended be punitive in nature. The Juvenile Justice System is built to help and treat juveniles, not simply punish them.

The entire system is completely different from the adult criminal justice system. Juveniles are not called delinquents or criminals because we do not want to stigmatize them with labels. The whole juvenile system is a world unto itself in that it differs from the adult system. Unlike adults, juveniles are not technically "convicted" of crimes, but rather adjudicated to be Wards of the Court.

If a minor is charged with an offense, a "Petition" is filed as opposed to criminal charges. Kids are not found "guilty" of anything theoretically because they are not technically charged with crimes. The functional equivalent of a guilty verdict is a finding by the court that the Petition is true, or sustained. If and when a Petition is sustained, the court finds the minor to be within the provisions of 602 of the Welfare and Institutions Code (on matters that are criminal in nature) and the minor is adjudicated to be a "Ward of the Court" as mentioned above. There is a lot of legal terminology that is very specific to juvenile law in California. Less serious matters referred to as "Status Offenses" fall under section 601 of the W&IC. These include disobedience to parents, curfew violations, truancy and running away.

By and large the juvenile system works reasonably well, and each case is independently reviewed and evaluated. Kids who have a good attitude and who demonstrate repentance or remorse for their behavior are generally treated very leniently. The kid who has never been in any trouble or commits a minor offense benefits from such a system because the system can say: we forgive you; go and sin no more. Even the cop on the street can do that without even arresting the kid if the minor is young enough and the offense is minor. Tremendous discretion is built into the system.

If a juvenile is charged with a very serious crime like murder, they can be tried as an adult under a variety of different legal circumstances. If the juvenile has been in the system a long time, is perhaps becoming older and committing more serious crimes with more frequency, the Juvenile Court judge may come to a determination that the minor is no longer suitable or amenable to treatment under the auspices of the juvenile court system. Examples of this would include crimes that are more sophisticated and behavior by the minor that tends to show a hardened attitude or disposition that is incompatible with treatment. If such findings are made by the Juvenile Court, the legal proceedings can then be transferred to the adult court system.

While the system is mostly fair, in my opinion, and full of mercy, compassion and leniency, some of these kids get too many breaks along the way. They say all the right things in court and produce tears of remorse like academy award nominees while standing in front of the judge with their attorney and parents, but their attitude sometimes mocks the entire criminal justice system. When they turn eighteen years old these heretofore minors become adults legally by law. A good number of them have unintentionally been misled by the system because the law is so lenient with juveniles.

These young teens reach adulthood not understanding well enough that they will be going to an adult jail in the real world, and that they will be held accountable to a much higher standard. I have transported many of these kids to both Juvenile Hall and the main county jail. Some of these kids have committed many crimes as juveniles but never really had to pay much of a price. All of a sudden they commit one serious crime as a young adult and now they are on their way to state prison. This scenario is reflective of the mother in the supermarket saying: Don't do that! Stop it! Mommy is going to punish you if you do that again! All of this is said time and time again with no consequences. Before you know it this young kid is slapped into next week and sent to state prison. In terms of the righteousness of progressive discipline this is intrinsically unjust. The human factor also plays in. There is never complete uniformity or justice with anything created and administered by mankind.

If we consider this same principle in spiritual terms we set some of these kids up and groom them for hell. This is simply one of a million reasons why I say sin is a deadly disease. Some of these kids would do far better if there were real consequences from day one. Like war, disease, famine and death, sin is always ugly; it does not have a "good" side to it as we may think in our foolishness; it leads to death.

After Juvenile Hall these kids go to the main jail and the first thing they learn to ask for is a "program." Programs are classes or rehabilitation efforts of one kind or another, either in the jail, or in a structured program run outside the jail, which are designed to help inmates overcome various weaknesses, which play a contributing factor to their incarceration. Examples of this might include basic educational skills, anger management, other mentoring forms of discipline and self-control, and the ever-ubiquitous issue of drug and alcohol addiction. These programs are very therapeutic and helpful and even efficacious for those who honestly and diligently apply themselves. In that context, there is nothing wrong with these programs, as they are tremendously helpful for some people. But like everything else, the potential for abuse is always present.

People who go to these programs do so in lieu of spending more time in jail or instead of going to prison. Every child molester, murder or rapist in the county jail would go to one of these programs if they could, and it always amazed me how many of these guys "found Jesus" when they thought it could help them get out of jail sooner. Good judges don't allow every Tom, Dick or

Harry to go to these programs, nor do judges become easily swayed by insincere inmates who have "found" Jesus. Good judges know from experience that too many defendants lose Jesus faster than they found him.

What kills me is humanity's insincerity about sin and our personal feelings about accountability for each of our own lives, and I am including myself here also. None of us want it. We want mercy and forgiveness but no consequences. This reflects the very nature of sin itself and gives us a glimpse of why it is nefarious and deadly. The fruit of sin is not repentance. Sin leads to cover-ups and further sin.

Some of these kids who get sent to county jail come from Juvenile Hall. By the end of their first day in county jail they have learned to ask for "programs." I found it to be pretty amazing!

"Hey, Deputy! I need a program; you got a program for me, dude?" a prisoner would ask.

"Yeah," I would answer, "I got a program for you: try our *obey the law program*; and by the way, remember my name is 'Deputy,' not 'dude.'"

Sin is a deadly disease but that is not the half of it.

The arrogance of man is itself another by-product or symptom of sin. We think others will be caught, judged and punished but we won't. We flatter ourselves into thinking we won't have to worry about accountability because of our powerful position or status. We seem to think the spiritual law which tells us that sin will lead to death and that, whatever we sow we shall also reap, will not apply to us. This is what every seemingly successful, yet arrogant man has thought from the recent fall of Governor Spitzer of New York, to Richard Nixon, President of the United States, to King David, King of Israel. Understand also these principles apply to all aspects of sin and not simply the sin of sexual immorality. Your weak link may have nothing to do with sexual infidelity. Sex just happens to be an easy example to understand. Your issue could be money or power and control over others. It doesn't matter. Sin is a deadly disease.

The sophistry and guile of sin leads us to avoid thinking about our own responsibility and need to repent and ask for forgiveness. You need a wonderful savior. We allow ourselves to get legalistic and think bold thoughts such as: a loving god would not send people to hell, at least not for minor sins, and mine weren't that bad. The ones you are thinking about may not be the sum total, but your pride in not seeing your need for a savior is a killer. A loving God would not send people to hell. I think you are absolutely right! When the evidence is presented it will show that Jesus did everything including dying on the cross for you. Unlike the police, Jesus would not kick the door down to your residence; nor would he force his way into your heart. The door to your heart does not need a dead bolt. A thin curtain will serve just fine. Simply closing your heart is enough to keep him out. Jesus said: But whosoever shall deny me before men, him will I also deny before my Father, which is in heaven (Matthew 10:33). Jesus has offered you forgiveness and eternal life and you want nothing to do with it?

It does not have to end this way. Jesus stands at the door of your heart and knocks. You can open the door and invite him in. If you choose not to do so, then remember that when you stand before him and ask if a loving God would send anyone to hell, consider that his answer will be: No, sir! You have done this to yourself by the consequence of your choice. I sent my only son to die in your place to pay for the penalty of your sin, but you rejected this priceless gift, so now you will pay for the wages of your own sin. Remember the words of Jesus: *By your words you will be justified, and by your words you will be condemned* (Matthew 12:37).

Your sin needs to be dealt with and paid for! Who is going to pay for it? I hope it's not you, because you can't afford it! If you haven't dealt with this issue then do it now. Put this book down, get on your knees, repent and ask for the Lord's forgiveness. What can wash away your sin? Nothing but the blood of Jesus! You need a wonderful Savior that can save your soul, and who is willing to walk by your side and guide you in life. Invite the Lord into your heart and ask him to make you a new person. It's the best *program* you'll ever find! When Jesus enters your heart he will turn your life upside down, and inside out, and when he does this, you'll realize how wonderful he is and you'll want to surrender your entire life to him and claim him as your friend and Savior.

Why not start right now? Serving the Lord instead of other things will bless your life richly beyond what you can fully understand right now. The pursuit of other *things* will ultimately destroy you in the long run. If you sincerely ask God to come into your life Christ will answer your prayer and help you turn your life into something far more meaningful and wonderful than anything you could ever do on your own.

Hey, dude! Have I got a *program* for you!

What kind of program is it?

It's called eternal life, and it's only offered at the cross.

72

CHAPTER 3

WHO'S GOING TO MAKE IT?

This subject is intrinsically sensitive. I am speaking of when time is no more. I am speaking of your eternal destiny. When time is no more as we currently fathom it, time will then become endless. Where do you think your soul is headed when it comes to the issue of eternity? Your spiritual destiny is a subject that you can have absolute confidence and peace of mind about. Walk through this with me.

As I mentioned, all of us are on either one side or the other of Jesus, just like the two thieves on the cross who were being crucified alongside of Jesus. Your destiny with Christ boils down to a decision that no one else but you can make. It boils down to the decision of whether you sincerely ask Christ to forgive you, and give you a new heart. Becoming a new creature in Christ is not the same as simply saying I hope I go to heaven. Whether or not the Lord invites you into his Kingdom is based on whether you invite him into your life and ask him sincerely to forgive you. Whether or not you accept his gift of forgiveness or have anything to do with him is a decision; one that will be made irrespective of whether you do it now, or you wait until you are unable to do anything about it. That also would be, in itself, a decision. I urge you not to wait until it may be too late. Too many people think, *I'll do it later* but never get the opportunity *later*.

Sometimes I like to think, we've come a long way, baby! The industrial revolution gave us machines to manufacture products much faster than we could by hand, piece by piece. We not only have electricity, we have laser beam technology and we understand fission and fusion. Medicine has, for all practical purposes, eliminated the disease of Polio and mortality rates have decreased. We live in a current age of technology and information and the human genome has been mapped. We have actually learned over time that tobacco companies manufacture a product that causes cancer, and that smoking is not a healthy thing. It took a long time to get to this point.

When I was growing up people argued about whether tobacco caused cancer or not because two people in the United Stated lived until they were almost 100 years old and they both smoked, but never had cancer. When I was in the Army cigarettes were so cheap they practically gave them to soldiers, thereby marketing the product for years to come. Americans allowed companies to market tobacco products to our children and suggest to them they were cool, independent, and rugged if they smoked.

Tobacco companies were happy to argue that there was no proof that cigarettes caused cancer, and they were partially correct in their position; not because of the truth of the matter, but because no one had actually done any hard scientific investigative research to prove the point. The facts have subsequently proven that nicotine is as addictive as heroin and more deadly than heroin in terms of lung disease. Science did not fail us back then. What failed was our own honest effort to pursue scientific clinical studies, which would subsequently reveal the truth about cigarettes.

There is a spiritual lesson here that goes beyond cigarettes and cancer. If you put your heart into it you will find that God hasn't failed us anymore than science has. Our lack of passion, hunger for truth, tenacity and only a half-hearted Laodicean pursuit of God have produced our own systemic failures. It is a mistake to blame God or science for our failures or lack of knowledge.

The FDA requires nutritional information and expiration dates on various foods now. On the bag of potato chips I just opened it had a label on it that read, "0 grams Trans Fat." I surmised that this must be a good thing; these chip are healthy, so I plan on eating the whole bag! Forget the nutritional labels! We have come along so far that we now put warning labels on products. Cigarettes, for example, should have a warning: *These lung rockets will kill you dead.* If you think I feel good about having quit smoking, you are right. Giving up nicotine addiction and the potential for all the misery it brings was a smart thing. As good as that was, it pales in comparison to how wonderful it feels to know that my sins are forgiven and to know with confidence where my soul is going.

With all the medical research taking place with genetics there will be major breakthrough developments in the coming years. Many are hopeful that we will find cures for diabetes and a host of other diseases. I recently read about a staggering medical breakthrough in which animal cells were used to grow a new, functioning heart in rats. Although this does not mean you will be able to buy a new heart at Walgreens any time soon, the research and understanding of how the body works and how science can feed the tissues with instructional information to repair itself, is mind boggling. There is new understanding and ongoing genetic research into aging. Hopefully there will also come a cure for Alzheimer's disease. The Bible tells us that in end times there will be increased knowledge. I see it and read about some of it on a regular basis.

In the political world we have come out of the dark ages where black people and women were both slaves and neither could vote. Today, either one could run for President! I am not suggesting our struggles for equality are over, because they are not, but the facts speak for themselves. The American people elected Barack Obama to be President of the United States. Many thought they would not see anything like this in their lifetime. In some respects, we've come a long way, baby.

On the other hand, in some ways mankind is very slow in learning anything; at least that was the thought I had about myself after having lunch and eating those potato chips today. I was just stupid! Ouch!

We are learning that we need to think globally and "green," a phrase that did not even exist twenty-five years ago when I was growing up. We are starting to acknowledge that the countries of the world need to work in cooperation with each other and that we can't collectively trash the planet, nor preserve it without working together in some fashion. It took a rock singer named Bono to bring AIDS awareness to political leaders.

I love some of the new T.V. commercials that promote education and awareness to young people about smoking. One of the ads that I thought was great is a series of bites that show seemingly young, healthy people in different places in their life, struggling with tobacco and nicotine addiction. One healthy looking guy says, "It's hard to quit." The next clip immediately flashes to a guy that is apparently gasping for air, and he says, "It's hard to breathe."

This juxtaposition of not quitting and the ensuing consequence go back and forth. Another actor in the commercial says, "It's hard to quit," and again the next picture flashed to another guy of similar age who says, "It's hard to get out of bed or even walk." Another actor says, "I just don't think I can quit." The next frame shows a doctor looking at an X-ray and he tells his patient, "I don't think I can operate," insinuating it's too late and that the patient will die. Finally, the last photo clip shows an emaciated man sitting in a wheelchair with an oxygen tube hooked up to his face who looks terrible, and he says something intelligent such as, I didn't expect this! It is a fabulous commercial, very well done, with a powerful message for our young people.

I sometimes think we've come a long way. If we keep this up we will be teaching our children in a few hundred years that sin is destructive and that ultimately, like the emaciated man in the T.V. commercial, it leads to suffering and death. I wish there were some good commercials, which conveyed the message that God is good and his son is the cure. Those of us who believe it need to so let our light shine that we become a living commercial that demonstrates this message. God help me to do that!

Why are we so disinterested in the cure?

Like the rock star Bono eluded to in an interview with Bill Hybels, it is not so much an issue for him (Bono) of not appreciating the message of Jesus, but rather the many, so-called Christian followers, who incessantly talk about right and wrong, goodness and evil, but do nothing to overcome injustice, poverty, hunger or disease. We talk the talk but we don't walk the walk, and we don't put our money where our mouths are. Many people see only the hypocrisy of religion. Good caring people, maybe even Bono, come to the conclusion that all spiritual things must be phony. That is one reason why some are disillusioned by the cure. We see only the worst of religious hypocrites, but not the goodness of God.

I have yet to meet anyone who does not like good things. I have never seen even an inmate in the jail who did not have some appreciation for some forms of goodness. For example, prisoners can clearly appreciate goodness or grace, when deputies in the jail offer it to them in the form of dignity and respect. Likewise, I have never seen anyone who does not like good food when they are hungry. It is not *good things* or *goodness* itself that people question. It is confusion about how to obtain it.

God is good and if you come to his table of goodness or invite him into your life you will not be disappointed. Every time I think about this it just blows me away. God is good. You are going to like him. The psalmist, David, said, *O taste and see that the Lord is good* (Psalms 34:8). If you like good things, you are going to like God.

What is the problem? One thing is that both good and evil exist. It's all around us and does not take that much imagination to see some of the evil that exists in the world. Satan is evil and he wants to create confusion about whether God is actually good or not, based largely on the many bad things that happen all around us. How could a good God allow such things to happen? Another thing is that Satan wants to create as much confusion and doubt as possible about how people can become saved and have the promise of eternal salvation.

One of the biggest lies Satan has ever offered is designed to create confusion over this very issue: as long as you "believe" in God you will be just fine, or in the alternative, that decent people or "good" people, such as ourselves, don't have to worry about such things, because a loving God would not send "good" people to hell. Of course, the operative word here is "good" and Jesus said, there is none "good" except God.

Every inmate in the jail is there because of disregard for the law or, in some cases, confusion over doing or obtaining some form of a good thing, but going about it the wrong way. Usually it is blatant disregard, but ignorance, confusion and a lack of wisdom are also big contributing factors. By and large, Christians could do a better job of modeling good spiritual behavior so that people could clearly see and understand that God is truly good. We don't see God; we see his children and they don't impress us most of the time, so we don't give spiritual things much of a chance. Add to this that we are born in sin and we don't understand the things of God, and we are blinded by our own sin. The Bible describes this perfectly: *But the natural man receiveth not the things of the Spirit of God: for they are foolishness unto him: neither can he know them, because they are spiritual* (I Corinthians 2:14). This is another reason many are not able to see the cure.

There is a third reason. Satan is a liar, a thief, and a murderer and he comes to deceive and to destroy. The Bible tells us that but you don't even have to read the Bible to know this. Moreover, Satan is a cunning linguist.

He speaks to us with sophistry and specious logic and we buy into it because it sounds halfway reasonable; or part of what he says is actually true, so we think it is all true. When Satan points out that religion is phony and so are religious people, both of those are partly true. The closer is when Satan says, *You can't trust any of that stuff or God; God doesn't care about you; you need to be self sufficient and take care of yourself, because nobody else is going to take care of you but you,* and right then and there it sounds like sage advice and you buy into it. You don't stop to consider that God loves you so much that he sent his only son to die for you and more importantly, that you need God's help.

As we just mentioned Satan also wants to confuse us, and not just on one or two things, but he wants to do so with as many issues as he can when it comes to understanding the plan of salvation offered by God. He is the father of confusion. He twists and turns real issues around trying to misdirect us. For example, he might whisper in your ear, *If you follow God you are going to have to give up the good life and everything you love; no one else does that.* Nothing could be a bigger lie because God's ways represent the "good life." Satan's lies furthermore misdirect you from examining your own life and the issue of personal responsibility and he suggests to you that you should look at everyone else. Everyone else may be doing the wrong thing, but everyone else is not going to heaven. The issue of your eternal destiny is not based on everyone else, but rather on you.

Where do you stand with God and your eternal destiny?

Are you going to make it into heaven? How does that happen and how can one be sure?

Most of us with any common sense or judgment would never think of turning down free life insurance or medical insurance, if our employer provided it for us. A good insurance policy protects you and your family. Why would you not consider free eternal life insurance from Jesus who died on the cross for you?

Maybe you asked God to come into your heart years ago when you were a small child, as I was. Maybe your name is already written in the Book of Life but your status or relationship with God has changed and a lot has happened in your life since then. Maybe your relationship with him is so tenuous and weak that you are on the verge of needing spiritual CPR. Not thinking about this or dealing with it is a decision, and a dangerous one at that. Yesterday is history, today is a gift, and tomorrow is a mystery. You don't know about tomorrow or what it holds for you. You may never get to take care of it later. Life is uncertain.

Jesus spoke about many important things including heaven and hell and our future. On one such occasion he spoke of a man who seemed to have everything going for him including financial success. *This man decided to tear down his old barns and build bigger and better ones, thinking to himself: I have much goods laid up for many years; enjoy the easy life, eat, drink and be merry. But God said unto him, You fool, tonight your soul will be required of you, then whose shall all these things be?* (Luke 12:16-20).

If you are currently saved and on your way to heaven but only because you are hanging by a thread from the skin of your teeth, you need to make things right with God and you should put this book down and do it right now. Open the door of your heart and ask God to give your life a fresh start. Make things right with God. Rededicate your life to God.

If you don't know the Lord, you also don't know if you have another month or even another week or another day. You could be in the prime of your health and be killed in an accident tomorrow in any one of a hundred different ways. Don't let your eternal destiny become a matter of choice by default. If you were in a spiritual court of law, how could you argue that you want the insurance company to pay for the cost of your soul because, even though you had no policy, you were thinking about getting a policy later on in life? Do you think that kind of logic is going to stand up in the courts of heaven? It won't stand up anywhere.

We often look at those who have a lot of money, as people needing next to nothing. They have everything, right? This perception is understandable if we are looking at what earthly things money can buy. On the heavenly side of the equation we eventually realize that money cannot buy someone a place in heaven. It might be able to buy anything on earth, but it can't pay for your eternal soul. Jesus spoke a parable touching on money and eternal matters. The Lord's words dismayed his disciples. Jesus was contrasting worldly and heavenly riches when he said that on an earthly level it was more possible for a camel to go through the eye of a needle than for a rich man to enter into the Kingdom of heaven (Luke 18:25). The surprised response of the disciples is exactly what I felt. Wow, how then can any of us make it? Jesus' answer was simple: *The things which are impossible with men are possible with God* (Luke 18:27).

It is not that money is evil or that good people can't have it. It is the love of money that the Bible says is the root of all evil. Money is such a powerful tool that it often becomes a corrupting force in the lives of people. People often end up loving money more than God and the priorities of their heart get turned around. On a purely earthly level, money can buy almost anything and provide such a wonderful lifestyle and comfort, to say nothing of the prestige, power and influence, that all these things blind most people to their need for Christ. Jesus was indirectly talking about the sinful condition of the human heart. His words go to the issue of our destiny and his entire mission on earth. We all need *new* hearts, and of course Jesus was not talking about medical organ transplants which were not yet available back then.

The reason we all need new hearts is because we are all born in sin. The Bible says, *for all have sinned and come short of the glory of God* (Romans

3:23). The solution to this problem is simple. We simply need to recognize our need for God and ask him to come into our hearts and forgive us and save us. The Holy Scriptures are perfectly clear about this. *If we confess our sins, he is faithful and just to forgive us our sins, and cleanse us from all unrighteousness* (I John 1:9). If you haven't done this before and you are not quite sure what to do, well, here it is: Do it, my friend! And you can have the confidence in knowing that you are forgiven, and a new creature in Christ because he promises that to you. *For whosoever shall call upon the name of the Lord shall be saved* (Romans 10:13). These are wonderful promises from God to you. *If thou shalt confess with thy mouth the Lord Jesus Christ, and shalt believe in thine heart that God hath raised him from the dead, thou shalt be saved* (Romans 10:9).

If you know right now that you would not make it into heaven if you had to walk into eternity today, then this chapter is for you. If you examine your own heart and come to the conclusion that you don't know the Lord, then this is a perfect time to ask him to come into your life. Acknowledge your sin and failures, repent and ask for forgiveness, and ask Christ to come into your heart and make you a new creature. It is that simple. Even if you happen to be surrounded by people right now, you can still do this. Just close your eyes and quietly pray.

Who's going to make it? Those who have sincerely repented and asked Jesus to come into their hearts will make it. Those who have died to their old carnal nature and sinful ways and who now have new a heart in Jesus Christ will make it because they have been forgiven. This spiritual transformation occurs in our lives when Jesus does his work of forgiveness. Jesus described the process of salvation as "being born again." The apostle Paul described it, as becoming a *new creature* in Christ (2 Corinthians 5:17).

This change, which occurs in our lives when Jesus comes into our hearts, results in a total transformation of our character and our entire outlook on life. The change is profound, if it's real. It's like having a new heart, one that wants to follow purity. This was what Jesus was talking about when he said: *You must be born again.* The ensuing cultivation of that spiritual change makes it possible to love the unlovely and to forgive those who we would not otherwise forgive. It makes it possible to love our enemies and to think of others above our own interests. Believe me, it goes against everything that is human in my flesh. Salvation is a miracle itself, because it produces change in our human nature that defies analytical assay, understanding or quantitative measurement by science.

Are you really growing spiritually?

Our walk with the Lord is an ongoing process of growth and development. If there is no visible or measurable growth of any kind, we need to be concerned about that. This potentially can lead to further deterioration, atrophy and even death. Intervention is required. There comes a point where alarm bells need to go off in your head if you are still spiritually drinking baby milk instead of solid food, when you are thirty years old in the faith.

If your baby did not develop physically in height, stature, weight and intellect, you would soon discover that terrible truth. If such a problem should come to your attention then one would need to deal with it. If your child did not learn how to walk, hopefully, you would not wait until the child turned twelve years old, before taking the child to a doctor. The absence of growth is serious and can lead to death!

Jesus gave the parable of the sower to warn us about these conditions. *Some seed fell by the wayside and the fowls came and devoured the seed; some seed fell upon stony earth where there was little soil depth and when the sun came the seed was scorched and it withered away because there was no root depth; some seed fell among thorns and the seed was choked; but other seed fell into good soil and brought forth fruit, some a hundredfold, some sixtyfold, and some thirtyfold. Who hath ears let him hear* (Matthew 13:4-9).

Most living things, except maybe weeds, require cultivation. You do not want to let your spiritual life rust away like a bucket of bolts in salt water and never do anything to feed yourself or nurture your faith.

New babes in Christ are just like small kids who have to learn how to walk. There is nothing wrong with being a new born babe in the faith. New Christians need support and nurturing just like all of us do, including mentoring by those who have walked in the faith for some time and who are themselves mature. New Christians have to learn to develop their spiritual maturity, wisdom, and their gifts. In the process of doing that they can sometimes make mistakes just like the rest of humankind and we need to be patient, longsuffering, and forgiving toward them just like Christ has been to us.

You can't judge a book by its cover. Appearances are deceiving. Goodness and character are best judged by content. Jesus said, *A good man out of the good treasure of his heart bringeth forth that which is good; and an evil man out of the evil treasure of his heart bringeth forth that which is evil: for out of the abundance of the heart his mouth speaketh* (Luke 6:45).

Jesus described the same principle with a different parable saying: *Ye shall know them by their fruits. Do men gather grapes from thorns, or figs from thistles? Even so every good tree bringeth forth good fruit; but a corrupt tree bringeth forth evil fruit. A good tree cannot bring forth evil fruit, neither can a corrupt tree bring forth good fruit. Every tree that bringeth not forth good fruit is hewn down and cast into the fire. Wherefore by their fruits ye shall know them* (Matthew 7:16-20). Pretty powerful words!

These principles may help us to evaluate ourselves for the presence or absence of the fruits of the Spirit in our lives. Is there credible evidence of Christ in your life? We can examine ourselves in this light. Is our faith and character in Christ real? Do we know him? Has he made a difference in our lives? Does it show? Do we produce good fruit?

If we are truly born again in Christ we need to reflect or mirror some of these character qualities. Do we need to do a chromosome test on you to determine what kind of tree you are? We all fail from time to time, and need fresh forgiveness and Christ's healing power to restore our lives. We all need ongoing wisdom and guidance. The Lord is gracious, patient, longsuffering and full of forgiveness when we stumble or fall and he loves to help us regain our footing and restore our souls. So, while we all make mistakes daily, we still should predominantly be displaying the fruits of the Spirit, if we are born again. That's the goal, to thrive and produce fruit for the Kingdom of heaven.

Falling on your face does not make you lose your faith or relational position with God. Failure alone does not mean you somehow automatically stop being a Christian. Failure alone does not define who you are. For example, there is a difference between having lied about something and being a liar. If you are defined as *being a liar* that suggests that this is representative of who you are, like a profession which you practice. There is a big difference. Jesus rebuked Peter and called him "Satan" (get thee behind me, Satan) but that did not mean Peter was doomed to hell. God will forgive you when you ask for it. That's why I do so frequently. I make a ton of mistakes. God will help you along the way and walk with you if you invite him to do so.

Some things just can't be bought or earned

Simple sociology teaches us that we have to get along so we don't all kill each other over parking spaces. We learn to observe certain moral values for survival. Civilization creates basic government and we develop basic laws saying that we should not steal, cheat, rape or murder each other. Because we observe two out of three of these, we think we are not so bad.

Good citizenship, hard work ethics, concern for others and a host of other good qualities, which you probably have, will never by themselves get you into heaven. Otherwise you could earn your way into heaven by being a decent person. It's not only the sin you see in your own life, but also the sin you don't see that will kill you. Nice people don't necessarily go to heaven. People who have been forgiven of their sin because they have a personal relationship with Jesus will go to heaven. Just admiring Jesus won't get you saved. Much of the world admired the healings and miracles Jesus performed. Believing that Jesus exists or admiring some of the wonderful things he did will not get you saved.

Understand that none of these things, like simply believing in the existence of God, changes our character or nature, and we are still born in sin. We forget that. We compare ourselves to others. In doing so we conclude that we're not *that* bad. After all, I am not a criminal. Sin is a terminal disease and it doesn't matter if the guy next to you has it, or not, because you have it! Your sin won't be judged by what someone else did. You will be judged by whether your sin was forgiven or not. That's why many a criminal will go to heaven. The record in heaven will forevermore show their sins were forgiven, and their criminal history was simply one of those forgiven sins.

The fact that you are not a criminal, but rather a nice guy and a tax-paying citizen does not mean your soul is saved. You need Jesus! Regardless of how nice a guy you may be, we are all born in sin and the measuring stick for eternal salvation is not whether you gave to the Red Cross, bought cookies from the Girls Scouts or did some other fund raiser, nor whether you sustained a criminal conviction. The eternal question is also not whether you "believe" in Jesus. Satan believes in God. Believing in God is a small part of the equation. Remember, believing in God and being eternally saved are two completely different things.

Do you know Jesus as Lord and Savior? Have you asked for Christ's forgiveness and asked him to come into your heart? All the other stuff is just learning how to grow and develop maturity and productivity.

Why is Jesus so important? Because the cost of sin is more than you will ever realize, in your own human understanding. The Holy Spirit must open our eyes to this fact. God is a just and perfect God, who hates sin and he demands a penalty for it. Sin has to be dealt with! This is what defines, in part, God's character and makes God so wonderful, because he is just and uncompromising. God doesn't bend or excuse the rules or violate his own moral standards. When sin entered the world, God did not suspend the death penalty for sin; he sent his only son to offer his life as a ransom for our sin.

Are you sure of your salvation or have you just fooled yourself by wishful thinking or delusion? In other words, is it real? *Where's the beef? Show me the money!* If you are truly born-again, your character will reveal the image of Christ. You can't have one and not the other. You can't be baptized in Jesus and have nothing but Satan flowing out of you. Can you fall or make mistakes along the way or just have an occasional bad day? Yes!

Consider the words of Jesus. An evil man out of the evil treasure in his heart bringeth forth that which is evil: for out of the abundance of the heart the mouth speaketh. A good tree cannot bring forth evil fruit. Godly hearts produce good fruit.

These comparisons are brought up for the purpose of looking at our own hearts and not for the purpose of judging others. We are instructed to not judge others because we need to leave that to God Almighty. We should judge ourselves and examine our own hearts with the word of God and ask the question, am I going to make it? You will only have to answer for your own deeds and words and no one else's. This critical analysis is for self-introspection. The words of Christ work like a mirror enabling us to look into our own soul and measure our character. How am I doing? Are my ways pleasing in your sight, Lord? Are there any fruits of the Spirit being manifested in my life? How does my spiritual maturity look? Have I lost my faith or am I well grafted in the Vine?

When people fall in love with each other they want to be together all the time. They talk to each other incessantly. They talk to their friends about how wonderful the person they love is. My father couldn't stop talking about Jesus to his coworkers. That's how it is when you love Jesus; he is on your mind all the time and you feel so passionately about him that you naturally want to tell others about him. People who fall into this category of faith are almost always in some visible stage of growth and development and it is not difficult to know this because it shows. Their good deeds and works and their inner spirit are all producing visible fruits. It's like being happy; it shows. Perhaps more importantly, their behavior conforms to their talk, which is to say they walk the talk. They practice a fair amount of what they preach.

Conversely, simply telling others that you love the Lord, or even telling the Lord that you love him doesn't, in itself, necessarily make it so, or make it meaningful. You might have a faint pulse, but are there other credible signs of life? This category of believers concerns me. Do your words and conduct reflect Jesus? If the fruit of the Spirit is *never* manifested in your life, and no one seems to ever witness evidence of it, and your love for Christ appears to be stagnant, lukewarm or anemic, then you should be concerned about the status of your own spiritual life. If you have lost nearly all interest in Christ, your faith is in jeopardy.

Having a weak or tenuous relationship with God does not mean you have no relationship at all, nor does it mean you are on your way to hell. But, when someone is so ill that they are on the verge of needing CPR, we generally call for an ambulance. It is appropriate for your friends to be concerned about your health, just as they would if you collapsed on the ground and your breathing became shallow. Maybe your good friends should lay hands on you and start praying for you. Prayer can be a spiritual I.V. that allows the Holy Spirit to resuscitate you.

People that fall into this category of believers are on shaky ground. It is very difficult to tell sometimes if they are dead or alive. Just as a good doctor could not simply look at the outside of your body and tell you whether or not your condition is terminal, so it is with your Christian friends or spiritual advisors. The definitive MRI results of your soul can only be answered by the Holy Spirit.

There is a difference between manifesting good health or poor health and being sentenced to hell or doomed to hell. We are all on our way to hell until we meet Jesus, get forgiven, and get on the right track.

It is completely appropriate to judge and discern character, good behavior and godly lifestyles. We don't want our children exposed to child molesters because we fool ourselves into not using wisdom, or because we deceive ourselves over the Lord's commandment that we should love others. You can love the child molester, but not his behavior, and you can pray for him, but not let him baby-sit your children. We have to have wisdom and make some reasonable value judgments about people, in order to be safe and protect our children and families, but we also need to be careful not to misjudge others or jump to conclusions that everybody, except you and me, is going to hell.

There is a difference between evaluating good and bad behavior, being observant for the presence or absence of righteous character and good fruit, versus being hypocritical, holier than thou, and obnoxiously judgmental about others when, half the time, we don't even know any of the surrounding facts. We should not condemn those around us because they aren't as wonderful as we want them to be, but we also should not be ignorant regarding our own standards of acceptable behavior, or ignorant over solid biblical truth. Let's not be confused about what constitutes righteous or unrighteous fruit! We need to know what the Lord's standards are for our own lives, but not for the purpose of beating our friends up with our self-righteous, smug attitudes. It's permissible to fairly and righteously judge behavior based on facts. Jesus was very clear about this moral issue when he said: *by their fruits ye shall know them* (Matthew 7:20). Just don't be smug and self-righteous about it, because we are to love and forgive one another, too. At times, this becomes a tough, balancing act and it's the very reason why we need the Lord's wisdom. Know and understand what constitutes sin, but don't be judgmental or unloving toward the sinner. Recognize good fruit from evil fruit but don't be unkind to the produce salesman.

It is not the job of Christians to judge people and try and figure out who's saved and who is not. That is God's responsibility. It is the job of Christians to love others. Regardless of where you are in this spiritual journey, we should examine and judge our own hearts using sound biblical standards and principles. What Jesus taught us on this subject was how to recognize good fruit and bad fruit, along with the knowledge that good fruit does not come out of evil hearts anymore than bad fruit comes out of good hearts.

The spiritual illustration is intended to help us better understand spiritual health and illness. Just as your nurse may be able to tell you and the doctor that you have a temperature of 102 degrees Fahrenheit, this alone does not mean you have a terminal illness, and that you are going to die. The temperature is a symptom of illness.

On a spiritual plane, God's Holy Spirit can definitively diagnose the status of your soul and lead you to a state of mind where you start feeling concerned about where you stand eternally with God. Just like reliable, scientific lab work might show the presence of deadly bacteria in your blood, which could be life threatening, so the Holy Spirit can convict us of our secret sin and draw us toward the cross so as to prompt us to seek forgiveness.

The Holy Spirit will also use the written word of God to convict us of our sin, and draw us to Jesus for the purpose of seeking forgiveness through repentance, but there is a caveat to all of this. The Holy Spirit will never contradict the word of God. In other words, if you know you are living in sin based on the word of God, don't fool yourself into thinking that the Holy Spirit is going to tell you that this is O.K. because of changing cultural times that we live in. God's word will never change and if you manipulate his word, it will no longer be God's word. Satan will tell you that it's O.K. and that you can live in sin or any other way you want. Satan will never tell you to accept or follow God's word. If you are open to the things of God, and inviting the Lord to show himself to you, and your need for him, his Holy Spirit will do that, and impress upon you the need to open your heart to Christ and ask for his forgiveness.

Just as the nurse cannot simply look at you and say that you are going to die today because you have a high temperature, so the same is true with Christians. No Christian can look at you and say that since you struggle with alcohol and drugs that means you are going to hell. A good nurse or a godly person might both be able to tell you that you are sick as a dog, based on visible, objective, measurable symptoms. On the other hand, Jesus, the Great Physician, is able to not only see your heart at the deepest level, he is also capable of healing you and forgiving you of your sin. The eligibility factor for this is simple: you have to be sincere; you have to truly repent and ask for Christ's forgiveness. When we do that, Christ also helps us change our old ways.

I don't know who will be going to hell, but I can measure my own soul with the criteria we have already discussed, the divine word of God, and by examining my own heart with the help of the Holy Spirit. There will be surprises for many on this subject. The Bible speaks of it. *Not everyone who says Lord, Lord, will enter the Kingdom of heaven, but he who does the will of my Father, which is in heaven* (Matthew 7:21). These are powerful words. Think about them. If we don't sincerely repent and we never change our sinful ways, forgiveness will not occur. We must love God in Spirit and truth, Jesus said. In other words, it can't be a fraudulent act or game.

Trickery, duplicity and insincerity

There are some who will do seemingly good deeds, perhaps just like Jim Jones, and impressive tricks, but their true motivation, when the truth is revealed in heaven, will not have been the will of our Father in heaven; it will have been the will of their father which is in hell. Jesus spoke on this very topic saying: *There will be some who will ask, Lord, didn't we preach and prophesy in your name, cast out devils, and do many wonderful works? When these things are asked, the Lord God will reply, I never knew you: depart from me, you workers of iniquity* (Matthew 7:22-23).

Some will play the game so well that they will fool or convince many people here on earth, but they will not convince God because he sees deep into the heart of each person and can tell who is sincere and who is not. There is a big difference, you see, between knowing about Jesus, and actually knowing Jesus personally. There is a difference between believing in Jesus and surrendering your will to Jesus and making him your Lord and Savior.

You can use the word of God as a two edged-sword dividing asunder the truth from evil and confusion so that you are not fooled by the words of others or by your own conduct. What I want to do is have you see the important scripture and biblical truth that will guide you with insight and spiritual wisdom and understanding, so that you can measure the condition of your own heart. The combination of these things along with your own open heart and honesty should enable you by the end of this chapter to have confidence about your destiny, or about what you need to do.

If your heart and mind are open to examine this important eternal issue, God's word has plenty to say about it. Openness and honesty toward God is the entire key to having faith and confidence about your eternal destiny. God is not in the business of tricking people. He speaks plainly and tells us how to be saved. He is trustworthy. If you ask him with sincerity to come into your heart and you mean it, he will.

The remaining few words of this chapter are meant to be a failure analysis of behavior from an analytical perspective of insincerity, hypocrisy, unbelief and disobedience. These are things that people do to shoot themselves in the foot and cause failure. The purpose of the proceeding review is not to make anyone fearful, but just the opposite, to show that courage and faith and honesty with God can help us be victorious in any circumstance. If your love for Christ is real and sincere, you have nothing to worry about in terms of the Lord turning his back on you, or casting you into hell.

If you think you could possibly fall into that terrible category, then know that the remaining words and emphasis of this chapter are to help you identify and overcome those very pitfalls. God wants you to succeed! He sent his only son to the cross to give his life for you. Ask Christ to come into your heart. A good portion of Bible scripture is provided to help us see the failure of others so that we can avoid making the same mistakes. That is what this chapter is all about, overcoming failure by prompting you to examine either the presence or absence of a relationship with Jesus.

It all boils down to what is truly in the heart. If we say that we love the Lord, but we don't love others and nothing in our life reflects Christ, we deceive ourselves. Do we leave the impression with everybody we come into contact with that we love evil more than righteousness? Does our life reflect the real deal or is it all a big sham? Do we produce any spiritual fruit in our life? Do we obey God's commandments? Do our deeds and thoughts reflect the values of Jesus? Most importantly, have we asked Christ to forgive us for our sins, and are we committed to actually following Jesus? Are we living our spiritual lives with Christ like we are still deeply in love with him, or, as though we are separated, and on the verge of a divorce? Jesus said, *for where your treasure is, there will your heart be also* (Luke 12:34).

Is my love for the Lord real?

If we evaluate our hearts and try to become transparent, we should ask ourselves this simple question: is Jesus still the most wonderful thing that ever happened to me? If you need to take a long time to ponder and answer that question, you need to bring yourself into God's presence and ask for a thorough tune-up and servicing, or at least an oil change.

If I were on the witness stand in court and an attorney were to hypothetically ask me if I was a liar, a cheat or a thief, it might bother you if I took too long to answer such a question. Even if I were to facetiously reply, "Well, not today," that might make you laugh, but such an answer might disturb you if it required too much deliberation, for such a basic question about character and honesty. You still would not know what was is in my heart and a follow-up question would be in good order. A good attorney would surely ask more questions.

"Well, Officer," the attorney might ask, "when was the last time you stole anything?"

If I answered, "The last time I can remember stealing anything was when I was a small child," such an admission might make you feel better, knowing that my bad behavior wasn't yesterday, and it didn't involve robbing a bank.

Say, the attorney then asked, "Officer, why did it take you so long to answer the question?"

I might answer, "Your question was compound and poorly worded Counsel; you essentially asked me about lying, cheating and stealing so it took me a long time to reflect on all three of these things."

The judge would agree and sustain my objection and tell the attorney to rephrase the question. This tit for tat still does not provide a definitive answer and all the legal mumbo jumbo might annoy you. This is not what you want to hear. This is almost like real life.

"Are you a Christian, or not? Where is your soul headed; can you tell us? You can't even answer these questions, Officer, can you?" snaps the attorney.

I contentiously ask, "Which question are you referring to now, Counsel?"

The attorney pleads, "Your Honor, please instruct the witness to answer the question!"

The judge replies, "Well, you did ask three questions, Counsel."

The attorney acknowledges the Court's remark with deference and formulates a new question: "Alright, Officer! Have you lied today about anything?"

Again, the response time is way too long before any answer comes. The attorney becomes obviously annoyed and relentless.

"I'll ask you once again, Officer! Have you lied today or not?"

At the risk of annoying the judge, I might then respond with honesty and a little wit, by answering, "I told my wife she looked good this morning before I kissed her good-bye and left for work, and that was a lie Counsel; she looked terrible. That's the only lie I've uttered today."

If you want to know where one stands on any particular issue you need to ask questions. We need to ask ourselves some of these important questions. If you ask yourself important questions about eternity and you don't like the long, pondering wait before an answer comes out of your thoughts, then you need to reassess the status quo of your soul. The more uncertainty that appears, the more you should be asking questions. Are you rock-solid or just so, so? If you had to unexpectedly leave and go into eternity tonight, are you comfortable with where you are headed? Are you going to make it into heaven? Nobody can better answer this question than you can.

Is your heart truly set on following the Lord, obeying him no matter what the cost, and serving him no matter what the price? The sad fact is while most people will be quick to say they would want to go to heaven, many will not truly serve or follow the Lord. Many are blinded by their own sin and desire, and deep down in their heart, they do not want to follow or obey. Jeremiah the prophet spoke of this blinding condition of the heart saying, *The heart is deceitful above all things, and desperately wicked: who can know it?* (Jeremiah 17:9).

Who better understands all of this than God himself? *I, the Lord, search the heart; I try the reins, even to give every man according to his ways, and according to the fruit of his doings* (Jeremiah 17:10). *The fining pot is for silver, and the furnace for gold: but the Lord trieth the hearts* (Proverbs 16:3).

You will never know for sure how deep your relationship is with someone until your love is tested. This is a principle of life. If your love is so lukewarm that you are open and available for a better deal if one comes along, God will see this and the truth will prove itself out when adversity comes along. God is very much for you and not against you and he tells us this repeatedly throughout scripture. His words will endure forever. The weak link is our words. When we tell God how much we love him, think not that God will not test you to find out just where you stand on that very issue.

God tested Abraham with this and told him to offer his son Isaac as a sacrifice unto the Lord. This, you will remember, was Abraham's only son for whom he had waited a hundred years. In obedience Abraham stretched forth his hand and took the knife to slay his son. And the angel of the Lord called unto him out of heaven, and said, *Abraham, Abraham, lay not your hand upon the lad, neither do anything unto him: for now I know that you fear God, seeing you have not withheld your son, your only son from me* (Genesis 22:10-12). *God further said, because you have done this thing and have not withheld you son, your only son, I will bless you and multiply your seed as the stars of the heaven, and as the sand which is upon the seashore* (Genesis 22:16-17).

The Lord tests each of us with this same principle. The stakes may be different but he asks all of us similar questions; will you trust me? Will you obey me? Do you love me? Is it real? When adversity comes will you abide in me?

Is your relationship with Jesus rock solid? Or, does the Lord just fill a small place in your life that you reserve for one or two days in the year like maybe Christmas and Easter? Do you go to church on those days mainly to honor your mother or some other family member, or is it based on your deep love for the Savior?

If we don't have a real transformation in our character that penetrates all the way into our DNA, the whole spiritual thing might be just show, and no substance. How real is your faith day-in and day-out?

Who is going to make it? *he who overcometh shall inherit all things; and I will be his God, and he shall be my son* (Revelation 21:7). *But the fearful, and unbelieving, and the abominable, and murderers, and whoremongers, and sorcerers, and idolaters, and all liars, shall have their part in the lake which burneth with fire and brimstone: which is the second death* (Revelation 21:8).

I find the above passage very sobering. This dirty laundry list of those who are cast into the lake of fire includes not only those who we might expect, but also the unbelieving and the fearful.

I would like to opine a couple of thoughts about these two categories of people who do not make it. If not taken in proper context, I believe Satan could do what he does best, create confusion and torment for you over these words. That is not the purpose or plan of Christ. Every other passage in the Bible from beginning to end has these words, designed to encourage us and help us overcome our fears: <u>be not afraid</u>, spoken either by angels, prophets or Jesus himself. The Lord is not hiding around a bush outside your house waiting for you to make a mistake, or detect your fear, so he can cast you into hell. *For God sent not his Son into the world to condemn the world, but that the world through him might be saved* (John 3:17).

God's plan is to help us overcome fear and be victorious. Hear the words of Jesus: *The thief comes only to steal, kill and destroy: I have come that you might have life, and that you might have it more abundantly* (John 10:10). Christ is love. When we are in him, *perfect love casts out fear* (I John 4:18).

We all experience fear. As a police officer I did many times. Developing our faith in God will help us overcome our fear. You will notice the scripture above says: *he who overcometh shall inherit all things*. The scripture also states that the *just shall live by faith* (Romans 1:17). In another passage it says, *without faith it is impossible to please God* (hebrews 11:6). Our trust and hope in God is based on faith. If we could put it in a test tube we wouldn't be talking about intelligent design. Faith is a way of life and it is largely a decision: I choose to believe and follow Jesus. When I see the miracles he has done in my life and I feel his presence in my spirit, my faith continues to grow and get stronger. Each answer to prayer increases my faith.

One of the best examples that come to my mind of the "fearful" not making it is found in the Old Testament. Consider the following. The children of Israel were delivered out of the hand of Pharaoh in Egypt, with many mighty miracles performed by the hand of God. Israel was delivered from Pharaoh's army, where God split the Red Sea in half so that Israel could escape, and buried Pharaoh's army in the Red Sea when the walls of the water returned. The children of Israel were given manna from heaven, water from the rock, a pillar of fire and a cloud to lead them by day and by night, and victory over all their enemies, including when God brought down the walls of Jericho. The Israelites where brought to the land which God had promised their fathers, Abraham, Isaac and Jacob.

A reconnaissance team was sent into the land to assess it. When the team returned they brought back fruit from the land including a cluster of grapes from a branch that they carried on a pole between two men; they also brought pomegranates and figs. They described the country and terrain as a land that "floweth with milk and honey," but also said there were giants in the land. One might think that after being in the desert for so long these people would jump at the chance to eat grapes the size of baseballs.

The scripture tells us: *All the children of Israel murmured against Moses and Aaron: and the whole congregation said unto them, would to God that we had died in the land of Egypt! or would to God we had died in the wilderness! And wherefore hath the Lord brought us unto this land, to fall by the sword, that our wives and our children should be a prey? were it not better for us to return into Egypt? And they said one to another, Let us make a captain, and let us return into Egypt* (Numbers 14:2-4). They also talked about stoning those who had the courage and audacity to suggest that they enter the land and possess it. [An amazing story!]

After all the miracles that God had performed for the children of Israel, they allowed fear to so grip their lives that it became the exclusive motivating factor in their decision making process. In a singular, momentous event, fear and unbelief, expressed through the power of choice, over-powered prior histories of victory, critical analysis and all desire to persevere. Fear can be overcome. We can ask God to help us overcome it. They chose not to do so. This whole thing was a choice. Hear the words of God from scripture: ....*to him that overcometh will I give to eat of the tree of life, which is in the midst of the paradise of God* (Revelation 2:7).

After all God had done for these people it was like the ultimate slap in God's face to deny his mighty works and faithfulness toward them. It was tantamount to spitting in God's face and blaspheming his mighty name by saying essentially, you can't be trusted; you brought us here to murder us in the wilderness.

God allowed these people to wander another forty years in the wilderness, one year for each of the forty days of reconnaissance. Many, if not most, of the original people who had fled from Egypt died in the wilderness and their children inherited the Promised Land.

So, consider the preceding account of the Israelites ignoring God's servant Moses and the courage of Joshua and Caleb (Numbers Chapters 13 & 14) in refusing to enter into the Promised Land. Use this as a perspective in understanding the heart of God when he speaks through scripture to us about the fearful and unbelieving. Who is going to make it? He who overcometh! God is for you, not against you. Nothing will please him more than to hear his children cry out unto him for help in overcoming their fears.

The issue of unbelief is also important. Understand there is a big difference between struggling to have faith, *more faith*, or the choice of not believing. When Jesus was ministering to those around him, there were crowds, which followed him everywhere. While he was in the midst of these people, many of them, the scriptures tell us, would reach out that they might only touch the hem of his garment; and as many as touched were made perfectly whole (Matthew 14:36). These people were healed by virtue of their faith in Jesus, not because of something spoken by Jesus to them.

Not everybody has this kind of faith. A father had brought his demon possessed son to Jesus' disciples to be healed. The evil spirit would cause the child to violently tear at himself, gnash his teeth and wallow on the ground foaming at the mouth. The disciples could not cast the evil spirit out of the boy. The father explained this to Jesus saying: Often the evil spirit would cast the child into the fire and into the waters to destroy him: but *if* you can do anything, have compassion on us, and help us.

Jesus picked up immediately on his qualifying word, "if" you can do anything. Jesus said unto the man, *If you can believe, all things are possible to him that believeth.* The ball was now back in the father's court. Jesus understood that faith, or the lack of faith, was an issue here. What follows are some of the most beautiful words you can find in the Bible. The father cries out with tears, "Lord I believe, help me with my unbelief." Jesus cast the evil spirit out and the child was healed (Mark 9:17-27). The father was not rebuked or put down because he struggled with unbelief. This man acknowledged his weakness and insufficient faith and asked for the Lord's help even with his unbelief. That is what you and I can do every time we are crippled with fear, doubt or unbelief.

All of Satan's roadways lead ultimately to hell but some of the landscape along the way looks deceivingly good. There might be some lovely golf courses and water falls or rolling hills. He wants you to look at cosmetic things, not substance. So it is with sin. We intuitively know that a common cold is not nearly as dangerous as pneumonia. A broken finger is nothing compared to cancer.

While all sin ultimately leads to hell if not forgiven, one sin in particular is catastrophic in my mind, and in some ways more dangerous than others, because it is so blinding, deceitful and beguiling. That sin, of course, is false pride. I am not speaking of the kind of pride we might have in completing a task that was done well, which met standards of excellence; a well executed, skilled or detailed, thorough job, that we are not ashamed of. I am speaking of arrogant pride. Perhaps the most dangerous sin of all is not recognizing our need for Jesus. I don't think anything scares me more than this. We can feel so comfortable with ourselves that we don't see our need for a savior. If you are fooled into thinking, whatever sin I might have is so superficial, I am not that worried about it, then you have placed yourself in a most precarious position. The sin of fear or unbelief can be overcome. If you are content in your darkness, and your pride makes you want nothing to do with Christ, you are in a catastrophically dangerous mind-set that has eternal consequences.

The Bible says this about being satisfied without Jesus: *And this is the condemnation, that light is come into the world, and men loved darkness rather than light, because their deeds were evil* (John 3:19). If you love darkness more than light, this is as dangerous as it gets my friend! Nevertheless, if you are capable of even acknowledging this, you can ask God to help you see your need for him and he will hear that prayer.

In evaluating the concept of who is going to make it into the Kingdom of heaven, we discussed our need for Christ's forgiveness toward us, but there is another element that is important to consider. In modern day Christianity we sometimes overlook this subject. In fact, pastors, who sometimes don't want to offend their congregations by preaching too much about sin, don't preach enough about it. I am speaking of repentance. True repentance involves more than just seeking forgiveness. It also embraces the act of inwardly turning away from our sin and wrongdoing and changing our behavior.

If we study the Bible we see that almost every prophet you read about spoke about repentance. John the Baptist preached: *Repent, for the Kingdom of heaven is at hand* (Matthew 3:2). We are to repent from our wrongdoing and turn away from our sinful ways.

Jesus spoke about this too, and upbraided the cities wherein most of his mighty works were done because they repented not (Matthew 11:20).

Simply asking God to bless us and keep forgiving us is not enough. Jesus forgave the adulteress but told her go and sin no more. Jesus did not say feel free to live any way you want and just keep checking in with me so I can forgive you. I'll set up some appointments for you. The whole reason Jesus came was to forgive people of their sin, but this also requires repentance on our part, for this to be meaningful. If you are not sorry for your sin and only asking for forgiveness, and there is no desire to change anything in your heart, then your request for forgiveness is tantamount to asking God to bless you while you keep right on sinning. That, in turn, pretty much translates to, just bless my sin, Lord. I'm having a great time and I have no desire to stop or turn from my sinful ways.

One could just continue to live in utter sin and simply keep on saying, day in, and day out, please forgive me...again. We would become so casual about the whole thing, soon we would start to say oh, by the way, please forgive me, like a mere afterthought. Eventually we would stop asking for forgiveness because, we would reason: *it's your job to do that for me.* Without repentance and the changing of our ways, forgiveness may not occur. You will remember that only one of the two thieves being crucified with Jesus was remorseful and repentant in spirit. The other railed on Jesus, "Save yourself and us, if you are the Christ."

Jesus spoke of his return and said: *As the days of Noah were, so shall also the coming of the Son of man be. Then shall two be in the field; the one taken the other left; two women shall be grinding at the mill; the one shall be taken the other left* (Matthew 24:37-41). Not everybody is going to make it. Those who never really had a personal relationship with Jesus will be left behind.

Who is going to make it? The answer is: he who has repented and whose sins have been washed away by the blood of the Lamb; he who truly loves the Lord, in spirit and in truth; he who overcometh. If your love for Jesus is real and sincere, your position with him is also secure. Jesus promised he would never leave or forsake us. His words will forever stand: "Lo, I am with you always, even unto the end of the world" (Matthew 28:20).

As you think about your soul, remember that other things in your life, far less important, were most likely well documented. We usually put such things in writing and often in the presence of witnesses. We draw up contracts to protect our property and our assets, so as to ensure our legal rights as far into the future as we can. These contracts don't just simply appear out of thin air all by themselves because we happen to realize that we need them. Similarly, having a relationship with Jesus and having the benefit of his forgiveness does not occur just because you happen to daydream about it for a few minutes. Becoming a member of the family of God and having a relationship with Jesus is the result of *choice*. It's a consensual thing. If you don't invite him in, nothing happens. It's like admiring a beautiful woman. Simply admiring her won't make her your wife. You have to invite her into your life for starters. You also don't marry her without exchanging words. Words have to be exchanged at the altar and promises have to be made. It's the same with Jesus. Words have to be exchanged. You have to sincerely invite him into your heart.

Things happen for a variety of reasons, the worst of which is because we abdicate or do nothing, and a default judgment is entered against us; or, things can happen because we thoughtfully enter into contractual agreements. Such arrangements are usually manifested in the form of carefully drawn up words, which are memorialized in written covenants, contracts, or agreements. When time is of the essence even oral agreements can be made and they are considered binding. For something as serious as your eternal soul, it would be good to have a solid contact. Again, words are important and they define the conditions of your contract. More importantly, words reflect what's deep in your heart, *for by thy words thou shalt be justified, and by thy words thou shalt be condemned* (Matthew 12:37). Whether your words reflect a heart of defiance or one of repentance, they shall be recorded, *for whatsoever ye have spoken in darkness shall be heard in the light; and that which ye have whispered in the privacy of a closet shall be proclaimed upon the housetops* (Luke 12:3).

So, if you simply want nothing to do with God, and you reject your *spiritual constitutional rights* for his love, compassion, forgiveness, his grace and all his wonderful blessings, then you will end up walking alone in your own darkness and your sin will lead to damnation. Sin is a fatal disease and it leads to eternal death. I didn't make this up. These are the words of Jesus (Mark 16:16/ John 3:18). I simply want to point them out and emphasize them because, whether we like it or not, our sin will be dealt with and paid for, in one fashion or another, either by forgiveness or by default. But always remember, you have spiritual rights! Don't throw them away. If you don't invoke your spiritual rights, you'll end up paying for you own sin, and that would be far worse than making the mistake of a *lifetime*, it would be *the mistake of all eternity*.

Aside from the issue of judgment, I want to tell you how wonderful it has been for me these last fifty-three years to walk with Christ in my life. He has provided sustaining power in my life to overcome. I feel his Holy Spirit and guiding hand in my life. Therefore, I revel not only in the past, for the goodness of the Lord shown to me, but also for the joy which has been set before me presently, and for the things which are to come. I await with great anticipation for the Lord's return.

As you honestly examine your spiritual destiny, perhaps you realize that the closest you have ever come to making any connection with Christ, was simply *wishing or hoping there will be forgiveness* when the Day of Judgment comes. Don't risk eternity and disappointment on something this important. Wishing and hoping is for the lottery. You need to sincerely ask for forgiveness and be willing to surrender your life to Christ. If you make a decision to follow and serve him, the Lord will help you along the way. As I mentioned early in this chapter, I have never met anyone who did not like good things. This is as good as it gets! This is something you will never regret. Why not invite Jesus into your heart, right now? There is great power in walking with Christ. Jesus can help you to become more than you could ever be in your own limited strength and he can bring about a joy in your life that is profound.

CHAPTER 4

IF GRACE IS FREE, WHY DON'T I FEEL BETTER ABOUT MYSELF AND MORE SATISFIED?

This is an important spiritual issue for me. Jesus said that he came that we might have life, and that we might gave it more abundantly (John 10:10). If you are anything like me, I don't always feel good about my earthly self or my spiritual life. Usually this boils down to not living up to my potential and the absence of productivity and spiritual fruit. If I were the mighty warrior the Lord wants me to be, why don't I feel more like a conquering child of God who can handle anything? Am I the only one who struggles with these thoughts?

I was driving home from Orchard Supply and contemplating the weak side of my own human nature, and that sin is so beguiling that we don't see it in ourselves, and when we do, we look the other way, as though that might suggest we didn't really see it or, worse yet, that in a delusional way, it doesn't exist, so God won't see it either. Children do this. *Timezies*! Remember that? In the middle of a game children will call "time out." All the rules are temporarily suspended. I'm safe because I called time out at the critical moment of accountability. Saved by the bell.

My cat does this. He will run and hide under the chair and look at me from under the chair as though the rules no longer apply if I can't see him. The cat even peeks to see if I am looking towards him or not. Does any of this fallen nature have a ring of familiarity? *And they heard the voice of the Lord God walking in the garden in the cool of the day: and Adam and his wife hid themselves from the presence of the Lord God among the trees of the garden* (Genesis 3:8). The thought of all my failures and the truth of knowing I could not trust my own flesh felt overwhelming to me. I also felt a sense of despair. How's a guy supposed to make it?

I belong to a small home group of wonderful people who love Jesus, just as I do. We all share our failures with each other and we support each other as we attempt to walk uprightly before the Lord. We pray for each other and we make efforts to practically share our love with others in our community and thereby fulfill the two great commandments.

Our home group was sitting together and talking about our faith and the things of God. Someone said God doesn't expect anybody to be perfect. Without batting an eyelash, I whole-heartedly agreed. As soon as the words slipped out of my mouth I remembered that was not exactly what the word of God had to say about the subject, at least in terms of our pursuit of discipleship.

Internally, I felt slightly embarrassed, like the Vice President undoubtedly felt when he spelled potato incorrectly. I would have settled for that but it was almost like Jesus was sitting there and he gave me an affectionate look that said: Come on Malmin! Give me a break; that's not what my word says. The look alone would convey the message without saying so much as a single word. A lot of things are conveyed through the eyes of another and sometimes words aren't necessary.

Part of my feeling was almost guilt because I had been perfectly happy to agree with the statement, but only because I had forgotten what the word of God said about this very important subject. It was like all of a sudden, in a split second, the light bulb went on and I realized that my taking this position gave me a lot more leeway to be imperfect and not even try to walk the walk. Who expects perfection? It's unreasonable, so why try? I forgot what the standard was. It wasn't just a momentary lapse of memory. Achieving the objective is a different issue altogether than simply acknowledging the standard set before us by Jesus. It is a commandment.

Technically speaking, God probably doesn't expect anyone to succeed at being perfect on a full time basis because he knows we will all sin even when we are trying not to. In retrospect, that was what my friend was most probably trying to convey.

Nevertheless, the spiritual standard which was set and the commandment which Jesus gave us was: *Love your enemies, bless them that curse you, do good to them that hate you, and pray for them which despitefully use you and persecute you.* I struggle with loving my wife the way I should and the way in which she deserves to be loved, and she is not even my enemy, although sometimes I treat her as such. And if you thought those words were not hard enough, here's the killer: *Be ye therefore perfect, even as your Father which is in heaven is perfect* (Matthew 5:44-48).

As I continued driving home from Orchard Supply, I found myself thinking about this standard and my inability to even get close to it. I had even forgotten what the standard was. I felt my spirit being willing but the flesh unwilling. I felt so utterly helpless to control my own behavior. I felt water in my eyes and I asked God, in prayer, how can I ever do anything perfectly before you? A beautiful thing happened instantly for me. I felt the love of the Lord suddenly upon me all at once and my mind was opened to these words: several small steps make an entire day! This was the Lord speaking to me. I also visualized a kind word I had spoken to someone earlier in the week, which served as a reminder: a very small, yet perfect act of kindness. I realized that every time I forgive someone or practice random acts of kindness, those all reflect small, yet perfect steps of love. Several small steps make an entire day! The standard is high and Jesus commands us to do the impossible! If we try in our own strength it is impossible, yet, with God all things are possible! They become possible when we walk in the Spirit. When we do fail, God's grace sustains us.

Examining my thoughts and putting them into words helps me sort through and acknowledge my own tough questions or feelings. Doing this helps me have a dialogue with God. I struggle with this at times because I don't know where some of my discontentment or anger comes from. I have to examine by thoughts and feelings and I frequently end up thinking: where did that come from?

Imagine how wonderful it was, before sin came along, that Adam and Eve walked and talked with God in the garden in the cool of evening. We can do that with the Lord anytime we want to be in the Spirit with him, right now, and in the near future there will be a time where we can do it with our new bodies in heaven. I wonder if Adam and Eve were experiencing some of the same thoughts I just expressed? I wonder if Adam asked Eve if she felt the same as he did? Why do I feel compelled to hide?

Since we often settle for less, it's probably a good thing to be a little dissatisfied, since we only tap into a small percentage of our potential, and we lack the vision to imagine or see what we can be in Christ. We only surrender a percentage of our total being and energy to God. We have such a death-like grip on life that we are afraid to let go of it, so as to die in Christ and become more than we could ever be on our own. Like the iceberg, most of our potential is under the surface level of the water and we don't even see it. Being discontent to manifest only a small portion of our potential is a good thing. Our faith should motivate us into the pursuit of greater things.

There is an old Christian adage that says God doesn't create junk. We are wonderfully and fearfully made and even though humankind has suffered from the fall and the curse, we still see the tremendous potential that is lying dormant in ourselves and in others. That is a good thing. When we see potential, that enables us to practice possibility thinking. Possibility thinking promotes faith. Faith promotes works. Jesus said that all things are possible to him that believeth (Mark 9:23). You will notice this was not a metaphor or parable. His words were not: All things seem possible.

We often hear theologians say that God created mankind with a vacuum or yearning that only God could fill. Our fellowship with God brings about a sense of completeness to our being that we cannot experience without God. If what you have with God is actually real and you walk the walk, then you will also love others. The scripture says that if we say we love God but hate our brother, we deceive ourselves and we are liars because we cannot love God and not also love our brother (I John 4:20).

When we love Jesus we begin to see the needs of others all around us. If this awareness makes us lose a little sleep at night, that reaction is a precious response in God's eyes. When I talk about need, I am not just talking about Africa. I am also talking about the coworker right next to you, the one in the cubical on the other side of your office, and your next-door neighbor. If you see the needs of a dying, hurting world all around you, then you should not be content in simply living the so-called good life, pleased with your life to the exclusion of others. Viewing the world this way through the eyes of Christ may produce a subtle form of discontentment, which we don't even realize, quietly bubbling under the surface. If this represents your state of mind, fall on your face and thank God, and ask him to let you never become satisfied!

Examining grace, service and cost

We are supposed to partner with Christ and become his hands and feet. Jesus said, "Feed my sheep" (John 21: 16). So, what's the problem? Well, we get too satisfied with the things of life, including our own comfort, so we do everything within our power to preserve our good life, rather than give it up, surrender it, or share any of it. We don't fully understand the cost factor of walking with Jesus but if we do, we usually make excuses for it, so as to avoid the issue.

One of the ways we do this is by drawing a fallacious conclusion with our theological thinking regarding grace. We overemphasize that since grace is free, we don't have to work so hard or discipline ourselves that vigorously, because it's *free, praise God!* In the alternative, one might prefer to take the easy way out and phrase it like this: God doesn't expect anyone to be *perfect*. Boy, does that sound good! Like apples and oranges, we take that comparison of grace and somehow apply that to a totally different issue of service, sacrifice and cost. We walk away thinking servanthood must be analogous to grace and thereby draw the conclusion that we don't have to do anything, because grace is free.

Our fallen human nature or flesh, being what it is, reveals a propensity to resist anything that will cause us to deny ourselves and pick up our cross and follow Jesus, and the excuse we sometimes like to fool ourselves with is that *grace is free*. Jesus did it all on the cross, so I don't have to do anything, or precious little. The practical application of this ultimately boils down to a mistaken belief or mentality that I also don't need to *serve* others, least of all, endure the cost of suffering or pain for anyone else, because Jesus did all that stuff. Those hungry people in Darfur need to simply seek God's grace. The words of Jesus, "feed my sheep," get thrown right out the window.

Christ's wonderful grace is provided to us and it is free; we cannot purchase it. All of this is true but it is only half of the story. *Receiving Christ's* grace is free, but grace cost Jesus dearly by virtue of offering himself as a ransom for our sin. If you follow Jesus it will also cost you as you offer grace to others.

So, please understand that grace doesn't mean we don't have to do anything or make any sacrifices, or endure any suffering, because Jesus did it all. Jesus calls us to follow him and do as he did. I can lie on the coach and eat pizza all day long and become useless. I can tell my pastor that I can't help anyone in my neighborhood or be bothered with any of the world's problems.

We don't usually talk that bluntly because we prefer to sugarcoat our words, but our mentality can easily reflect our thoughts of poor theology. I don't need to do anything then! Jesus did it all on the cross, and his grace is sufficient, so there's no need for me to help that elderly lady down the street paint her house. If you really want to sound spiritual and self-righteous, tell your pastor that you will "pray about it." If your pastor is really sharp, he or she will quickly remind you that we don't have to pray about doing the right thing. If the pastor bothers you again, tell your pastor you don't *feel led* to help that old lady down the street...or anyone else for that matter.

As laborers we need to harvest the vineyard fields for the souls of others until Jesus returns. The harvest is great and the laborers are few. Jesus did not say live the good life and party until I return. Jesus said: *let a man deny himself, and take up his cross and follow me* (Mark 8:34). If we love one another as he loved us, and we follow in his footsteps, it is going to cost us something.

Turning the other cheek and not retaliating when men speak all manner of evil about you involves the cost of discipleship and it requires the grace of Jesus. Walking with Jesus is a wonderful privilege but it will cost you something here as well! Doing the right thing usually costs something. If you suffer persecution for doing the right things before your heavenly Father, you too, will then suffer for the Kingdom of heaven. This kind of suffering for the sake of righteousness doesn't feel good, but it produces good. This kind of discontentment or discomfort, which comes because of suffering for the sake of the Lord, is a good thing.

I am not advocating a new doctrine about grace. I believe God's grace is not only free, but it is sufficient to meet our needs. Nothing can diminish the wonder or beauty of God's grace. I simply want to point out that the availability of grace does not eliminate all our difficulties or adversity. Walking with Jesus, serving him, dying to our own flesh and offering God's grace to others will not be without cost or pain. The grace part of the equation may be free, but suffering with Christ and giving of ourselves in service to others, as he did, is never without sacrifice or pain, nor is it without joy and reward.

In police work we need to serve our community as public servants and treat people with dignity and respect and also protect and defend their civil rights. That sometimes is a tall order when you deal with child molesters, rapists and murders. All of these folk will remind you of their rights just in case you forget them. If we relentlessly pursue justice and enforce the law, we make some people unhappy along the way. I quickly came to understand that I wasn't doing my job if I never received any complaints or unfair criticism along the way. It is not our job to make everyone happy.

In a spiritual sense the same applies. Jesus' primary mission was not to make everybody happy, but to sacrifice his life for the sin of the world and to draw us to repentance. Happiness follows because of our repentance and Christ's forgiveness of sin. The wonderful blessings and joy that can follow are by-products of righteous living, obedience, Christ's redemption, grace and generosity. The nexus of joy and happiness that follow often come from obedience and service. You aren't representing Jesus if you don't experience some adversity and pain along the way. The pain and adversity come when we start walking toward the cross. Pain and adversity come when you start sacrificing yourself and your rights. We all have the right to be self-centered and preserve our own way of life. One road leads to death, one leads to life.

If you are a pastor and you are not occasionally making some people in your congregation uncomfortable, you either aren't preaching Jesus, or, you are not preaching about sin and repentance. The road to our redemption begins with the work of the Holy Spirit in our lives. Our discontentment and recognition of our own sin should draw us toward Christ and lead us toward repentance. Repentance should naturally lead to behavior modification. If all we do is eat and feel good about our salvation we are not serving others.

Hardy physical exercise produces sweat and a little pain. The same holds true on a spiritual level. Both of these are good things even though they may produce some level of discomfort. The great apostle Paul, who endured more adversity than most of us will ever comprehend, boldly wrote, "Rejoice in the Lord always: and again I say, rejoice!" (Philippians 4:4). Adversity means you're still in the fight, and it means you aren't dead yet and you may be doing something right if there is a little discomfort and pain along the way. If you are not experiencing some form of conflict and adversity, you are either hiding under the bed or you are already dead, but you just don't know it.

Do cops ever get their uniforms dirty or torn up? My mother used to ask me when I was a child if I had been rolling in the dirt. If you have been rolling in the dirt it shows. When this occurs, those who know you well by your fruits will ask, "You've been serving Jesus today, and involved in warfare, haven't you?" A little blood on your spiritual uniform is a badge of honor. Unlike a baseball player who hasn't yet been in the game, their uniform is spotlessly white and clean. You can tell who has been stealing bases and scoring by the dirt on the front of their uniforms. It's metaphorically beautiful! You need to get out of your comfort zone and into the trenches. Sometimes adversity will come in cycles or seasons. If you are in a time of wonderful prosperity, health, peace, joy and productivity, enjoy it with humility and accountability, but rest assured, it also represents the quiet before the storm. Get mentally prepared for your daily spiritual warfare and be prepared to get your uniform dirty. Be a warrior for Christ!

If you thought our walk with Jesus is just a journey about our salvation, without any kind of cost, you should know that it is not. That is why I made a distinction between grace being free but service and sacrifice not being free. If cost is an issue, it is only fair that you count the cost. The issue of cost requires resolution. In the same way that we have to count the cost of building a new home, we need to do the same in how far we go with Jesus. This is one of the reasons some Christians never get too terribly committed to their spiritual walk. They talk the talk but they don't walk the walk. The cost is more than they care to invest.

What I can tell you about my own journey is that I have never been disappointed with God's goodness toward me. I have often been disappointed with myself. I have also never met a godly person that I respected who ever told me they regretted walking with Christ because the journey was too hard. Likewise, I have never met anyone who has said they regretted giving too much to the Kingdom of God. Nothing that Jesus could ask of us will ever be too much. My biggest fear is that of standing before him wishing I had done more! I don't ever want to regret any aspect of my service unto the Lord. I want to run the good race the apostle Paul spoke about. I don't ever want to look back at my life and feel like I was half-hearted with any talent I had or any possession I could have shared. There are few things in life worse than regret.

Examining the issue of stewardship

Not long ago I heard an excellent sermon on the subject of giving and sharing of our resources. In the course of the message the speaker parenthetically said the same thing we hear other pastors say about church tithing trends. Those who do not give far out number those who do. Some of these figures are sadly disturbing.

Research on tithing trends and giving from around the country reveals that church tithing has fluctuated for more than thirty years. Unlike the song Frank Sinatra sang, "That was a very good year," churches across the United States had no such good year. In 1968, the average church member gave 3.1 percent of their income. Evangelicals gave 6.15 percent, almost double but way below what God asks of us. By 1985 giving by evangelicals dropped to 4.74 percent. By 1990 the average church member gave only 2.66 percent of their income.

By the year 2001, mainline denominational members gave only 3.17 percent of their income and evangelical denominational members were giving 4.27 percent. By contrast the percentage of adults who actually gave any amount of money in 2000 was only 12 percent and by 2002 this number dropped to 6 percent.

Just think of it! For any given year, in over a thirty-year period, only 12 percent of United States church members gave money of any amount and the amount they gave never exceeded 6.15 percent.

The sad truth of this research shows that over these thirty-plus years the income of U.S. Christians increased while the amount of our giving decreased. (The Scandal of the Evangelical Conscience, by Ronald J. Sider; p. 20-21; Baker Books Publishing 2005).

During this thirty-plus year period of time, 88 percent of so-called Christian believers gave nothing! So when the issue of faithfulness is brought up, why do we wonder why some perfidious believers spend their entire lifetime in the desert, waking around in circles as the Israelites did, lamenting about the delicious leeks back in Egypt? God blesses those who walk in faith. God is trying to deliver us from the bondage of Egypt and some of us want to go back home.

An attorney representing Satan would argue that organizationally, no church in the United States actually tithed during this period of time. Whatever pitiful amount was given did not even meet the definition of tithing. So, if one could say you are either pregnant or you are not, then the same might be said of tithing, either you do or you don't. Throwing a token twenty-dollar bill in the offering once in awhile is not tithing; that simply represents a diminutive and delusional effort to relieve guilt.

Thank goodness God is merciful and not ruthless as we are when it comes to money matters, because most of us, if the shoe was reversed, would try to sue God in Small Claims Court. Imagine the wages and penalty fees our infidelity could bring! Imagine if interest was factored in and our tithing debt was imputed unto us like arrears in child or spousal support. If we define tithe, as most theologians do, as being ten percent of all our first fruits, then giving less than ten percent would constitute some *level* of giving, but it would not deferentially or definitively constitute *tithe*. Therefore, it could be argued in the pejorative that, except where faithfulness was demonstrated by individuals, there were no entire churches or organizational church bodies in the United States that truly tithed in this thirty-plus year period of time. I, too, also fell into this horrible category where entire years elapsed in which I did not truly tithe, or, if I gave anything, it did not meet the definition of tithe. Token loose change that we give to some homeless guy panhandling at the baseball park does not constitute tithing; it constitutes nonfeasance. I felt convicted about it when I considered how good God had been to me, and how little I had given back to those in need all around me.

Let me frame it another way. If Jesus asked the senior pastor of every church in America: Is my church, which you lead, faithfully tithing? What would the pastor say? Well, how do you define tithe? Is that 10 percent of the gross or 10 percent of the net? Or, maybe we would ask what constitutes "faithfully"?

Research study by John and Sylvia Ronsvalle concluded that if only the self-proclaimed Christians within the United States, not including Europe or other continents, were to simply tithe, this would generate one hundred and forty three billion dollars a year. It has been estimated by United Nations studies that, in addition to current aid, it would take roughly seventy to eighty billion dollars a year to provide access to essential services like basic health care and education for all the poor of the earth. Ronald Sider points out that if American Christians did no more than just tithe, this would pay for the entire bill and still leave between sixty to seventy billion dollars a year to spread the gospel of Jesus Christ around the world. (The Scandal of the Evangelical Conscience by Ronald J. Sider, p. 22, Baker Books Publishing 2005)

What I find so disturbing about these figures is the thought that eighty-eight percent or more of any congregation, anywhere on the planet, could be so disengaged as to contribute nothing at all to the Kingdom of God. We are talking about members who ostensibly believe in the principles, values and doctrine of their own church, not some opposing political party. How can that many people give so precious little? I find this to be quite amazing, but it also gives me a greater appreciation of how we tenaciously cling to money and that the "love of money" is not some metaphorical blemish that applies to Europeans or some other continental group of people but not Americans.

What makes me so passionate about this is not some personal desire to make you feel guilty to the point that you no longer even want to follow Jesus. It's actually, just the opposite. I don't view tithing failure as some ultimate sin that God could never forgive or that it's intrinsically worse than murdering your neighbor. It's neither of these things. I've been guilty of this myself and I know that God loves and forgives me. He will forgive you too, if you ask him.

God wants to teach us to be both full of wisdom and also be recklessly courageous and full of faith to give ourselves in love to others and not be afraid of dying or of not having our own needs met. This whole thing boils down to getting a glimpse of what it is that Jesus has done for us, and of loving him so much that we want to give our all, like an athlete that performs in the Olympics. I'm not saving myself for a later event. This is the event!

I want you to see how wonderful Jesus is and not later look back at anything in your life and realize that you cheated the Master, the Prince of Peace, out of your financial resources. Money is simply an important piece of the pie, but the principle is not limited to money. The principle here, is represented by the entire pie.

Don't be satisfied with your own mediocrity, your lukewarm affection, or with giving Jesus your leftover bread crumbs; give him your whole life and all your energy and all your resources, and that will be a modest beginning. Sing songs of praise to him at the midnight hour regardless of whether you find yourself on the mountaintop of life, in some prison or jail, or some other pit of darkness. Dance with majesty before the Lord! The Lord has redeemed you! Your circumstances don't dictate who you are! Show some enthusiasm and joy! If you can't do all this in one leap, welcome to the club, but we all need to get engaged in the pursuit of surrendering our lives back to Christ. This has nothing to do with whether we *feel* like celebrating or not. Put one foot in front of the other and take a step in faith. Ask God for help. He is faithful and just and delights in giving his children wisdom, understanding, character, faith and courage. God is good beyond our ability to fully understand it. If we didn't praise God the rocks would cry out! (Luke 19:40).

Sing a new song unto the Lord as though your voice alone represented the world's largest choir and musical production, performed exclusively for the Lord of Hosts. Let your energy and enthusiasm raise the roof like that of world-class symphony conductor Gustavo Dudamel. Shout with fervent joy and dance before the King of kings and show him your moves! Do it with holy respect and passion like you mean it! This goes ways beyond ten percent!

I saw a Giants Vs Padres baseball game last week and the Marine Corps had about 1600 of our finest sitting in the upper grandstand seats of right field at Petco Park in San Diego. The Marines were neatly dressed in their uniforms and hats. During the game the crowd got the "wave" rolling all around the upper decks of the stadium and when it came to the Marines, they threw their arms upward in a rolling motion, to simulate the wave and simultaneously got on their feet and let loose with a "Hoo-rah" that rocked the stadium. It filled my heart with pride. Such praise is befitting of our King. I want that kind of praise and honor to rock the courts of heaven with our love for the Lord and our willingness to serve him even in harm's way. It should come from the heart and not be limited to our money or any other part of our resources. The whole pie belongs to the Lord. We don't have to wait till heaven gets here to start a party. When we give, we should stand up and do a little spiritual wave and shout Hoo-rah, for the joy that stands before us! Our private prayers and songs of praise should rock the gates of heaven like the voices of 1600 mighty warriors at Petco Park.

Our collective failure as Christians, including my own, makes me feel grieved to realize how little we have given. We need to look at giving as something that goes beyond simply paying the pastor a decent salary. Pastors typically have set salaries that are predetermined by the governing board of directors for their church. Pastors don't get paid on the basis of commission like used car salesmen, although sometimes we might wonder about that. If I promise not to preach too much about sin or repentance, or make you feel uncomfortable, and I promise to give a steady diet of "make me feel good sermons" will you raise my salary? It makes you wonder why some pastors only preach the *feel good* doctrine of prosperity. Are you an enabler or a leader? Are we holding each other accountable to Christ and each other?

For those who may wonder how a church budget generally works, all the money that comes into a church through membership giving, or from other donations, gets distributed to a variety of programs that the church board members have voted on or agreed to support. Everything is done through some form of membership representation or church-like-democracy. If you are a member, you can be assured that all your money does not go to the pastor. Some of the money goes to funding children's Sunday school programs, the choir perhaps, and usually a host of other valued ministries that the church membership has voted on and agreed to support.

Not tithing is like being a member of a family that loves and supports you in wholesome ways, but you take advantage of their love and support without offering anything in return. You become strictly a consumer who never gives back anything to the needs of others. When such behavior gets mirrored from the heart in this manner, it can be summarized with the following type of thinking: *I'm an independent operator and I refuse to help the team financially in any fashion. I'm not a team player. I'm a one-man show. I'm not giving squat to anybody! I'm two years old, selfish, and everything I get my hands on is mine!* This always gets euphemistically stated in much more polite language but it reflects that which comes out of the heart. *For where your treasure lies*, Jesus said, *there will your heart be also* (Matthew 6:21).

God still loves you in spite of your confusion, but as you start to grow up, you will eventually come to the understanding that it's not all about you, and your love for others will motivate you into carrying a small portion of your own weight and responsibility. That two-year-old mentality lacks social reciprocity.

Even non-Christians who might be just seekers who attend church and want to learn more about Jesus and his promises, come to a place where common sense says someone has to pay for a pastor, the building, the electricity, air conditioning and heat. So, they reach a place, if only on an intellectual level, that makes them feel like they want to contribute something, even if they only think of it as a "show" at first.

What I was trying to share earlier is that when this love for Jesus becomes a profound thing from your heart, your desire to want to give back should become automatic, instinctive, genuine and sincere and no one should have to tell you to do this, nor beg you to do so. If you see the need you should want to give if you are walking side by side with Jesus. If you see the need and couldn't care less about it, then your heart isn't where it needs to be. Giving comes from the heart and less from the mind. If you are unable, for whatever reason, to give with a heart full of love and thanks, you need to pray about this issue and ask God to change your heart.

What began to profoundly change my life in this area was the recognition that I was not giving from my heart freely or joyfully and that my love for Jesus was not nearly as stellar as I thought it was, nor as I wanted it to be. I confessed it and asked God to help me by circumcising my stony heart. The day I prayed that prayer I felt so low and absent of faith and courage, that I only put two dollars in the offering, but I wept over it with sincerity, and I asked God to do that "little thing" with my two dollars that he did with the five loaves and two fishes. I asked God to increase my capacity to give more in the future. God has been honoring my prayer ever since that day and my faith and capacity to give has increased, as well as my joy. My heart is learning to become more passionate about giving. You probably detect some of that in my writing.

Prayer changes everything! Until I offered that prayer, my heart was unwilling to examine this subject because it was too painful. My heart was aching but the door to that room of my heart was shut. It was only because I allowed the subject to be brought to the table and examined with honesty that I felt convicted, and only because I prayed and asked for help, did anything change. It is entirely possible to go through your whole life with little secret compartments, hidden like illicit love letters in your heart, that tell God, you can't have these *little areas* of my life; I won't surrender this one, small, little thing. If we are not careful, we will take these secrets to the grave with us. God will never open your letters or your heart. Only if you open the door will he come in and change your heart. If you are willing to undergo surgery, he will circumcise your heart, and he will help you overcome your deficiencies and fears. There is room at the cross for you! Everything seems to begin with honest dialogue (prayer).

105

Think globally. Your family or local church may be doing fairly well because you are truly blessed. Don't be fooled into thinking, well, I don't need to contribute. My church needs are already being met. We're doing fine. Without realizing it you are getting into the mind-set that it's all about me. It's not all about you! This is the very point most of us miss. Jesus said, "Feed my sheep." There are people outside of your world or neighborhood who don't have clean water to drink. If your home church is doing fine, increase your missions giving to include Darfur.

Sometimes there are plausibly logical reasons that come to mind for not giving. I don't like giving money to an alcoholic who is going to drink the gift away and further kill himself. That's why I prefer giving to reputable organizations that know how to assist the alcoholic with a sobriety program, and distribute gifts with both love and wisdom. This rationale of withholding our gifts can apply at a global level if we only look at it with dispassionate, business-like thinking, wherein the bottom line is not whether souls are being touched, but whether our efforts are cost effective or not. We can rationalize that giving to countries that can't manage their own affairs is like pouring precious water into a rusty can with holes in the bottom of the can. We conclude it is a waste to do this and we might be tempted to accept the premise of collateral damage, as though there were a certain number of people who will just have to perish because we don't have enough life rafts or mosquito nets to hand out.

Be careful with this type of thinking because it will provide you with every logical reason you could ever hope for, in finding arguments for not giving. Remember what the word of God teaches about our endeavors: *Whatsoever ye do in word or deed, do it in the name of the Lord Jesus* (Colossians 3:17). *Whether therefore ye eat, or drink, or whatsoever ye do, do all to the glory of God (1 Corinthians 10:31). And let us not be weary in well doing: for in due season we shall reap, if we faint not (Galatians 6:9).* Reorient your thinking. We are not just giving to some country; rather, we are giving as unto the Lord. We are not just giving to someone who perhaps does not deserve it, because we didn't deserve God's grace or forgiveness; we are giving as unto the Lord for the purpose of feeding his sheep and fulfilling the second great commandment (love others).

This goes back to the issue of cost and sincerity. You can't do the right thing and serve Jesus and not have it cost you anything. If you are a Christian and you don't contribute anything financially to the Kingdom of God, you are not doing your job!

I'm not sure it's possible to intentionally live a lifelong pattern of not being a part of the solution and claim Jesus at the same time. If you literally can't give because you have mismanaged your finances so badly, then you need to carefully examine your heart on this issue, but more importantly, you probably need to re-examine your choice of lifestyle.

If you married the girl of your dreams would you not treat her with love and affection, and be a faithful provider also? If you were blessed to have beautiful children in such a marriage, would you not feed them? You can't justly argue that you only support your family emotionally with kind words, but you won't support them or share your wealth and resources with them, or otherwise properly care for them with food, clothing and shelter. Such thinking would be unconscionable and despicable.

Why should we think of our relationship with Christ any differently? The Lord wants you to love your family but others as well. If you intentionally left your children destitute no one would listen to your excuses if you told us how much you love them. The same is true spiritually. You can't love God and hate the world and close your eyes to those who are suffering and starving.

We will be judged by our words and by our deeds. We can't say we love God if we hate our brother. Remember the words of Jesus:

> *For I was hungry and you gave me food; I was thirsty and you gave me drink; I was a stranger and you took me in; naked and you clothed me; I was sick and you visited me; I was in prison and you came unto me. When did we do these things? Inasmuch as you have done it unto one of the least of these, you have done it unto me* (Matthew 25:35-40).

These scriptures offer a great way to reorient our thinking so that we are not giving to *just* some country, cause or undeserving person, but rather as unto the Lord himself. As we begin to look at giving the way Jesus views it, we should also get rid of the "deserving" or "undeserving" qualifiers that we sometimes attach to our giving. We need to love people who are unlovely and hard to get along with, not just nice people, or deserving people.

As you ponder these powerful words, please don't think of them as simply some eloquent, or artistic metaphor. Ask God to let the truth of his word soak deep into your heart so that it motivates you to serve others with such honor and dignity, that your Father in heaven will be proud of you. You can do this! Why not become a Mover and a Shaker? Be someone who makes things happen! Get in the game! The stakes are eternal! Picture the person you love the most on this planet, dying in the desert of thirst. Now, visualize someone giving them a drink of cold water from that rusty can filled with holes that were plugged with mud-clay. Think about how their life would be saved and how you would feel about that. Now, go and do likewise. Did you notice that it was unnecessary to ask how the person got into the desert? Were they hiking or was it an airplane crash? If the water saves their life, it won't matter if it came from a rusty can either. Did it matter when it was the one you loved?

Some people get fed pretty well at their local church by their local pastor, but they send a substantial portion of their tithe to some fancy T.V. evangelist who, I can assure you, won't fly out to your city to pray for your wife in the hospital, nor will the T.V. evangelist conduct funeral services for your son. I'll bet the T.V. evangelist also won't counsel your daughter who may be contemplating an abortion, but if he were willing to, you wouldn't be able to afford his fee.

I could not imagine eating at my favorite restaurant but never leaving a tip for my food server. Conversely, I could not imagine eating at my favorite restaurant, but then walking across the street and leaving my tip at a different restaurant because I really like the waitress over there, or because the T.V. evangelist eats over there. If you practice exchanging gifts at Christmas time, would you tell your children that you have no gifts for them this year because you gave all your gifts to the children across the street?

Most of us would not think of cheating the food server out of their tip at the restaurant where we eat. Most people that I know who eat out leave a minimum of 15 percent and often more for their waitress or waiter, yet often people don't think twice about not tithing at the church where they are spiritually fed. You should tithe at the church you belong to and attend. Don't refrain from becoming a member because you think legally I won't have to tithe if I never become a "member" of that church. The prophet Malachi asked the question: would a man rob God? The Bible describes the practice of withholding tithe as stealing from God. See what the scripture says about this and the incredible "I double dare you" offer that God makes to people (Malachi 3:8-11).

The spiritual principle of giving and reaping what we sow is so fundamental, reliable and proven that even business corporations understand that giving back to the community and to the poor is like loaning money to God. Giving is good business and it can produce both personal and corporate blessings because it represents a sound principle (Proverbs 19:17). You can't do the right thing and not have God bless you for doing it. God has promised to take care of us. Go figure! Corporate America gets it better than most Christians do!

If you can't leave your food server a decent tip you should not be eating out. Stay home. You probably need to eat corn flakes once in awhile! These folks work hard and without tips they would not make a living. Think about your giving to God. He deserves your best, not leftovers, loose change or your old blue sweatshirt. A gift that cost you nothing means nothing! Abraham could have offered God your kid as a sacrifice instead of Isaac, but that would not have cost Abraham anything, nor would it have tested Abraham's faith.

This all boils down to the same thing I said about loving your wife and your children. It's simply not limited to them. Would you go out to dinner with anyone if, time and time again, they never offered to pay the dinner bill, and just left it up to you? The truth speaks for itself. No hyperbole is necessary to explain it. You either do the right thing or you don't. If you have been sitting on the bleacher seats, or in the church pew, watching the game, but otherwise doing nothing, I encourage you to get directly involved in the game of life. It's a game of life and death, and what you do, or fail to do, will make a difference.

If you fall into this category and you feel badly about not giving back to God a portion of your substance and all of your blessings, that is a good thing, because you should feel convicted! That feeling of guilt or conviction may be the work of the Holy Spirit softly whispering to you that God can help you to become more than you will ever be on your own, if you surrender all of your heart, your gifts and talents to him.

One thing is certain. If you feel guilty about this, that means you are struggling to do the right thing and your heart is open to this, otherwise you wouldn't care at all. If your heart is already as hard as a rock and you are almost dead now, then you might not feel any guilt. If you care about doing the right thing, and you are struggling with this issue, then you can choose to do the right thing, especially with God's help. Ask God for his help! You will feel better about yourself just as I did about myself. Learn to give more. If you don't think about this and deal with it, your behavior won't change.

Understand that God still loves you dearly and irrespective of what you may think about others trying to steal your money, God is not one of them. God is a gracious Father who loves to bless his children and bestow gifts upon them, but he also wants you to learn how to give because it reflects his ways and his own spirit of generosity to others. He gave his life for you and he wants you to give your life in service to others also. Spiritual maturity requires that we grow up a little and learn to trust God with the small stuff first. He who is faithful with little will be faithful with much (Luke16:10).

This isn't something I made up. These are the words of Christ! God wants to shine through you to the world but he needs to win your heart first. He wants us, his children, to represent him well. God is not cheap and he doesn't want us to live like we are either. God wants his children to reflect his generosity. Your character needs to be developed, along with your understanding of God. God wants you to understand his character. Jesus said: *Take no thought, saying, what shall we eat? or, what shall we drink? or, how shall we be clothed? For all these things do the nations of the world seek after: and your heavenly Father knows that you have need of these things. But rather seek first the Kingdom of God and all these things shall be added unto you* (Luke12:30-31).

God does not personally need your money. Others all around you do. We are to be the hands and feet of Jesus to a lost and dying world. Jesus wants you to do what he did; give yourself and your resources away so that others might live. Jesus wants to minister to those who are in need, but his plan is to do that through you, because he wants to develop your character and enrich your life.

The Lord is not experiencing a cash flow problem this month. He wants your heart, not your money. If you surrender your heart completely, the Lord will automatically have your wallet also because the two are attached at the hip. Giving is a byproduct of spiritual faithfulness. Jesus described the principle perfectly: where your treasure lies, there will your heart be also. He wants you to learn to give to others and to trust him that he will supply your needs. He wants you to learn how to swim and survive in stormy seas, but he also wants you to learn that it's possible to walk on water if you trust him. Peter walked on water even if it was just for a few moments. The Lord isn't trying to steal your money. You need to learn to give it away and trust him that he will not abandon you for feeding his sheep or loving others with your assets. You can't out give God!

There is no single thing beside money, except for maybe life itself, that I see people clutch so tightly and hang onto so fiercely. The *love* of money is the root of all evil. That is why Jesus said it would be easier for a camel to go through the eye of a needle than for a rich man to enter heaven. If we can't be trusted with money, we are delusional to think we can be trusted with other things.

We cling to money like we are going to need it when we get to heaven to pay for association fees on a condo. I have news for you! God doesn't have condos or "fixer uppers" in heaven; God has mansions! Think bigger! Don't limit how big God can be in your life. Ask God to help you start thinking bigger and with greater boldness. Take a risk in Christ and start living dangerously! Start with simple obedience to God's word.

Most of us who are in reasonably good health, at least if we have no respiratory illnesses, don't think twice about whether there will be an ample supply of air to breathe tomorrow morning. Most of us never think about running out of air unless you are in the Navy working in a submarine out at sea. We don't worry about the ocean running dry next week and we don't worry that God hasn't provided air for us to breathe. We might be worried that mankind has screwed the air up, but there still will be plenty of it, even if it's dirty air.

Why do we worry so much about money? You are not taking it with you, wherever it is that you are going. We seem to be able to trust God that he can forgive us and save our souls, but we can't trust him with *our* money! What is wrong with this picture? Dear God, help us to understand we are mistaken to think it's *our* money or that we can't trust you. We act like God might not meet our needs if we give a small portion of it to the poor. Dear Jesus, Wonderful Savior, forgive us for not even knowing what your word says. Would you be curious to know how God views giving to the poor? Just read his word...just this one time and don't ever do it again; it might bless you or open your eyes! Read Proverbs 19:17.

It all belongs to God if you are his child. Everything we have belongs to him if he is Lord and Savior. You need to get your mind set straight on this. Nothing belongs to you! It can all be taken away from you in the blink of an eye. I knew a good officer on the SWAT team who was in his mid thirties and in good physical shape. A valve in his heart ruptured and he was dead before he hit the floor. His wife was upstairs and her a thud on the floor downstairs. She called his name out and got no response. She walked downstairs to investigate and found him on the floor quite dead. The autopsy report revealed he died instantly. Every breath of air you take is a gift from God. Remember that and stop being so arrogant about your empire! It all belongs to the Lord and you should consider it the greatest honor one could ever have in this lifetime, to be a servant and steward to the Lord of Hosts! You don't own anything, not even your children. They are blessings and gifts from God and you should be thankful for each moment that you have with them, but always remember they are not your property; they belong to God, just like everything else you manage.

If we closely examine some of our thinking when it comes to the subject of giving, we will most likely discover fear. If the Great Physician sliced our hearts open with a scalpel to examine what was inside our hearts, many of us would fall into a category that would show a desire from within to give. For many, the ultimate issue is not opposition to giving or sharing of resources; it's fear that our own needs won't be met if we give generously of our resources. We don't ruminate about why we don't want to give, but often it boils down to fearful thinking. If I give too much of my resources away, *there won't be anything left for me.* It is a lack of faith and trust in God. And, everyday that you are not saturating your mind with the things of God, Satan whispers this lie into your ear, that you will not have enough if you give it away. Individually, we need to confront this fear and ask God to help us overcome it.

Your actions speak louder than your words. Nothing in life speaks louder than behavior. If you think about it, this represents Jesus. He went to the cross for us. Aren't you glad Jesus did not walk away from the cross because the cost was too high? At the Last Supper, Jesus lifted the cup, knowing what it represented, and gave thanks. This is my blood, shed for you, Jesus said. Think of it! As he held the cup, he thanked his Father for the opportunity of suffering that he was about to experience at Calvary for you and for me (Luke 22:17-20).

Bill Hybels describes the issue of tithing and giving as a heartfelt issue that we need to put into the perspective of the bloodstained cross and what Christ did for us. Hybels points out that if we make the decision to give from this perspective, we give differently. (Bill Hybels' sermon: "The End of Financial Folly;" www.PreachingTodaySermons.com; A Resource of Christianity Today International).

Unbelievers sometimes do not understand all of our spiritual language, but they do understand the concept of good stewardship. The world also clearly understands that the ability or failure to manage money speaks louder than any holy talk or other credentials we might offer in most cases. The world cares less about what you say and more about what you do. How's your credit? How's your tithing?

The inability to manage money can be a job breaker. For example, you may not be hired by some agencies if you have not managed money well. You won't get a government Top Secret clearance for sensitive work of any kind if you can't manage your financial affairs. If you had trouble paying your taxes, you may have trouble with Senate confirmation hearings.

The world doesn't care about your religious view unless you are a terrorist. The business world, to a lesser extent, but clearly the government, both have concerns about whether you pose a liability because of how you have handled money matters in the past. Past performance is often viewed as the best predictor of future performance. How you handle money is huge! If you have an interest in any field of work that requires a security clearance, expect your background to be scrutinized closely by the government. The absence of good financial stewardship has been proven to be a factor that causes some people to be more of an employment liability than an asset. People who get into financial trouble are often susceptible to various forms of manipulation and sometimes these people can be induced to sell government or corporate trade secrets to foreign powers. People that fall into this category may become an excellent source or target for bribery and extortion. It doesn't mean that you would do any of these bad things, but it puts you at a huge disadvantage if you have a bad credit rating and you are perceived to be an employment risk.

How you handle money can affect your testimony for Christ. Your testimony is not going to mean anything to the world if you get arrested and jailed for Federal income tax evasion. I use this example because I actually knew of an ordained minister, preaching Jesus and his redeeming power, who was willfully not paying any income tax over a substantial period of time. This is contrary to Bible scripture and common sense. Jesus even paid taxes because he came not to overthrow the government but to overthrow sin.

I suppose you could write books in prison on how to become financially independent or perhaps you could write a theological paper on why one would not need to tithe on money that was illegally earned. That might be provocative, don't you think?

I am speaking about principles of good stewardship. How you live reflects the presence or absence of character. One does not have to love God in order to follow this logic because most decent people already understand it. My testimony and your testimony mean absolutely nothing if we both go to jail for lying, stealing, cheating or otherwise mismanaging money.

Like evidence offered in the courtroom, an assay of scientific scrutiny, or an expert witness examined with vigorous cross-examination, the truth either stands up under bright light or it collapses, just like our testimony about how well we know and follow Jesus.

Money is huge and that is why I am emphasizing this so strongly. It is an area of weakness for many people. The subject is not limited to Christianity or religious principles of faith. Stewardship also represents "good business" and reflects trustworthiness.

Jesus spoke more about money than most other subjects. Jesus understood the earthly power and influence that money brings and all the corruption that can come along with it. Most people could not handle the temptation that could be brought to bear on them over money matters. Judas Iscariot betrayed Jesus for thirty pieces of silver.

Why is money such a big deal?

- money is a powerful tool
- money unlocks earthly doors
- money can buy judges, presidents and countries

- money can buy people: over 800,000 people a year are sold into slavery and prostitution according to Homeland Security estimates
- money is the last stronghold
- money is the deal breaker
- money reflects the priorities of our heart
- money is security
- money is peace of mind
- money represents unspeakable earthly pleasure
- money represents your children's inheritance
- money buys a 5,000 square foot villa but not the empty tomb
- money is the weak link between you and Jesus

The love of money is the root of all evil (I Timothy 6:10). Other than that, it's not that big of a deal, right? Are you kidding? There are few things that speak as loudly about your walk and character as money. You may not have a problem with money because you are faithful to God and perhaps your struggle is with something else. The fact is the vast majority of Christians struggle with stewardship. I have had problems with money, some of which were beyond my control and some that were not. I am no better or more righteous than you are and my failure at this is partly why I write about it. Looking at where we are and seeing where we need to be is the first step in turning financial conflict and adversity around.

If you are in such a position, it may very well be that you are so far into debt because of mistakes that have been made that it may take you several years to get out of your current situation. If this represents your situation, I would encourage you to honestly take a hard look at your finances. Seek sound advice and help. Make a decision and a commitment to turn things around.

Beside credit consolidation and a number of other practical things you can do, one of the best strategies you need to look at and be very honest about is so simple that I am almost embarrassed to even say it, but you need to live within your means. Doing that is far less complicated than most people make it out to be.

There are more excuses on the table than Carter has pills, but people save next to nothing and live in homes that are far more expensive than many can afford. Then they blame everything on the stock market and economic conditions. Don't live in a million dollar home if you should be in a modest condo. If you can't save a little money as you go along, you are doing something wrong, most likely living above your means. I don't care how much money you make or don't make; I have never seen an alcoholic who didn't have enough money for just one more drink. Even if they did not actually have the money, they could always manage somehow to obtain the money, even if that meant begging for it or stealing to obtain it. If you can't put a little aside every month for a rainy day, economic hard times or famine, you are not doing everything you can to manage your financial affairs.

113

If you lost your job and have become unemployed by no fault of your own, Jesus understands that and wants to help you get back in the work force because he knows what you have need of before you even ask. If you have children, Jesus knows and cares about the fact that you need to feed your children. Ask God to help you find work. He is faithful and he wants us to learn that it is possible to walk in faith, practice good stewardship and still succeed. If, on the other hand, you are having trouble paying your bills and you are not tithing because of your yacht payment, then get rid of the yacht.

Not all failure or adversity is your fault and nothing that I am writing is intended to remotely suggest that it is, however, more often than not, we don't practice the right principles to begin with, such as living within our means, tithing and putting aside money on a regular basis through savings for a rainy day. The unfortunate, honest truth is that most people, yet, not all, live in debt up to their eyeballs and most Christians fall into the perfidious eighty-eight percentile of those who don't tithe at all. If you are unemployed now, ask yourself if you were faithful to God with your tithing and stewardship when you did have a job.

If you have had any part or role in your own financial failure because of mismanagement of resources, examine that and be honest with yourself and with God about it. Stop making your financial failure so complicated. Most of the time it is not complicated and it boils down to simple arithmetic, *Vis à Vis*, budgeting. If you practice living on the edge by overextending yourself or your investments to the point that if anything goes wrong you will be facing financial collapse or disaster, then maybe you need to reassess your mission statement and redefine what constitutes good business and faithful stewardship.

Righteous living does not require a Harvard MBA degree. You may remember Mr. Hammerwall from Chapter One who sent money to my parents in the jungles of Brazil. I can assure you the only degree this dishwasher had was from the University of Hard Knocks.

God doesn't want people to lose their homes or have them repossessed through foreclosure, but he also doesn't want us living so far beyond our means that we can't tithe, pay income tax or property taxes, or have two dollars in our pocket to buy popcorn at the movies. It's not God's plan for any of us to fail, or have us face the possibility of jail because of financial mismanagement. Good financial asset-management is all about the principle of managing our resources and practicing good stewardship through sound judgment, common sense and integrity. Even Jesus paid taxes when he was asked to do so and he told us to give unto Caesar that which belongs to Caesar, and unto God the things that are God's (Matthew 22:21).

If you know in your heart that you have not been doing everything you can to be a good steward, start turning things around. Stop making excuses if you are part of the problem and ask God to help you do a better job. Do your part by getting rid of those "things" that you know are impeding you and make a commitment to live within your means. Remember, God doesn't shoot people in the feet; we pretty much do that to ourselves.

This is the time and place to change your behavior and take ownership and responsibility for your financial affairs, and ask God to help you learn to trust him more, and start doing your fair share of giving some of it away! Remember, as I have to frequently remind myself, it's not *yours* anyway! This is what repentance is all about. Start by simply being honest with yourselves and with God. After asking for forgiveness and help, what follows should be a change of behavior. Consider how eager God is to help his children when they ask him for righteousness and character!

You may well experience a new joy you haven't had before by giving faithfully to the works of Christ with your first fruits. Don't give your left-overs. Give of the cream of your crop, your very best! This is the *principle* God wants us to learn as his children. God gave you his very best; he gave his only begotten son as ransom for your soul.

So, why don't I feel better about myself or more satisfied? Some of that dissatisfaction comes from our failure to understand and follow spiritual laws and principles, and some of it comes from failing to fully surrender our lives and resources to Christ by walking faithfully in obedience. Asking ourselves this question is important, but exploring the real reason for the discontentment is far more important. We may not like the answer but we should not reject the truth simply because it tends to make us feel uncomfortable. The truth may be we are selfish and unwilling to pay the cost of serving others, if it goes beyond giving cookies to homeless people during the Christmas season.

Again, Jesus did not come to earth simply to make people feel good. Feeling good is a wonderful, serendipitous by-product of grace and righteous living; however, Jesus' primary reason for coming into the world was to save lost souls by offering his life as a ransom for our sin. That's why the scripture says you were *bought with a price*, referring to the *cost* that Jesus paid on the cross on your behalf. Some of that hard-to-define, unconscious, discontentment that we can't quite put our finger on may come from the Holy Spirit, given to us so that we become motivated to serve the needs of others as Christ did. The Spirit whispers in our ear, there is more to life than what you are experiencing. Open your heart to the gentle voice of the Holy Spirit. God wants to use you and partner with you. Those in need of Jesus and his pragmatic power are all around us.

One Franciscan benediction I recently heard touches on this issue of giving our lives away in service to others with this eloquent prayer: (unknown author)

May God bless you with discomfort
At easy answers, half truths and superficial relationships
So that you may live deep within your heart.
May God bless you with anger
At injustice, oppression and exploitation of people,
So that you may work for justice, freedom and peace.
May God bless you with tears

To shed for those who suffer pain, rejection, hunger and war
So that you may reach out your hand to comfort them and
To turn their pain into joy.
And may God bless you with enough foolishness
To believe that you can make a difference in the world,
So that you can do what others claim cannot be done,
To bring justice and kindness to all our children and the poor.

Some of this lack of fulfillment comes from being too absorbed in our own comfort. Sometimes we simply get too satisfied with our own surfeiting or, as I like to sarcastically refer to myself, I become satisfied with *my own lovely self*. We don't usually describe our lives that crudely; we like to refer to our good living as well deserved and having the rich quality of being content or otherwise blessed. It sounds less selfish because it's the fruit of our labor.

At the same time we often lack the full joy of the Lord. We feel kind of miserable and unfulfilled but not *that bad!* We want the joy and fulfillment that is ostensibly possible in Christ. We want the good life! We want to walk with Jesus at times, but we don't really want to walk toward the cross, certainly not for the purpose of crucifying our sinful flesh, nor for the purpose of offering our lives as a sacrifice for anyone else. We want our cake and we want to eat it, too. We want Jesus and we want to become whole, but we don't want to go too deep with this stuff, or face our own pathology.

Herein lies the juxtaposition of conflict. Jesus said: *If any man will come after me, let him deny himself, and take up his cross and follow me* (Matthew 16:24). I find it hard to deny myself even a single meal. I don't want to give up anything. I want the meal (super-size it) and the cake for dessert! This conflict over living or dying is what we struggle with and why we cling so desperately to life. Our flesh is at war with our spirit. It's what the apostle Paul wrote about. The flesh does not want to die, and that is the same reason why we don't want to tithe or give our lives away in service. We are all very much into preserving ourselves, rather than giving our lives to save others, and this is one of the reasons we lack deep fulfillment.

That *feeling good, euphoric stage* comes after going to the cross, after giving your life to others; after walking in obedience, something which seems to have a cost all its own. Too often, we are withholding part of, or all of, ourselves and our resources because we are afraid of our own cross. Jesus said that whosoever will lose his life for my sake shall find it (Matthew 16:25).

Everyone's battle looks slightly different. For some, life's biggest struggle consists of losing weight. I need to lose more weight myself but I've had a horrible time trying to make it happen. It never used to be this hard. When I worked out I could eat anything and everything, and I did. I can't do that now. My metabolism in younger days used to burn those calories right up. Now, if I eat two grapes I could put on five pounds. I need to take better control of my eating habits, yet I really don't want to, so there you have it!

I struggle just like everyone else. Weight loss is a legitimate issue. I already confessed to you about the potato chips I ate. The fact is, I don't want to ever stop eating potato chips, but I want to lose weight. I want to be just like Jesus but I don't want to eat less.

I look at other people sometimes and secretly think of them as being pathetic. When I look at myself I sometimes gasp and think, wow, you got to do something about this dude, but I somehow manage to forgive myself. I'm not sure how that is possible but it seems to happen quite frequently. If I look at someone else I may think of them as being undisciplined but I rarely look at myself this way. If I look at myself in the mirror, I think I need to get another mirror; this one doesn't work right. I am pretty much a self-righteous hypocrite and I am sure that Jonah and I could become best friends. We could both watch Nineveh burn to the ground while eating a combination pizza.

It is more complicated than you even think. I already lack humility and I don't have an ounce of compassion in me. I could have been a disciple! Wait a minute; I am a disciple! Wow, that's a scary thought. This is getting ugly. I actually have the willpower to do just about anything I deem myself to be capable of doing, providing I put my heart, soul and energy into the effort. In an absurd sort of way I am half afraid to lose weight. If you think I am hard to live with now, wait till I slim down. I can see it already. Yet, I feel guilty for making excuses. I wouldn't accept your phony excuses if I caught you speeding. You would probably get a ticket even if you were the Pope. Why do I accept my own phony excuses? For the same reason you do: because the flesh is weak, and I am no exception to this rule.

I want to lose weight and I am actually doing so but I don't want this little victory to be the only dominant goal in my life to the exclusion of other things. Taking care of my body and taking care of my spirit do not have to become an issue of it's "one or the other." I need to do both. Having said that, if I should fail at one of these endeavors, or if it boils down to the fact that I can't sleep at night, I would rather have the reason be, that I care more about the lost souls of dying men and women than I do about whether my butt looks too big. Nevertheless, I want to lose weight and be a good disciple, too.

My perception is that too many of us are too self-absorbed in our own issues and problems. It isn't a matter that our problems are not real. They usually are, but when compared to others, our problems often seem far smaller. I remind myself of this when I see members of our Armed Forces coming back from Iraq with permanent brain damage and missing limbs. It makes me realize that my weight loss battle is more manageable than I realized.

The needs all around us are great! The laborers are few. We should be a little distraught. We need to sacrificially give of our time, money and energy until it hurts. People are drowning, burning, starving, thirsting and grieving in deep despair and not enough of us are aware there is a problem. If we stop focusing on ourselves so much and we redevelop our passion for Christ, two things will happen: the joy of the Lord will become our strength and our awareness of the needs of others will consume us with a burning passion to serve others and feed the Lord's sheep.

Other earthly pleasures are nice, but they become less important as we sacrifice our rights. For the joy that was set before him, Jesus endured the cross, despising the shame (hebrews 12:2). If you are anything like me, I have not had to "endure" that terribly much of anything. I want to start doing more and giving more.

There is a great joy that comes with service. If you have ever had the wonderful privilege of saving, or helping to save, someone's life you will know what I mean. There is something indescribably special about living on the edge of life and death that brings an appreciation for life itself. It will make you feel alive! Lying on the couch might become boring after this. If you live through one of these things, it changes you in some ways. It becomes a defining moment in your life when you are willing to pay the ultimate price to help someone. What follows is a profound sense of gratitude that the person you helped to save made it and so did you. You not only appreciate the value of their life, but your own as well.

I can tell you that at times in my career where I have put my life at risk I never had any regret, or ambivalence as to whether I did the right thing, or not, neither during the incident or afterwards. These things seem to happen in a split second and you don't have an hour to think about the choice you are making. If we had that much time to think about this stuff, none of us would ever do the right thing.

The decision to serve the Lord should be just like going to work. Before you leave the house for work, make the decision to give your all to the Lord, up to and including your life, if it should be required of you. There is no greater gift than that a man lay down his life for another. If you accept this premise, and make that decision, everything else falls into place. Later in the day when you run into Goliath, you won't have to deliberate about it all day because the thing involves some personal risk to your life. You already made that important decision before you left the house this morning. Now it's just a matter of saying Lord, be with me as I do this. The biggest battle most of us will ever face is simply making the decision to follow Jesus.

I believe with all my heart that spiritually the same principle applies to all of us. I have never felt like I was doing too much for Jesus. The thrill of doing the right thing overtakes you in the moment and your *rights* become inconsequential; you simply don't care about your rights at that time. The joy, which I experienced, following each of my own events, was profound and euphoric. I did the right thing! It felt wonderful! Service to others is something you will never regret. This is what produces that *feeling good stage!* The joy of which I speak doesn't precede the cross, it proceeds the cross.

When we commit ourselves to this kind of service we will naturally adjust our mind-set more toward Kingdom business. By that I mean, we can learn to, and choose to, stop sweating the small stuff, the dirty dishes, or the minor argument you had with your son or daughter. Eternal issues become more important. If your life hangs in the balance I can tell you that you won't be worrying about the scratch that someone put on your car. Life takes on a whole new meaning. I believe that is exactly what Jesus is calling us to: an exciting dance with life and death and servanthood.

Our source is the Lord if we put all of these things into eternal perspective. Everything we "own" or think we own, including every breath of air we take, belongs to the Lord. We are simply stewards.

Living a balanced life

Why don't I feel better about myself and how come grace isn't making me feel any better? We know what we believe at the intellectual level, and sometimes even at the deep, heart-felt level, but why is it not working for me at the gut level of everyday living?

Another common reason I believe this happens is because we don't live a balanced life physically or spiritually and we don't set boundaries. Part of living a balanced life is getting enough rest. It is literally amazing what a good night's sleep does for one. Having said that, it is also important to recognize that you can't burn the candle twenty-four seven and deplete yourself, like a college student, then expect one good night of sleep to re-energize your whole being.

Sleep deprivation is so commonly understood to be effective in breaking people down that it is used by the military to interrogate suspected terrorists. We do it unintentionally to ourselves. Take good care of yourself. Jesus understood this principle and that is why he devoted time to prayer and rest. His walking on the water was not intended to be a circus trick, but rather reflected time he spent alone with his heavenly Father restoring his spirit. If you don't take good care of yourself, you won't be of much help to anyone else.

In police work one of the really important things that we have to teach rookies is how to successfully drive a patrol car, day in and day out without crashing. As an FTO (Field Training Officer), I would remind recruits to avoid the mentality that if they did not get to the emergency before everyone else, the world would end. That sounds simple enough, but in this line of work your arrival at the scene of a crisis can literally mean the difference between life and death. The rookie understands this. When a fellow officer yells for help on the radio, we all understand that can mean life or death. We want to rush to the officer's aid so that the officer does not get injured or end up having to shoot someone. We don't want anyone to die. If you drive too fast to that call or take your turns too hot you are going to crash, and then you become of no use to the officer that needed you the most. Humbly understand and appreciate your limitations. Don't frantically throw all wisdom out the window because the cause is just.

Lots of research taught us that if we can inculcate that principle of wisdom into a rookie and they can make it through an entire first year of street patrol without crashing, then they have an excellent chance of going many years without crashing if they practice the principles they are taught. Teaching young officers how to pace themselves in code three driving (emergency lights and siren) is just one of the many important things an FTO tries to teach recruits.

Sound wisdom has widespread application at all levels of life. Our spiritual lives are no different. Sometimes the most spiritual thing you can do is simply go to bed and get a good night's sleep. If we don't recognize our own limitations and need for rest, we can start to unconsciously live like the world can't survive another day without us. Set boundaries for yourself and others. Take care of yourself and be kind to yourself. Don't be afraid to ask for help. If you start thinking nobody can do this task except me, you are setting yourself up for failure and setback. No matter how wonderful you actually are, you can be replaced. This should remind us to practice humility. But even if there was some truth to the assertion that no one can replace you because you are the best person for the job, and God picked you for the assignment, the principle still applies. Moses comes to mind.

If your burdens are causing you to sink like a parachute that is on fire, it doesn't really matter how this came to be. What's important now is how to overcome the immediate crisis and save your life. Once you stabilize your fall then failure analysis might be helpful.

God gave Moses the daunting job of leading the Israelites out of Egypt. In his quest to serve God faithfully and diligently Moses reached a point where he was completely overwhelmed by bearing the personal conflicts and issues of all these people. They came to him day and night like fighting children complaining that Johnny took my bicycle and he won't give it back to me. Moses tried to do it all himself. What is fascinating about this story is that Moses not once asked God for any practical advice about this issue, ostensibly because he did not want to bother God with trivial matters. Here we see the doctrine of "don't ask, don't tell." If we don't ask, God doesn't tell. It took Moses' father-in-law, Jethro, to volunteer a solution to Moses for this onerous problem in the form of sound advice: delegate these burdens (Exodus 18:12-24). Jethro probably never went to seminary!

Sometimes we can stretch ourselves so thin that we put ourselves into exhaustion and thereby create our own demise. We need to set boundaries and sometimes say "no," I can't do that or take that project on because I am overcommitted already. For example, if you are a full-time caregiver to someone, such as a family member suffering from Alzheimer's disease, you need all the help, support, and relief you can get on a regular ongoing basis. This kind of service to others is intense and the weight of it is emotionally and physically draining. The last thing this caregiver needs is for someone to ask them to teach a Sunday school class or head some committee. This person needs a two week vacation for every two weeks of service they provide. Of course they don't get that but they deserve it.

Focusing on things above

Sometimes we simply get weary from non-stop adversity and the cares of this life. The cares and issues we deal with are usually real enough, and we get overwhelmed with the load and choked by the cares and burdens of this world.

In so doing we simply overfocus on our problems and we don't take our eyes off the problems. We start forgetting that there is nothing too difficult for God. We become tired and fatigued and we forget to look upward. The solution is to get your eyes off horizontal matters of earth and look upward toward heavenly resources.

It is hard to have a perspective that our earthly struggles and suffering are temporal, but Paul describes the solution to this problem. *Therefore we look not at the things which are seen, but at the things which are not seen: for the things which are seen are temporal; but the things which are not seen are eternal* (2 Corinthians 4:18).

We orient ourselves to the things we can see, touch and understand with our senses and that leads us to focus on the earthly side of things including our feelings. This problem is so real and common that I can say I don't think I have ever met or known any Christian who does not get discouraged or worn out with overcoming the world with all its burdens. Just plain, simple life makes it possible to become weary in well doing. It happened to Job for very obvious reasons, but it happened to all the great ones, including Elijah and King David, and it happens to you and me.

Some people might feel that they are not inclined to be confrontational or warrior-like because it does not represent their makeup, personality or style. That's perfectly O.K. because we are all members with different gifts and talents but we are all part of the same family. We don't all want to be the same nor do we need to be. God uses you because of your individual uniqueness, talents and abilities. You don't have to be someone else; just be yourself.

The last lieutenant that I worked for in the Sheriff's Office used to tease me relentlessly at times and usually in front of all my peers. On one such day I was working at the security checkpoint at the entrance to the Hall of Justice. The "LT" (pronounced "el tee" in police lingo) walked past me and then, almost as though he was doing it for effect, abruptly turned around and approached me as though he had something very serious or urgent to say. He smiled at me and looked me straight in the eye and affectionately said, "Remember, Malmin, we wouldn't even talk to you if we didn't like you! I pick on you because we like you." I laughed because I knew he meant it.

God loves you just the way you are even with your faults and weaknesses. We look at how we are and get discouraged. God looks at how we are but sees what we will be. We look at ourselves and see failure. God looks at us and sees possibilities and untapped talent and potential. We look at ourselves and think we are the least of all our family or coworkers. God looks at us through the work of Calvary and sees us as overcoming conquerors.

We tend to underestimate our own value and potential. We look at our own strength and we tremble. God looks at us and says when I anoint you, you will become a mighty vessel and warrior. Mother Teresa was such a warrior. And so are you! You just need to have the scales removed from your own eyes so that you can see. Christ does just that when you turn to him and let him empower you.

These are principles of faith that work, not tricks. But your mind-set or attitude is all-important. When we think victoriously victory comes as no surprise. If we think in terms of defeat we expect it, but worst of all, we accept it. Our thinking greatly influences whether we succeed or fail. Our thinking reflects what comes from our heart. It's what we are willing to accept, victory or defeat, life or death. King Solomon wrote: *For as he [a man] thinketh in his heart, so is he* (Proverbs 23:7). Jesus spoke of this also saying: *out of the abundance of the heart the mouth speaketh* (Matthew 12:34).

When the ten members of the reconnaissance team returned from the Promised Land, Caleb and Joshua calmed the people and said, *Let us go up at once and possess it, for we are well able to overcome it.* There is that word again that Jesus speaks of: he who overcometh.

But the rest of the team (eighty percent) brought an evil report, the scripture says, and reported: *there are giants in the land who are stronger than we and we were in our own sight as grasshoppers, and so we were in their sight* (Numbers 13:30-33).

Here again, we see mind-set and attitude. We look at ourselves as being inadequate for the job. Well, of course, if you are looking at your own strength! What made the report "evil" was not factual information about the enemy but an attitude of defeat, which translated into thinking that God was not big enough to help them overcome their battles. Caleb and Joshua viewed their strength as coming from the hand of the Lord based on his promise regarding this land, and God's many prior acts of power and victory, and they looked at the whole situation through the eyes of courage and faith. Be careful who you listen to! Be careful of how you allow your thinking to run wild.

When I was in the Army I was deployed to Germany. I was stationed in the Big Red One. That is a famous infantry division. The Big Red One's motto was written on a sign that greeted visitors as they entered our compound. It read: No Mission Too Difficult. No Sacrifice Too Great. Duty First! Underneath these words the sign read: The difficult we do immediately; the impossible takes just a little longer.

All things are possible for those who have faith. The Big Red One is a faithful group of men and women with a "can do" attitude. This attitude permeates from the infantry soldiers to the mission support personnel up and down the chain of command. Shouldn't those of us who know Jesus be living and thinking this way?

You have heard of the battle of Gideon. Gideon was not a Navy Seal or Airborne Ranger by today's standards. In fact, he probably wasn't much to look at and the scripture tells us that when Gideon spoke to the Lord he described himself, not as the biggest, the bravest or the badest, but as being the least in his father's house. We look at ourselves and we see inadequacy. I'll bet he couldn't do that many push-ups either! Little runt! But look at how God viewed Gideon. *And the angel of the Lord appeared unto him, and said unto him, The Lord is with thee, thou mighty man of valor!* (Judges 6:12-15).

Mother Teresa probably weighed not much more than one hundred pounds on a good day, but she was a mighty warrior of valor also, and in her quiet, unassuming way slayed Goliaths all around the world. I look forward to having a cup of jo with her when I get to heaven. Mother Teresa was herself a giant who personified the love of Jesus to the marginal and lowly.

King David slew a lion with his bare hands and killed Goliath and cut his head off. David was not unaccustomed to danger. In the book of 1st Samuel we read an incredible story, the kind of which you would normally see in a well-crafted movie these days. David and his men return from a trip back to their home town to find the city had been burned and their wives and children had been kidnapped and taken hostage.

Talk about a bad day! How many people do you know that have had family members kidnapped? The scripture says David and the people wept until they had no more power to weep. One would think the situation could not get any worse but it did. David's men wanted to blame David for everything that had happened and they were ready to stone him. I wonder what I am going to have for dinner tonight and David has to wonder if he will ever see his family alive again or whether his own men are going to kill him. Here is this mighty warrior who is down in the pit of hell with discouragement, loss and grief most of us could never even imagine (1 Samuel 30:1-18).

What does David do? The scripture says that David encouraged himself in the Lord his God (1 Samuel 30:6). After this David inquired of the Lord. If most of us just did these two things our lives would be better. David inquired of the Lord: Shall I pursue after this troop? Shall I over take them? The answer was yes and David was successful and all were rescued.

Life is just full of adversity, and enough death, illness and bad news to make anyone sick to their stomach. Not once does God tell us to put our heads in the sand and live in a mental state of denial; just pretend it isn't so. Not one of us is spared from the difficulties of life either. In fact, God did not spare his own son. Jesus said: *In the world there shall be tribulation but be of good cheer, for I have overcome the world* (John 16:33).

I am not sure that we should ever be too satisfied with earthly things. Things on earth are a mess. I don't trust earthly governments because they all fail. I have learned that I can't trust my own flesh because it fails daily. I am persuaded that God's enduring love and promises will never fail me. And what could possibly separate me from his love?

The apostle Paul answers this for all of us who put our faith in Jesus: *Who shall separate us from the love of Christ? Shall tribulation, or distress, or persecution, or famine, or nakedness, or peril, or sword? As it is written, for thy sake we are killed all the day long; we are accounted as sheep for the slaughter. Nay, in all these things we are more than conquerors through him that loved us. For I am persuaded that neither death, nor life, nor angels, nor principalities, nor powers, nor things present, nor things to come, nor height, nor depth, nor any other creature shall be able to separate us from the love of God, which is in Christ Jesus our Lord* (Romans 8:35-39).

What thrills me everyday of my life is that Jesus is real, trustworthy and wonderful. This is not my permanent home. My home is built on the Rock of Ages. The prophet Isaiah described the government that I am affiliated with when he spoke of Jesus saying: *For unto us a child is born, unto us a son is given: and the government shall be upon his shoulder: and his name shall be called Wonderful, Counselor, The mighty God, The everlasting Father, The Prince of Peace* (Isaiah 9:6-7).

Guarding, nurturing and preserving our mind and spirit

Our spiritual success and much of life is simply a battle, or war, over thoughts and words, which we choose to entertain. We engage in this war whether we realize it or not. Feed your mind with material that is wholesome, and which will build you up and motivate you to follow and do the things you know God would want you to do. Avoid the things that simply give you ulcers, suck you dry and rob you of victory. Meditate on the things of God. Encourage yourself in the Lord, as David did. Read the word of God. Engage yourself in short conversations of prayer with the Lord throughout the day. Nurture your spiritual life. Serve others. Do these things and you will have a rich life!

Let me give you an example of something that is, in itself harmless, but which can rob you of your victory and peace of mind, if you entertain the subject. Civic responsibility is something we should all care about. Abdicating your responsibility by not voting does not promote your interests and it leaves important issues up to everyone else except you.

Yet, some folks spend more time worrying about immigration than they do reading God's word, praying, or seeking how to become better servants or how to overcome their own deficiencies. Politics present important issues, which need to be addressed, but they should not give you ulcers. You will never find complete joy or peace of mind that Christ gives by worrying about politics and, if this subject robs you of your joy in Christ, or makes you hard to live with, then maybe you should spend less time agitating yourself with this subject.

No matter who goes to the White House in the next elections, or the elections thereafter, earthy problems will not disappear and you are not going to suddenly be satisfied! Don't look for spiritual satisfaction with earthly things. Scripture makes it clear that we should focus first on the Kingdom of God when looking for answers to our legitimate needs. Jesus said, referring to our earthly needs, that we should seek first the Kingdom of God and all these things will be added unto us (Matthew 12:31). What you allow your mind to constantly dwell on will either lift you up or tear you down. Jesus did not say ignore other important issues. Jesus said your Father in heaven knows what you have need of before you even ask. We forget both of these principles. In doing so we may allow ourselves to become too agitated over all the many earthly issues around us. If we start thinking that the pursuit of these other things might bring us inner peace and satisfaction, we will be sadly mistaken. We need to find a place of balance where life's legitimate problems don't rob us of our joy. We lack divine wisdom, strength and energy. We need to continually nurture our body, mind and spirit and stop trashing ourselves. This will enable us to serve others better.

Unless you have the right temperament, patience, focus and perspective, earthy politics may only serve to agitate your mind and give you heartburn. If you enjoy politics and you are well suited for it, you may have a rewarding career in this field just as I did in law enforcement. If politics, on the other hand, do nothing but rob you of your joy and peace of mind, then you should probably devote yourself to something that will lift your spirits and enrich your life. We need good people in politics just as we do in other professions. But don't let politics, your job, your relationships, or anything else rob you of your spiritual destiny. If *other things* are cheating you out of the rich life Christ wants you to have, then get rid of them. Seek to have balance in every aspect of life. Safeguard your mind and spirit against those things, which tend to be destructive to your well-being. The apostle Paul writes that whatsoever things are true, whatsoever things are honest, whatsoever things are just, whatsoever things are pure, whatsoever things are lovely, whatsoever things are of a good report; if there be any virtue, and if there be any praise, think on these things (Philippians 4:8).

We are not to walk around being filled with anger, defeat and misplaced judgment. Vote your conscience and spend the rest of the day praising God and walking in victory like you are a child of the King! The joy of the Lord should be our strength and we should not be living in fear or constant tension. Jesus spoke about men's hearts failing them for fear and about devastating earthly conditions and he said: and when these things begin to come to pass, then look up, and lift up your heads; for your redemption draweth nigh (Luke 21:26-28).

It is wonderful to know the Lord and be satisfied in his Spirit. This is where our satisfaction should be derived from, not ourselves, our occupation, our good works and certainly not from our political party. Our hope is in Christ. God is faithful and his words endure forever. Our sense of well-being and security should come from Christ. When troubles rise, we need to hasten to his throne.

When we put ourselves in his presence and take our eyes off of earthly troubles, we enter into a new dimension where our spirits are refreshed and our batteries recharged and our hearts become renewed and filled with faith so that all things become possible. Fear becomes dispersed and we experience joy. This is a holy communion that we can experience by drawing near to God.

There is a lovely song I grew up with as a kid that has these healing words:

> There is a place of quiet rest, near to the heart of God
> A place where sin cannot molest, near to the heart of God
> Oh, Jesus, blessed Redeemer, sent from the heart of God
> Hold us who wait before thee, near to the heart of God
> There is a place of full release, near to the heart of God
> A place where all is joy and peace, near to the heart of God
> Oh, Jesus, blessed Redeemer, sent from the heart of God
> Hold us, who wait before thee, near to the heart of God
> (Near To The heart of God / written by Tom Fettke)

Placing ourselves in Jesus' presence brings solitude, understanding, comfort, joy and peace. It changes everything. Jesus promised to meet us at our point of need. These promises are specific and they are real. Jesus said, "Peace I leave with you, my peace I give unto you: not as the world giveth, give I unto you. Let not your heart be troubled, neither let it be afraid" (John 14:27).

If you can bring yourself to a quiet place and shut the outside influence of the world out of your mind and come before the Lord in prayer and worship and a state of mind where you just acknowledge his saving power and greatness, anything can happen. When I do this it becomes a powerful changing force within my spirit. It takes my mind off myself and the other problems at hand and it causes me to refocus on God's profound love and his mighty hand and power to save and heal to the uttermost parts of my soul.

If I saturate myself in his holy presence, I begin to feel his Holy Spirit and that cleansing power makes me a new person. When I do this it represents a surrendering of my spirit and my will unto the Lord. The great apostle Paul wrote many wonderful scriptures for us and two more of them come to mind because they both describe the feeling of my inner spirit after I surrender my will to Christ in prayer. One is that "can do" attitude of Caleb and Joshua that Paul wrote of which says: I can do all things through Christ Jesus who strengtheneth me (Philippians 4:13). The other scripture is representative of total surrender because my will no longer dictates the outcome. Paul writes: For whether we live, we live unto the Lord; and whether we die, we die unto the Lord: whether we live therefore, or die, we are the Lord's (Romans 14:8). This is victorious spiritual thinking and mind-set. Lord, I'll take it whatever way you lead, even unto death; thy will be done. If you can pray this and mean it, it's a win, win, and as good as it gets! This is what Jesus prayed just before going to the cross: Not my will, but thine be done, Father.

You have to draw nigh unto the Lord and kneel before him in his holy presence and open your spirit unto him to make these things start happening. The substance of this type of prayer is based on submission to God's will, and the result or outcome which we prefer has little or nothing to do with how we feel. We don't pray: Lord, make all the pain go away, nor do we pray, make me feel good. We pray the prayer of surrender: Lord, not my will, but thine be done in this matter. We then abide by that prayer. It is not how we feel that is so important. What's important is our commitment and our faith. What's important is what we know. What we know is Jesus is trustworthy, enduringly sufficient, propitious, ever present in time of trouble, and he is the same, yesterday, today and forever. We know furthermore, not only because he promised us, but also by empirical evidence and testing, that he will never leave or forsake us. Reorient your thinking. Aim high. Stop focusing on the horizontal and go vertical. Look upward to appropriate your strength. Rejoice in the Lord!

CHAPTER 5

WHAT MAKES THIS JOURNEY SO HARD IF I'M DOING THE RIGHT THINGS?

When I was sixteen years old I got a job working in a Shell gas station. I was able to work full time during the summer when I was out of school and part time during the school year. With the help of some wonderful people that I was staying with, I was able to buy a brand new Volkswagen bug. They trusted me enough to co-sign for the auto loan since I was still a teenager and unable to negotiate the contract without a parent or guardian agreeing to guarantee the loan. I was very grateful for the help this family gave me and also proud of my own accomplishment.

I took enormous pride in my new car. I waxed this car as though Jesus had given me secret dispensational permission to take it to heaven with me when the time came. Every month the car got waxed whether it needed it or not. Every wax job seemed to make the car look more brilliant, and the car even seemed to drive better. Isn't that funny how that works? One evening after completing another meticulous wax job, I got into the car, started the engine, and backed straight into a truck and smashed the right rear fender. The car was no longer ready for heaven.

The car looked terrible. Worst of all, I had no one to blame, except myself. This did not happen by virtue of my not knowing how to drive, or how to work the stick shift, because I had actually learned how to drive a stick shift pretty well in the jungles of Brazil when I was eleven years old. The problem with driving is there is more to it than just steering the car or shifting gears. The primary collision factor for me was simply backing up without looking carefully. I presumptuously considered it was clear to back up.

I wish I could tell you that this never happened again but I can't. On several occasions during my police career I have backed up and struck objects. Small objects like walls, trees and twenty-foot cement pillars in under ground parking garages and even fire hydrants have been known to suddenly and unexpectedly jump behind my car. I managed to chase bad guys in high speed pursuits all over the county at speeds in excess of a hundred miles per hour and I made many exciting arrests, without killing myself or anyone else, yet I couldn't back the patrol car up and make a three point U-turn without bumping into a fire hydrant late at night. Go figure!

Unlike my V.W. incident, all of these police "accidents" were very minor in nature and amounted to nothing more than very small bumps or scratches to my patrol car. The embarrassing thing for me was telling someone that I had shot myself in the foot again by backing up without looking. How basic is that? In each case, the same scenario applied. It's unbelievable! I presumptuously considered that it was clear behind me and unnecessary to look. What I find so amazing is that I can make the same embarrassing mistake over and over again, even though I know better. One should, presumably, learn a lesson from prior mistakes, wouldn't you think?

This human weakness, a state of mind in many ways, is representative of life in general. Metaphorically speaking, we shoot ourselves in the foot, but we do it over and over again. We do it spiritually also!

By and large, we live in a very orderly world that is governed by recognized laws of physics and scientific principles. The planets rotate and spin on their axes in just the right way, in a precise, balanced fashion. Science tells us that it would take only a slight disruption or variance of a couple degrees to throw the whole solar system out of kilter and Mr. Goodwrench would not be able to fix it. What is noteworthy is the precision and order of creation. The constant speed of light is 186,000 miles per second. Sunlight and water nurture all living things. In addition to their esthetics and food value, plants provide us with oxygen through photosynthesis.

The laws of gravity and physics work day in and day out and we don't have to worry that any one of these scientific principles won't work on Thursday afternoon. If your electricity fails it won't be because the science of electricity is unreliable. If you toss a rock up in the air, it predictably must come down. If you walk across the street without looking and step in front of a bus, you face the consequences of physics and kinetic energy.

The rain falls on the just and the unjust alike. If you back your car up without looking you are going to bump into something. While fire can be used to warm your home or burn it to the ground, most calamities are avoided by obeying the laws of science. NASA avoids space shuttle landings in severe, turbulent weather. If we observed and obeyed spiritual laws with no more diligence than we do the laws of physics, people would still fall off cliffs because of carelessness, and some people would still be electrocuted in the bathroom because of radios and hair dryers falling into bathtub water, but there would be far fewer needless deaths. If you can appreciate the simplicity, value and availability of a GFIC switch for your bathroom to eliminate electrocutions, imagine how well you might do if you follow God's spiritual laws and principles.

Just as the law of gravity applies to all of us, likewise, spiritual laws and principles apply to all of us. As the sun nurtures my lawn and roses, so the Son nurtures my soul. Moreover, it is not that anomalies don't occur, or, even evil for that matter, but rather that your heavenly Father knows what we are facing and what our needs are before we even ask him for his provision or assistance. Moreover, God has power over all things, including anomalies, life and death, and all evil, and there is nothing too difficult for God (Jeremiah 32:17).

Jesus said all power is given unto me in heaven and in earth (Matthew 28:18). Jesus commanded that we go into all the world and preach the gospel to every creature; and these signs shall follow them that believe; in my name shall they cast out devils and they shall speak with new tongues; and they shall lay hands on the sick, and they shall recover (Mark 16:15-18).

There is a television commercial that has been airing which sums up my feelings regarding what our spiritual attitude should be. It shows a young woman who has cancer and it depicts her still being engaged in life even while she routinely gets radiation treatments. The closing caption reads: I have cancer; cancer does not have me!

It is not a matter that adversity does not come along or plague us, but rather that Jesus has given us power and authority to overcome and be conquerors through him, in life and death. We simply have to get out of the classroom and the theoretical and get into the streets and apply our faith to real life situations. When we do so we can overcome all adversity, including all the works of Satan. He that overcometh shall inherit all things; and I will be his God, and he shall be my son (Revelation 21:7). We are encouraged to ask anything in his holy name and know that Christ will hear us, and that he will never leave or forsake us. Jesus said: *verily, verily, I say unto you, he that believeth on me, the works that I do shall he do also; and greater works than these shall he do; because I go unto my Father. If you ask anything in my name I will do it* (John 14:12-14).

Consider the resources God is willing to provide if we seek him. Israel had a well documented, perfidious history of walking in disobedience before God, but the message of the Lord to Israel through the prophet Jeremiah came these wonderful words: And ye shall seek me and find me, when ye shall search for me with all your heart (Jeremiah 29:13). In the New Testament we read that God is no respecter of persons (Romans 2:11). God loves everybody. For God so loved the *world* the scripture says (John 3:16).

God doesn't favor Democrats or Republicans, although I am amazed at how many people are confused about this issue. God is, in the purest sense of the word, an Independent, omnipotent God who favors those who love him in spirit and in truth and who obey him and walk justly before him. God doesn't play favorites, political games, or quid pro quo the likes of what we are used to seeing. His mercy and promises are for all generations for whosoever will come to him. There is neither Jew nor Gentile who has exclusive rights to salvation, and the only circumcision that counts or means anything is of the heart. It's not the flesh that is so important but the condition of the heart (Roman 2:28-29/1 Corinthians 7:19).

My point here is that the entire Bible is full of scripture that explains and gives examples of God's redeeming love, mercy and promises to his children. God's laws, ways, and principles are there for the taking! They apply to all of us; we simply have to claim them and appropriate his wonderful promises and have faith and courage to seize the moment. God loves all his kids and not just a handful of them. God is loving, merciful, forgiving and just. When we stray and wander away and get into trouble he hears our cry and sees our tears when we approach his throne in prayer. No key that I know of will open the door faster than our humility. It is like a golden key that opens doors in heaven. When we are broken and full of humility we are right where God can do something wonderful for us because we are at the point where we are willing to listen, obey and lean on him. Miracles can happen at this level because the battle of the wills is over. It's no longer our will but his will that we begin accepting, and this brings us to a place where all things are possible.

How do we get into so much trouble? There are lots of ways to be sure, but like Israel we wander away and our thinking falls into a mind-set that it is vain to serve God and it doesn't make any real difference (Malachi 3:14). If you follow the path of Israel, you see how they stray from God and God allows them enough rope to hang themselves, so to speak, and be taken into captivity. You might think that after several hundred years of slavery in Egypt they would be disinclined to go back down that road again, but that is exactly what happens. The anguish of their deprivation and the cry from their hearts always evokes a response from God. The prophet Isaiah gives a descriptive chronology of Israel returning to God: *Then shalt thou call, and the Lord shall answer; thou shalt cry, and he shall say, here I am. And the Lord will guide thee continually, and satisfy thy soul in drought, and make fat thy bones: and thou shalt be like a watered garden, and like a spring of water, whose waters fail not* (Isaiah 58:9,11).

Israel gets into trouble and eventually cries out to God for help. This reflects a paradigm, not only of Israel but one for us as well. Our battles are different but the principles are often the same. God allows us to experience the bread of adversity and the water of affliction because it ultimately draws us back toward God. When we call unto him there is often a waiting period before the answer or relief comes. The waiting period does a couple of things. God deliberately takes his time because he never gets nervous, especially over our limitations. God is all-powerful and all knowing. God wants us to ponder that and understand he doesn't fall off his stool just because we snap our fingers and ask him to intervene. The waiting period requires or fosters an attitude of patience and humility and it reminds us that he, alone, is God. The scripture speaks of this waiting period. *And therefore will the Lord wait, that he may be gracious unto you, and therefore will he be exalted, that he may have mercy upon you: for the Lord is a God of judgment: blessed are all they that wait for him. For the people shall dwell in Zion at Jerusalem: thou shalt weep no more: he will be very gracious unto thee at the voice of thy cry; when he shall hear it, he will answer thee* (Isaiah 30:18-20).

Another famous biblical passage that depicts this period of time of waiting on the Lord is described with these words: *Why sayest thou, O Jacob, and speakest, O Israel, My way is hid from the Lord, and my judgment is passed over from my God? Hast thou not known? Hast thou not heard, that the everlasting God, the Lord, the Creator of the ends of the earth, fainteth not, neither is weary? There is no searching of his understanding. He giveth power to the faint; and to them that have no might he increaseth strength. Even the youths shall faint and be weary, and the young men shall utterly fall: But they that wait upon the Lord shall renew their strength; they shall mount up with wings as eagles; they shall run, and not be weary; and they shall walk, and not faint* (Isaiah 40:27-31).

God has provided his only begotten son, Jesus, who took on human flesh and died on the cross to pay for the cost of our sin. Jesus promised he would return for us soon. For these brief moments in which we wait, we have been given the Holy Spirit to empower us, guide us, and lead us as we seek God's direction and help in our lives. Jesus said, "Lo, I am with you always, even unto the end of the world" (Matthew 28:20). If you read and study the scriptures and devote yourselves to what God's word has to say to us, you will find that it doesn't get any better than this folks!

God has done everything beyond what we could even ask to help us, save us, heal us and give us victory over every storm of life. If we have all these things at our disposal, why does failure occur so easily? Like the innocuous example I used in the beginning of this chapter, I crash my car repeatedly and shoot myself in the foot over and over again because I fail to practice the fundamentals. We do the same things spiritually. I do things which I know lead to failure and I become presumptuous in my own wisdom and strength. Consider the remedy from the word of God:

> *Trust in the Lord with all thine heart; and lean not unto thine own understanding. In all thy ways acknowledge him, and he shall direct thy paths. Be not wise in thine own eyes: fear the Lord, and depart from evil. It shall be health to thy navel, and marrow to thy bones. Honor the Lord with thy substance, and with the first fruits of all thine increase. So shall thy barns be filled with plenty, and thy presses shall burst out with new wine* (Proverbs 3:5-10).

These words are a recipe for your success. Follow them. You could have no more than an eighth grade education and be successful if you follow these godly principles. I am not advocating that anyone drop out of school, because we should devote our best efforts in everything we do, including our education and preparation for life. We are to love the Lord our God with all our strength and with all our minds, and we should do everything to the best of our ability and as unto the Lord. This includes developing our minds. Imagine what you can do with your mind through a good education if you apply it as unto the Lord. And whatsoever you do, do it wholeheartedly as unto the Lord, and not unto men (Colossians 3:23). And let us not be weary in well doing: for in due season we shall reap, if we faint not (Galatians 6:9).

Why is my soul despondent and downcast? Take your eyes off yourself and the problems you are facing and look upward. One of the biggest reasons we have problems with adversity and struggle with the load we carry is that we fail to appropriate God's resources, which are freely available to us. They that wait upon the Lord shall renew their strength! We don't wait on the Lord enough.

This human response to threatening stimuli is largely a mind-set. I prefer to think of it as a perspective or attitude that leads to discouragement and robs us of our faith and our vision. When we lose our faith we end up losing hope. When hope, faith, vision and courage are lost, we conclude that God is no longer able. This mind-set is pervasive and ubiquitous, but it's nothing more than the absence of vision in seeing God's power. God's power is real even if our vision is defective. Focusing only with the five senses implements a philosophy, which says circumstances rule. Circumstances rule only if you acquiesce. It's not what we feel or what we see that counts; it is what is unseen that matters. For we look not to the things which are seen, but at the things that are not seen: for the things which are seen are temporal [and circumstantial]; but the things which are not seen are eternal (2 Corinthians 4:18).

Imagine how much it might have helped Job if he had not been limited to horizontal gazing. Job had no idea there was warfare taking place in the heavenlies over his very situation. We have the benefit of reading the book of Job. Job did not have this luxury. It might not have made his suffering any easier, but psychologically it would surely have been easier to bear knowing that God was still on your side. Imagine the psychological edge you would have if you knew that your situation was a heavenly test of God's best servant. Wouldn't you want to know that God was pleased with you and that moments earlier he had been bragging about you. Have you seen my servant Job? Part of the testing is being blind to the real facts. It's called blind faith. But it's also an excellent reason why we need to look upward for our strength.

A friend of mine was telling me about a church service where a handful of believers were praying for a person possessed by a devil. As the believers prayed to Jesus to cast the spirit out, the evil spirit spoke out and stated: you wouldn't be so bold if all these others were not here behind us. To the naked human eye there was no one else behind them. Since there was no one else there except the few who were praying at the front of this small church, I believe the eyes of the evil spirit were able to see in the spirit world the angels surrounding them and feel the anointing pressure of the Holy Spirit descending. Don't be limited to your five senses when discerning spiritual matters. Be filled with the Holy Spirit and the Lord can remove the scales from our eyes so that we see.

When the king of Syria sent a great host of men with horses and chariots to capture Elisha, the prophet's servant saw only the enemy which had surrounded the city. The servant asked, "Alas my master, what shall we do?" Elisha answered, "Fear not: for they that be with us are more than they that be with them." And Elisha prayed and said, "Lord, I pray thee, open the eyes of the young man: and he saw: and, behold, the mountain was full of horses and chariots of fire round about Elisha." And when Elisha prayed the Lord smote the enemy with blindness according to the word of Elisha (2 Kings 6:11-18).

Focusing on circumstances rather than possibility thinking eliminates the dimension of faith. If you live and breathe, you will suffer with this human condition. We all struggle with it. What is important is that we recognize the problem and we make a conscious decision to look upward. Remember the tomb is empty. Remember the words of Jesus: *And all things, whatsoever ye shall ask in prayer, believing, ye shall receive* (Matthew 21:22). *Ask, and it shall be given you; seek, and ye shall find; knock, and it shall be opened unto you* (Matthew 7:7). *Be of good cheer, for I have overcome the world* (John 16:33).

If you want to overcome adversity start looking upward. When we stop trying to solve earthly problems in our own human strength we move into the spiritual realm, and this is where our strength and power come from. We need to tap into the power of the Spirit. The biggest battles we face in life have nothing to do with stature, human prowess, guns, armies or swords. For we wrestle not against flesh and blood, but against principalities, against powers, against the rulers of darkness of this world, against spiritual wickedness in high places (Ephesians 6:12).

When we look upward that changes everything. It is the very reason Jesus said that if you can believe, all things are possible to him that believeth (Mark 9:23).

When we trust God and walk in faith, the key is focusing on his provision and power to make things happen. This produces efficacy for God to do what he does best all the time, the impossible. Look to your source, your heavenly Father. Metaphorically, we look upward. The only reason we use this expression, upward, is simply because it is easy to relate to in terms of visualizing God being in heaven. That is good but don't limit it to that. Remember the words of David: *Whither shall I go from thy Spirit? Or, whither shall I flee from thy presence? If I ascend into heaven, thou art there: if I make my bed in hell, behold, thou art there. Yea, the darkness hideth not from thee; but the night shineth as the day: the darkness and the light are both alike to thee* (Psalms 139:7-8;12).

It just seems to be human nature to try and figure God out and put him in a box. The minute you think you have God all figured out and start thinking you know how he is going to accomplish something, you are going to be mistaken. If you think God is going to send the answer to your front door, he will come through the back door, or some other unexpected way. Don't get hung up with methodologies. Don't try and figure out how God is going to accomplish something because invariably he will fool you and do the unexpected. Use the word of God to judge or weigh something for righteousness and content, but don't limit how, when or where God answers prayer. Don't get hung up over day or night. God reigns over both. If you start thinking this way, pretty soon you'll be thinking God isn't with you if you fly on airplanes because Jesus said "lo" I am with you always. Oh, maybe you thought he said "low."

One of the sergeants I worked with told me this amusing allegory. You've probably heard it already. This guy out at sea had boat problems and his vessel was going down. He prayed and asked God to rescue him. God heard his earnest prayer and sent help to him, but the man died at sea anyway. When the man got to heaven he asked God why help didn't come. I sent a helicopter, a coastguard vessel, and a passenger cruise ship just to help you, but you waved them all off, said the Lord.

I don't know exactly why we do this, but it reflects how narrow our thinking can be. The story of the guy at sea waving off the lifesaving rescue offers because he is waiting to be saved by God makes me chuckle every time I think of it, but on the other hand it is not really all that amusing, because it is representative of peoples' opinionated view of what God's solution should look like. What was this guy looking for, a white angel with a twelve foot wingspan?

Why do we struggle with adversity? Why is the journey so hard at times?

If the answer we want isn't packaged the way we think it should be, we are too quick to rush to a judgment that it must not be from God, so we politely discard it away or decline the offer for help. I've learned that when my wife offers me a stick of gum it may be because I have bad breath. I need to accept the gum and entertain the sound advice of others. Good leaders don't surround themselves with only loyal "yes" people.

How many times do we entertain angels unaware? I don't know but what I do know is that God is in the business of helping people and he uses people to help people. He told us to love one another. That is why we are to both serve one another as foot washers but also exhort one another in truth. That is why the Lord commissioned us to go into all the world and preach the good news (the gospel) of Jesus to every creature. Sometimes that message should include repentance. That is why we are to be the salt of the earth and not hide our light under a bushel basket, but let it rather shine so that others recognize the source of our fruit or good works, our heavenly Father.

God also wants us to learn to become humble. Sometimes he uses imperfect people to speak to us and provide us with truth, wisdom or other guidance. Don't limit the answer to a motorcade of cops escorting Elijah to your house on a chariot of fire. Be open to someone as meek and humble and unassuming as Mother Teresa or, to someone such as one of your co-workers. God might even use an obnoxious fellow brother or sister in the Lord to help you. It's hard to accept truth or instruction of any kind when it comes from someone that knows less than you do, right? Remember, God spoke through a donkey to Balaam (Numbers 22:22-31).

Don't try and twist my words on this because I am not suggesting that you may think of your wife in a pejorative way. For example, in my case, I would do well to think of myself as the donkey and my wife as the angel of light, which I was too stupid to see on my own, but for the mercy of God. The fact that the answer comes from one riding on a camel wearing a turban doesn't mean the person must be a terrorist; the person might be an angel. Be open-minded and weigh all things.

Why is the journey so hard at times when you are doing the right things?

First of all, you may not be doing all the right things. The question itself is presumptuous. In addition to rejecting help because we don't like the way it's packaged or because the source doesn't look like an angel, human nature has a tendency, not always, but sometimes, for people to be arrogant, proud, and unwilling to accept sound advice or criticism. I am that way. Trust me! It annoys me slightly that my editor points out errors in my manuscript.

Allow me to illustrate the principle. The fact that you are a mighty prophet of God with faith so great that you can throw mountains into the sea may speak for itself in that regard, but as the scriptures say, if we don't have love, it profits nothing. Being highly competent and gifted in one area of life does not make anyone a master of all life. It doesn't make one, for example, a great husband, a great wife, or a great leader, maybe, just a good mountain thrower. My wife, who I can say with complete confidence loves me, recently told me that I am consistently impatient and moody, and that my anger can be so explosive that she is afraid to approach me with issues half the time because I am like a rabid dog. Is he going to bite if I ask him a question or maybe foam at the mouth? As you can see, sometimes my behavior fails any standard of excellence. In fact, every failure described in this book probably has examples of me in it. If my own wife is afraid of me, I am not the successful husband I want to be. So, if I go on and on about how great my faith is or brag about some other accomplishment, or I throw mountains into the sea, it pretty much means nothing. Without practical love, patience and forgiveness, these things mean nothing. I have a long way to go.

I considered my father to be a mighty man of God, and a giant in the faith. My father had tremendous faith for some things. When it came to his personal weaknesses he was just as vulnerable as the rest of us. In financial matters, for example, my father would occasionally say, "Well, you know, son, money doesn't just grow on trees!" We all think this way at times, and sometimes, for good cause. Such a statement might simply represent the fact that you don't have any extra money for non-essentials. The problem, however, is that we also practice this kind of thinking when it comes to more legitimate needs, or with things that we should be stretching our faith to believe for so that God can meet our needs. For the sake of argument, such thinking, if we apply it to ourselves, is either based on faith, courage, and God's leading, or it is based on human resources, thinking and limitations. On the natural, human level, such horizontal thinking inherently and implicitly would suggest that God might not be able to provide for some of our needs, and that potentially, there might just be something too difficult for God. My father would not think that

137

way when he was walking in the Spirit or practicing his faith and reaching out to God. He did this when he was viewing things in the humanistic, natural realm, looking at things by earthly standards and the circumstances around him, or the limitations of his personal checkbook.

I catch myself looking horizontally all the time. That is when I need to refocus and try and look toward God for solutions and remind myself that the answer could come from any direction, including from another brother in the Lord who God is using to speak to me. In the case of receiving honest, constructive criticism, I especially need to listen to the words of people who I know love me, and care deeply about me. Remember, there is nothing too difficult for God, but that also includes his methods of shipping and delivery. The best advice you get does not have to necessarily come from some prophet who looks like Charlton heston, playing the role of Moses in one of his great movies; it could come from your spouse, a co-worker, or a stranger.

Why is the journey so hard sometimes?

Sometimes we don't admit our limitations or lack of knowledge, nor do we acknowledge our need for help. More often than not this type of thinking is probably related to pride. We never think this way of ourselves, but our behavior reflects that attitude that I know it all. If you don't know anything about financial investments or financial planning, it would be wise to admit that to yourself and seek advice from a trustworthy source who knows far more than you do. That reflects common sense. You would not try and set a broken bone with sticks and plumber's tape when you know nothing about medicine and have no first aid training, unless you were in the jungle or bush and had no access to good medical technology and emergency services.

There is a great saying that became popular as public awareness began to grow in the United States regarding drunk driving. Lots of media advertising brought this to our attention: Friends don't let friends drive drunk or under the influence. As Christians, we should do no less. If we love people, we have a responsibility to say something when things are getting out of hand. Christians are to exhort one another and hold each other accountable in our faith. When the pastor says this, most people agree with it, or if we have a philosophical discussion about it, people tend to agree with it. Yet, for any of this to work, someone has to have the courage to speak up. We also have to submit to one another. In relationships, if no one ever submits, then none of this works and we will all be at odds with each other all the time. After attending a wonderful church service, a family could argue about which restaurant they are going to for lunch until no ones wants to go to lunch anymore. Love requires submission to others and a surrendering of our own desires for the good of others.

If a good friend is trying to tell you, don't do this, this is wrong; it's going to hurt you, or get you in trouble; I love you, please don't do this, let's talk about it; that would represent a plea to listen to reason and be open-minded and submit to wisdom and advice. Friends offer constructive criticism in love

138

and sometimes they get their head bitten off for offering it. Good friends listen carefully to friends and evaluate and weigh constructive criticism even though it may be hard to hear. This is a two way street. Ask the Holy Spirit to give you wisdom when to speak and when to listen.

Why is the journey so hard?

I believe some people have difficulty with authority in general, but all the more so with anyone who might be an authority figure. Some people are not teachable and they are contentious about everything. If you said the sun rises in the East, they would argue that there are likely exceptions, in spite of evidence to the contrary. Who does this guy think he is? He is no stinking scientist! I don't have to listen to you. Well, of course, you don't have to listen to anyone.

If you can't accept constructive criticism very well or at all, you are going to have problems submitting to whoever is in charge at any given moment, and you will most likely have trouble submitting to God's authority. You simply won't accept it. You will find yourself picking and choosing which portions of God's laws or teaching you think are worth following or paying attention to. Those who can't submit to others in leadership or get along with others will always find themselves struggling, and life may end up being a source of never-ending conflict. Part of that contentious conflict simply stems over who rules in your life. If you take pride in thinking that you submit to no one, because you are god of your own life, you are going to be surprised in the end, because every knee *shall* bow and acknowledge that Jesus Christ is Lord (Philippians 2:10-11).

Even God listens to people and what they have to say and it often changes the outcome (2 Kings 20:1-6/Luke 18:1-6). God can be touched by our humility and repentance (2 Kings 22:19-20). While God can't be deceived or tricked by insincere tears or emotional, manipulative outbursts, he does care about how you feel and makes this offer to you: come now, let us reason together... (Isaiah 1:18).

Why would someone not want to have sound, righteous counsel? Sometimes people are less interested in the truth than their own predetermined outcome. For example, an open, honest discussion of the various possibilities or options likely to be viable in any given conflict resolution might be distasteful to some who don't want to hear what is being offered to begin with. Their mind might be already made up and no further factual findings are needed or wanted. Don't tell me what to do; who do you think you are? Either these words or the body language that goes with them will tell you all you need to know. Well, I love you and I was just tying to be helpful and point out that you have other options. I wasn't trying to tell you what to do. I was trying to constructively explore what your options might be. Thanks, but I don't need your advice or help; I am quite capable of taking care of myself and I don't need anyone else's help, [let alone yours]. Look out!

Understand that people in this sometimes-angry state of mind are not necessarily interested in other viable options or the truth for that matter. They might not even be interested in your friendship at this stage if you don't agree with them or support their position. That's how people are. That's how we are with Jesus. Half the time some of us wouldn't want Jesus around us as long as we think we are still going to make it into heaven. I am not advocating that we run around giving unsolicited advice to others. Jesus didn't do that and neither should we. Don't presumptuously take liberty or intimacy for granted with someone that you do not have a strong relationship with.

Intimacy typically requires trust and that doesn't occur over one latte. But as we get to know each other at a deeper level, we also need to be honest and when the door to intimacy is opened, we need to be honest and truthful, and not just tell each other what we want to hear. I am speaking about friends who love friends. Friends don't let friends drive drunk. The body of Christ needs to hold each other accountable with love, truth and scriptural acumen.

If you are overly defensive and have difficulty with criticism, you are going to have constant tension with others. If someone is trying to gently tell you something important, listen and evaluate what is being offered. Sometimes it is more valuable to listen to criticism than to praise. Backstabbers and liars will tell you that you have no flaws and that you are wonderful and that your adulterous affair sounds exciting. Polite guests tell their host the meal was well prepared and delicious. Acquaintances tell you that your new dress looks lovely. Friends will console you when you are down and tell you that you are a good person. *Good friends* who love and who would give their life for you will tell you when you have bad breath or that your feet stink, or that you need more quiet time with Jesus. Good friends will also walk an extra mile with you in silence and stand beside you often without giving any advice.

Another reason we can make our journey harder than it needs to be is for the simple reason of disobedience. My good friend and I were talking in generalities about this and also about spiritual unfaithfulness. My friend was thinking out loud, as they say, wondering why some people who are not even trying to do the right thing, do so well, while others who are breaking their backs trying to get it right and be honorable before the Lord, struggle so hard?

I told my friend that from a biblical perspective we are spiritually admonished to not waste our energy worrying about anyone else or comparing ourselves to the apparent success of others. The Psalms are full of examples. King David wrote about this, that we should not fret over the momentary success of evildoers. We need to concentrate on our own behavior and not fall into the trap of judging others or allow ourselves to covet or be jealous of those around us. The one thing you will never have to account for when you stand before God will be the question of what someone else did with their life and talents. You will only answer for your own words and deeds. Parenthetically speaking, others don't always have it as good as you think they do.

I love my friend's question though because it is provocative. We need to examine our own hearts and judge ourselves according to scripture. How come I am not having success? The apostle Paul writes in scripture, "Prove all things; hold fast to that which is good" (1 Thessalonians 5:21). Am I walking in obedience before the Lord? Are all my ways pleasing in your sight, Lord? Am I following and incorporating sound principles and common sense along with obedience to the word of God? Or, am I bending the rules to suit my own agenda and purpose? Sound principles of truth hold up to bright light and close examination, and they don't change from year to year or day to day.

Think about this simple truth. If you know you are not submitting to God's *full* will in any area of your life or you are in some other way walking contrary to the word of God, then it's pretty hard to pray with strong faith for certain things because you know deep in your heart you are not walking uprightly in full obedience before God. Example: How do you sincerely ask God to bless you financially if you are robbing God of his tithes? How do you boldly pray for anything if you know you are not obeying God? Shouldn't you feel convicted about that issue? It is hard to pray the prayer of faith on any matter when you are practicing duplicity. Here is another example: How can you pray courageously the prayer of faith for God to heal one of your family members if you are cheating on our wife by having a sexual affair with an office co-worker? It is very hard to pray with faith and courage when you know you are walking in disobedience. Conversely, it is much easier to pray with great boldness and with greater faith when you can look toward heaven and say: God, you see my heart and know that I am doing everything I can to be faithful to you, but if there is something I have overlooked, Lord, show me. Please help me with this problem, Lord, and show me what to do.

In response to my friend's question about how the ungodly seem to do so well, I suggested that they don't. Their triumph and glory are only for a season, and often brief. You can't sustain an enduring life of success when you break or violate all rules of integrity or morality. Even crooks on the street understand this. The world has an expression for it that patterns spiritual truth. The Bible makes scores of references to this principle. One such reference states: Be not deceived: God is not mocked: for whatsoever a man soweth, that shall he also reap (Galatians 6:7). This principle on the street is phrased by the world as, "what goes around, comes around."

When we think of disobedience sometimes it is easy to think of the most flagrant examples of it, such as Jonah. God told Jonah to go to Nineveh and cry against the city, because their wickedness had come to his attention. But Jonah fled from the presence of the Lord on a ship toward Tarshish (Jonah 1:1-3). What becomes immediately clear is that this is an issue of total defiance and disobedience and not a misunderstanding or confusion over orders.

This makes me laugh a little when I think about the number of people I arrested in my law enforcement career for outstanding warrants. I was always amused at how many people felt compelled to tell me that the reason the court had issued a warrant for their arrest was because of a misunderstanding. You can't contumaciously respond to God as Jonah did and expect a room with a view. God might issue a warrant for your arrest. This also makes me think that we should soberly consider that when we stand before God to be judged, there will be no contradictions, false testimony or misunderstandings, only facts.

Jonah was thrown off the ship and into the ocean where he was swallowed into the belly of a whale. Actually, we don't know for sure it was a whale because the Bible refers to it as "a great fish." What is clear is that Jonah had three days and three nights in the belly of the fish. It must have been pretty wet and stinky inside the belly of a fish for that period of time. We can draw an inference from scripture that the fish experienced indigestion. The scripture tells us that the Lord spoke to the fish and that it "vomited" Jonah out onto dry land (Jonah 2:10). I suppose that Jonah never ate fish in a delicate cream sauce after this.

Think about it: no poolside cable T.V. or Internet, no air conditioning, no refreshments or Monday Night Football. Jonah's attention finally turned upward and he repented for going AWOL. You should read how sincere Jonah gets in just three days in a room without a view (Jonah 2:1-9). Once the battle of the wills was over, Jonah went to Nineveh and in spite of his personal anger management issues, a mighty victory of repentance spread throughout the city like wild fire! Obedience produced repentance which saved an entire city from destruction. Aren't you glad God came not to destroy the world but to save it?

I find this story just fascinating. Jonah was an unhappy camper. His life did not reflect any joy or contentment because he had the wrong focus. But I love the fact that the Lord could use this guy because sometimes I'm off track and I become just like him. Like Jonah, I love justice, and I want evil to be punished, but God wants repentance to have a chance before judgment. I love the Lord but I am basically a jerk without an ounce of compassion, just like Jonah. It helps me realize I don't want to be this way. I have to remind myself that I should be grateful that God came not to destroy me but to restore me!

What I opined to my friend is that the difference between the ungodly and the children of God is huge. What makes the children of God special is not their innate charm, intelligence, or goodness, because quite frankly most of us don't have any of those qualities and we are just as miserable as anyone else. What makes the children of God special is that we have been forgiven of our sin because of the work of Christ on the cross. Christians aren't better than anyone else; they're simply forgiven, and not for any good deed that they did. It's all the work of Christ. When we come to Christ, we do so through repentance and submission, and we acknowledge our sin and need for forgiveness. We become members of a family, the family of God. The ungodly and lost who have not been redeemed are not so.

David describes the ungodly as being like the chaff which the wind drives away. The scripture declares: *For the Lord knoweth the way of the righteous: but the way of the ungodly shall perish* (Psalms 1:4,6). God loves people and reaches out and wants to save the lost and often uses circumstances and calamity to draw people to himself so that he can save them and have them become members of his family. Once you become a member of the family of God, the Lord becomes your guiding heavenly Father. He guides you and leads you because you ask him to do so; he offers forgiveness because you ask him for it. God will watch over you as your heavenly Father and promote your growth and development if you ask for these things. You have not because you ask not (James 4:2). God also withholds things from you that would be harmful for you to have. As his child, God will lead you, protect you, and when necessary, even discipline you if you walk contrary to his will or direction. These are benefits that God extends to his children.

In much the same way a loving parent does, God loves, guides and trains his own children; with the major exception that God is just and righteous in every way. Only by your invitation does God walk with you and become involved in your life. He opens and closes doors that no man can open or shut. God sets obstacles in your way and may even allow a fish to swallow you so as to interrupt your plans. He knows the schedule of every cruise liner and he does not need GPS to locate you in Tarshish.

God may allow you to fail at times and utterly fall flat on your face so that he can teach you the proper way to conduct yourself, and surrender your will to him as his servant and disciple. The surrendering of our will to God is huge. You will never be on the same page with the Lord if your will is at odds with his will. It represents a blockbuster of an issue that allows God to lead and guide us, because we choose to follow his way, and not our own way. We give God permission to jerk our chain and put adversity directly in our path so that he has free will to mold us and accomplish his perfect will in our lives. He is the potter and we are the clay (Isaiah 64:8). When we get off track, God has our permission to get our attention in any way he sees fit to do so. Such direct intervention by God does not typically occur within the lives of the ungodly because they have no relationship with God to begin with. God strives with his children who claim him as their heavenly Father, and he guides and blesses those who love, serve and obey him in spirit and in truth. God operates in our lives only by personal invitation, and while the term lacks regality, he is also what civilized, decent people would call the perfect *gentleman*.

Our relationship with the Lord is based solely on consent. If you want nothing to do with God, then he won't force himself into your life. If you don't realize your need for God, that's a different story. God's profound love may pursue you. But generally speaking I would argue that God does not guide or bless those who want nothing to do with him. Since God is a perfect gentleman, he respects the rights of even the ungodly!

Does this mean the Lord will not help those who are spiritually lost or continue to be available to help them? No, it does not mean that at all. But it does mean there is a difference between ungodly people who don't realize their need for a Savior because of their own blindness and sin, and those who simply prefer darkness over light and who consciously choose to have nothing to do with Christ. Those who want nothing to do with Christ will not be forced to serve Jesus. It's a consensual thing.

God may block the path of the wicked or overthrow evil kingdoms on earth, but I don't see examples of the Lord sending whales to swallow nonbelievers as he did with Jonah. God seems to do that sort of thing with his servants. God may allow calamity to occur in your life so that he draws you to himself for the purpose of saving you, but if you make it clear to him that you don't want his guiding hand in your life, the Lord will leave you alone, if that's what you want. God isn't in the business of destroying people. We do that to ourselves. God is in the business of saving people (John 3:17) and he doesn't need to surreptitiously throw banana peels in front of nonbelievers who have trouble walking so they will slip and fall. Such things may actually happen but not because God is to blame for them. There is enough naturally occurring evil all around us that God doesn't have to manipulate people into serving him. More importantly, the work of Christ was and is so great that he will forevermore deserve and receive praise from those who love him and *want* to serve him, and pundits should be reminded that even the rocks would cry out if we failed to praise the Lord (Luke 19:37-40).

Sometimes God lets us crash and burn to bring us to our knees to humble us so that he can mold us and turn us into the fruit-producing children he wants us to be. When we crash like this, it's not because God is driving the car, but because we are driving and, moreover, unwilling to change course or listen to his direction. Therefore, the Lord may allow us in our obstinate ways, to do, as we will, so that he can show us his mercy, which endures forever. If you are going through such adversity, thank him for doing that in your life! Jesus said: *As many as I love, I rebuke and chasten: be zealous therefore and repent* (Revelation 3:19). *Thou shalt consider in thine heart, that as a man chaseneth his son, so the Lord thy God chaseneth thee* (Deuteronomy 8:5).

All disobedience does not fall into the severe category of Jonah and the fish. Like a well stocked produce store, there are lots of varieties to choose from. The bigger the issue the greater the consequences become. If you choose not to take an elective course in college that you felt the Lord was leading you to take, I am very confident that you will not burn in hell for not taking the course. Such punishment would be disproportionate to this hypothetical example. I could assure you that you would cheat yourself out of a blessing for not taking this course.

God always blesses obedience and you would cheat yourself out of the unseen future benefits that obedience would have brought. If you counted the cost and were able to see the future loss, you would not disobey to begin with. If you refuse to take a required college course, you won't graduate. Many have never graduated. The principles apply both academically and

144

spiritually. Some people turn the fifth grade into a career and become comfortable there.

Sometimes we just don't know what to do and we are even unaware that disobedience is a variable in our situation. It becomes both an issue of ignorance and disobedience. Failure is not limited to conscious or deliberate acts. If we violate spiritual laws, the result is analogous to violating the laws of physics or science. There are consequences. Godly spiritual laws don't just go away or stop existing, anymore than gravity does, because we fail to understand them. If you are not living a successful life you need to ask yourself why. If we are shooting ourselves in the foot, we need to ask ourselves how. Ignorance or lack of knowledge is a killer. The scripture tells us that: There is a way which seemeth right unto a man; but the end thereof are the ways of death (Proverbs 14:12).

If you are just doing the best you can and hoping for success, but you really are not sure what's right and what's wrong, you are destined for more failure than you necessarily need and certainly more adversity than you want. It really boils down to whether you are going to acknowledge and follow God's ways or your ways. This all boils down to fundamentals and basic spiritual truth.

If you want to grow and mature and become fruitful and have an overcoming, victorious life, there are certain fundamentals that you need to practice and embrace. Understand that everybody goes through hard times, trials and testing and the rain falls on the just and the unjust alike, but by and large, even if you are a spiritual giant, or especially if you are, life should not be one continuous living hell, day after day, year after year. We all have bad hair days and wish we were all doing something different and we all wish our problems would go away. Yet, if you are walking in faith and obedience and producing fruit, your life should be predominately victorious and full of joy and victory. If your life is not that way, start asking and assessing why not. Are you practicing the fundamentals? Ask the Lord to show you what you are doing wrong. What prevents you from overcoming?

Most of us will never go through anything the likes of what Job experienced, although we all relate to the story at some level. Most of us have difficulties and adversity because we cause our own problems, and we don't do enough to overcome the adversity, obtain help or foster our own growth. The agony of defeat is not because God has failed us. There are exceptions to almost everything it seems, and there are certainly some things that are totally out of our control such as the suffering that Job experienced. Job's trials are truly an exception to what most of us experience. I simply want to point out that failure to achieve success and victory is more often than not our own fault. It is a mistake to blame everyone else in the world for our failures. No one has as much to do with, or control over, your success as you do! When adversity rains down upon you, don't blame others. Examine it. The word of God tells us that the curse without cause shall not come (Proverbs 26:2).

I have been dealing with life threatening emergencies and crises for almost thirty years. I have been a hostage negotiator and have dealt with hysterical people of every kind. These events have included the most educated and successful people in our society such as doctors, lawyers, and engineers, all the way down the socioeconomic ladder to homeless people, children, and mentally distraught individuals who are suicidal and those under the influence of drugs and alcohol.

Many of us in law enforcement have seen more perversion, abuse, death, disease, sorrow, human failure and despair in a six month period than some folks see in a lifetime. The conditions these people face are real. The sorrow, depression, and hopelessness that they feel are very real to each of them. Two things that stand out for me in this are: the human condition and propensity for people to blame others for their problems, and secondly, that people can be seemingly incapable of helping themselves.

Of course, not everyone falls into these categories, but it is surprising how many do. Not one of these conditions, horrible as they are, come from some strange planet, randomly assigned to plague us without cause. Almost all of these problems are identifiable and treatable. Christians suffer from all of these things too, including the practice of blaming others. We all need help in different forms. We all need Jesus, especially Christians. Our attitude is itself an area in which we need to improve.

We need to be careful not to play the "blame game." Even if we have been wronged or victimized, we can't spend the rest of our lives lamenting that we lost an opportunity to be successful. Success is a journey, not a destination. We need to figure out what we believe and then live it and practice what we preach. If you are going through the fire and storm of adversity, do what you know you should do: seek the Lord, and wait upon him for his guidance. He will not forsake you. Stop asking Aunt Nelly what to do and stop thinking you might get some insight from the National Inquirer or People Magazine.

When we come to the place in our life where we realize that we need Jesus, we make a decision about what we are going to do with him. Do we ask for his forgiveness and invite him into our hearts, or do we keep him at a safe distance? For those of us who have experienced the wonderful joy of knowing Christ, we remember that our journey started by simply making a decision. The decision was to invite him into our hearts and to serve him and walk with him.

Our relationship with Jesus should grow and, as it deepens, we should begin to feel his Holy Spirit at times in our lives encouraging us, speaking to us, guiding us to walk in the light of Christ and steering us away from darkness. As we walk and become closer and deeper in our relationship with Jesus, we become more confident of our faith. Nevertheless, our relationship is based on the principles of faith, trust and conviction.

I can tell you that Jesus is real and that I feel his presence in my life in many other wonderful ways, but I can't put God in a test tube just so you have something to put under a microscope. God won't fit in a test tube because even the heavens cannot contain his majesty. However, if you are honestly looking for him, his beauty and his works are all around you, and his mighty works can also be seen in the lives of his children. How do I know this? On a good day I actually love some people who aren't all that loveable, and that is a miracle in itself because normally I'm selfish and self-centered and I don't care whether Nineveh burns to the ground or not.

I have never seen the back of my head. I have seen only the reflection of it through a mirror. I have never seen God, but I see the reflection of him through his children at times, and I feel his wonderful presence working on my stony heart, and I feel my heart begin to soften and change. If your heart is open and you are willing to try walking with him, you will see for yourself that he is real and wonderful.

Our faith simply begins as a decision to follow Christ. It's a simple decision. It is nothing more complicated than that. There is a song I learned in Sunday school as a boy that says, "I have decided to follow Jesus." It's a wonderful little chorus and I still love hearing it even today. The message is simple, yet profound. This act of faith needs to become a solid commitment to walk with the Lord every day of our life. If you ever want to get on solid ground spiritually and start growing and producing fruit for the Kingdom of God, you need to start right here. You have to make your mind up that you are in this for the long haul and your faith isn't up for grabs, depending on how you feel, if the weather changes or if something better or more pleasing comes along. There isn't anything more wonderful than Jesus, and if you are thinking there might be, that is the voice of the enemy.

Once you have decided to follow Jesus, you need to know what his plans are and what the rules of life are. If you don't know what the do's and don'ts are, you are never going to walk with much confidence or boldness because you will never know if what you are doing is actually right. We are not supposed to live in a state of confusion or fear. If you want to know what God is all about and build yourself up in the faith, you need to read the word of God, which is to say, the Bible. The Bible lays out God's word for us and provides many wonderful examples of right and wrong, and of failure and success. If you ever want to become a rock solid Christian, you need to accept the Bible as the word of God and be willing to accept it as the authoritative word of God for your life. It is the ultimate source of our truth for those who place their faith in Jesus.

For the word of God is quick, and powerful, and sharper than any two-edged sword, piercing even to the dividing asunder of soul and spirit, and of the joints and marrow, and is a discerner of the thoughts and intents of the heart (hebrews 4:12). This says it beautifully, succinctly and perfectly! The word is our source of authority. Jesus said of it: *heaven and earth shall pass away but my words shall not pass away* (Matthew 24:35).

The word will build you up and infuse you with the strength of Christ. The word will guide you and illuminate your path and give you wisdom and encourage you in not only your faith but in your real life battles. Many Christians struggle with adversity and the trials of life because they don't read the word or know what it says. If you don't know what the word says, you are shooting yourself in the foot. The word is like a spiritual I.V. that gives you the nutrition of God and charges your batteries up. If you don't know what the words says, you are going to flounder like a fish out of water. If you want to overcome adversity and develop a successful spiritual walk that is victorious and full of joy and which will enable you to bud like a tree in spring developing flowers or fruit, then you need to diligently read, study and meditate on God's word. I don't know of any godly person that I respect that would tell you anything different on this point.

We asked why the journey is so hard if we are doing the right things. One of the issues that attenuate our walk and faith we have already identified as disobedience. As pointed out, this comes in different forms and levels. Knowing what the word of God says will help you walk uprightly and honorably before God and shed light on what you should or should not do so that you are not walking in disobedience. I always find it fascinating to hear believers, who have walked with Christ for many years, say how the word of God continues to minister to them and open new areas of growth in their lives. Many believers share a common theme on this subject, that no matter how many times they read the Bible, the Holy Spirit has a way of not only making it fresh, but opening their eyes to new truths which they may not have seen in earlier readings. I concur wholeheartedly with their thoughts and assessments.

If you want to have spiritual success and have the blessings of God poured into your life, you need to accept and obey God's word. God's word does not change or evolve to accommodate changing social values or trends. Forever, O Lord, thy word is settled in heaven (Psalms 119:89). Do not be deceived into thinking you can tweak God's word or manipulate it into your own doctrine. You can do that of course, but it will no longer be God's word. Understand there are people all over the world who do this, but they will also answer for it.

God tells us to love one another, so some people then say that means I can sleep with anyone I want as long as I care about them and feel love for them. Such thinking represents a perverse manipulation of scripture and it does not reflect what is written in the word of God. The Bible is full of words, including those of Jesus, instructing us to repent of our sin, and obey: and, not only the Ten Commandments, but all of them! Jesus said, "If you love me, keep my commandments." We are to love God "in spirit and in truth," not through our own manipulation or duplicity. Those who intentionally manipulate God's words or his commandments and don't repent face serious consequences. Here are a few scripture references, which address this important issue: (John 4:24/14:15/Matthew 7:21-23/Revelation 3:19/22:11,14,18,19).

Remember, if God's word says something is wrong or forbids it, then it's wrong, and it will be wrong tomorrow as well as a thousand years from now.

The word of God states: *I am the Lord, I change not; Jesus Christ is the same yesterday, today and forever* (Malachi 3:6/hebrews 13:8).

Why do we struggle so with adversity of all kinds?

Many believers are...well, just that: believers, but not necessarily followers of Christ. We are to be not only hearers of the word, but doers of the word also. In failure analysis, I see that many Christians do not know what the word says to begin with, but what is even more disturbing is that there are plenty of folks who don't care what the word says. They have their own position about what is right or wrong or about how they are going to follow the rules. Some just make up their own rules. I can tell you for sure that making your own rules up does not work in the courts of California and it won't work in the courts of heaven. If you love the Lord, or that is where your heart is leading you, then read God's word. It will open your eyes to better understand not only God's character, but his love for you as well.

It is perfectly O.K. to pick and choose which type of fruit or vegetables you like to eat at the buffet restaurant because of preference, but God's word and his commandments don't fall into the pick and choose category. Don't confuse God's ways with your ways. It is neither your way nor your will that will ever please the Lord unless you are walking in obedience to the Holy Spirit and the word of God. The Lord's Prayer should remind us that it's not my *our* will, but *his* will that needs to be done.

The prophet Isaiah writes in God's word, *For as the heavens are higher than the earth, so my ways are higher than your ways, and my thoughts are higher than your thoughts* (Isaiah 55:9). If we are truly trying to surrender ourselves completely to the Lord, and faithfully serve him as disciplined disciples who rightly discern the word of God, then we can't simply make up our own rules as we go along. You can't be contentious and surrendered at the same time.

I was exchanging thoughts with a fellow believer about a spiritual principle and the person said quite honestly, "Yeah, I know the Bible says that, but I'm not sure that I go along with that or accept it." Another Christian said to me on a different biblical matter that in spite of what he knew the Bible had to say about the issue, he felt we should avoid pointing the truth of it out to others. Well, I know that's what the Bible says, but we don't have to identify that or go down that road, the believer told me. The implication was very straightforward. We don't have to acknowledge the truth, let alone walk in it or talk about it. You can't maintain an attitude of servanthood and a heart of surrender to God and still be doing your own thing and think that you are not going to feel conflict. You can't serve two masters the Bible says. But we actually try to play both sides of the fence. We serve God and practice obedience when it's convenient and we do our own thing if the cost of righteousness is too high.

When I was working the streets, I would often counsel young people on this subject in a generic way. You have to decide what you want out of life and where you want to go in life. You have to decide who you are going to hang with and allow to influence you. You can't hang with people that drink and do drugs and not expect that eventually you won't do the same. Who you hang with will either lift you up or bring you down. It's that simple, and even the world understands it. You can't serve two masters. I didn't develop this principle. These are the words of Jesus! *For either he will hate the one, and love the other; or else he will hold to the one, and despise the other. You cannot serve God and mammon* (Matthew 6:24). *For where your treasure is, there will your heart be also* (Matthew 6:21).

Why is the journey so hard at times?

There is a way which seems right unto a man, but the road leads to hell. We don't know what is always right and when we do, sometimes we choose not to follow the path of righteousness anyway. You can't play both sides of the fence, live recklessly and not get burned. When troubles rise we don't automatically inquire of the Lord or wait on the Lord. If the waiting is too inconvenient or time consuming we chuck that plan and either "solve" the problem ourselves, or we seek advice from some other person who may not even know the Lord, and we ask them what they think. Be careful who you listen to. Edmund Burke said that if an idiot were to tell you the same story everyday for a year, you would end up believing him. Trust in the Lord with all your heart and wait patiently for him. Rely on what the word of God says.

Another issue of adversity and discomfort that comes into play with our walk with the Lord is that, while our journey is sometimes harder than we wish it would be at times, it is not *that* unbearable most of the time. That is to say, our pain of mediocrity and disobedience isn't as bad as picking up our cross daily and actually following Jesus, or serving the Lord with all our heart no matter what the cost. As long as God doesn't stop us like a police officer for breaking all the rules, and demand accountability from us, we settle for that. As long as we can have Jesus and our sin too, we are just fine with life as it is. As long as the journey doesn't get any more painful or unbearable because of our duplicity and guilt, we often just stay the course because we like our plans better than God's plan. We deceive ourselves and talk to each other like used car salesmen of the worse kind, pretending to follow Jesus, but we don't obey his commandments, we don't love or serve others, and we talk to Jesus like we talk to ourselves, with complete denial regarding our behavior. Like the Frank Sinatra song, sometimes we are actually proud to tell our friends, "I did it my way."

If the truth be told, we can be quite satisfied with our own lovely selves. That's what my wife asks me sometimes. I'm not sure how this all came about, but it was another home improvement project that I worked on until the cows came home. After repeated failed attempts, I eventually got it right. I was so happy and pleased with my own self that we joked about it and laughed. We had so much fun being silly about it, that my wife now asks me periodically, "Is [sic] you happy with your own lovely self?"

While the concept of being pleased with ourselves might be innocuous at the human level, the same cannot be said if we apply it to our spiritual lives, but this is precisely what many do. We want the good life. We want God to richly bless us, our family and children and our business endeavors, but we don't want to go too deep with this spiritual stuff or take up our cross to follow the Lord. If the cost gets too high, there are plenty of dropouts who just walk away. I didn't work this hard to just give it away, right? If you play the game half-heartedly and your devotion is only lukewarm, don't expect an exhilarating finish. Likewise, if you are playing both sides of the fence, don't think that there isn't a conflict of interest in that. You can't serve two masters and be loyal to both. If you are catching yourself cutting corners with your spiritual life and devotion to the Lord, you need to take a hard look at that. If you can take or leave whatever the Lord has to say on issues that are important, I respectfully submit you are walking on thin ice. If you can figure out what part of Jesus' words aren't important, let me know. If anything I have written has made you angry or uncomfortable, then I consider that to be a compliment.

There are sections along the road of our journey that are just simply harder than others. The intensity is greater along with the demands. I just got an e-mail from my son yesterday saying hello. He is completing his third year of college and he was telling me how busy he is with school. He said he completes one thing and five other assignments are staring him in the face. By the time finals come, sleep is something you only read about that other people do.

When my mother was getting ready to pass on, she could hardly wait. She always loved to visit with me when I called and when I drove up to visit her, I would take her out for blueberry pancakes with whipped cream. She was focused on the future and not the present at that time. She said to me, "Mark, you have no idea what it's like to get old."

Well, of course I do! I stopped catching 18-year-old kids in foot pursuits when I was still only in my forties. The last one was quite memorable though. My partner and I from the San Mateo County Sheriff's Office chased some kid down the street from the Post Office and Roberts Market in Woodside, California, and I was sucking air as though I would have an apoplexy at any moment. My face was red and perspiration ran off my forehead like I had been swimming. We took the kid to the ground and got him handcuffed and I put out a "ten-fifteen, code four" on the radio, indicating we had our suspect in custody and we needed no further assistance. Well, the assistance, as it always does, came anyway.

The Sergeant got there in no time flat and I was still trying to catch my breath. The Sergeant took one look at us and started laughing. The Sergeant asked what happened and my partner told him the kid was wanted and had warrants for his arrest.

My partner then said, "The kid ran and we gave chase. Deputy Malmin came flying out of nowhere and threw the kid to the ground. We struggled with him briefly and handcuffed the kid."

The Sergeant kind of took me off guard because he asked the kid if it was all right if we took a picture of all of us together. I wasn't quite sure why he would ask that because we had the legal right to take the kid's picture regardless of whether he consented or not.

Nevertheless, the kid replied, "Sure, go ahead."

We got a Polaroid camera out of the trunk of our patrol car and we posed for a picture. The Sergeant told my partner and me to stand next to the kid and smile.

The kid suspiciously asked, "What is this for?"

The Sergeant replied, "I want a photo of the only kid in Woodside who couldn't out-run these two old farts!"

The Sergeant was very pleased with our work but also thought it was funny that we managed to even catch this kid. We considered ourselves pretty lucky, too.

Struggles, adversity and testing do not end when you graduate from college. All of life will continue to be an ongoing series of tests to the day you take your last breath of air. Why would you ever imagine that our spiritual lives would be any different? You might not be expected to chase an 18-year-old when you are in your eighties, but you may need to cast a few devils out along the way. Real battles are not only with guns but they involve the spirit world as well. Rebuking the devil and commanding him to leave or get behind you is a battle not any less real than any one of which I experienced.

Then, Jesus, being full of the Holy Ghost, was led by the Spirit into the wilderness to be tempted of the devil (Matthew 4:1/Luke 4:1). If God did not spare his own son from testing, you won't be spared either. God leads us, teaches us, cultivates and grooms us and tries us by fire until we are proven able and fit for battle and worthy to lead. This is an ongoing process and it doesn't stop just because you turned eighty years old. Get your spiritual patrol car out of the garage and put some gas in that rusty thing. Some young seventy-nine-year old chicken needs your faith, wisdom and encouragement to overcome what she might struggle with. You haven't reached your full maturity until either the Lord takes you home or you stop reaching for the stars. Get to work, pal! Time is wasting!

Are any sick among you? *Let him call for the elders of the church; and let them pray over him, anointing him with oil in the name of the Lord: And the prayer of faith shall save the sick, and the Lord shall raise him up; and if he have committed sins, they shall be forgiven* (James 5:14-15). In the Kingdom (of heaven) business there is no age restriction for warriors. Even the youths shall faint and be weary, and the young men shall utterly fall: But they that wait upon the Lord shall renew their strength (Isaiah 40:30-31). There is work to be done!

Some of the adversity we go through is simply a reflection of this spiritual process, and in that respect, it may have some of the components that Job experienced. Adversity doesn't mean you failed. It may mean you are a worthy warrior and God expects great things from you!

When terrible adversity comes, it may be that God has been preparing you for such a moment as this. Joseph was an example of this. Joseph was mocked by his brothers and called a dreamer. They conspired to slay him and throw his body into a pit. They took his coat of many colors and smeared the blood of an animal on the coat. The conspiracy was planned so that the brothers would return to their father Jacob and give him the bloodied coat and offer the explanation that some evil beast had devoured Joseph. *Then they said to each other: we shall see what becomes of his dreams* (Genesis 37:20).

The younger brother, Ruben, dissuaded the other brothers from actually murdering Joseph and, as an alternative, persuaded them to throw Joseph into a pit, which was empty and had no water. So they did this, intending to leave him there to die. Only because God had other plans, Joseph was not murdered, but was taken out of the pit and sold for twenty pieces of silver to passing merchants that were traveling to Egypt (Genesis 37:27-28). Most people I know would be upset if they lost their dental coverage. This would tip the scale.

Once in Egypt Joseph was purchased by Potiphar, an officer of Pharaoh, captain of the guard. *And the Lord was with Joseph and he was a prosperous man; and he was in the house of his master the Egyptian. And his master saw that the Lord was with him, and that the Lord made all that he did to prosper in his hand. And Joseph found grace in his sight, and he served him; and he made him overseer over his house, and all that he had put into his hand. And it came to pass from the time that he had made him overseer in his house, and over all that he had, that the Lord blessed the Egyptian's house for Joseph's sake; and the blessing of the Lord was upon all that he had in the house, and in the field* (Genesis 39:1-5).

There is a powerful message in this story that shows us we can be on top of life and have the blessings of God upon us and even in the worst of circumstances. What I find to be fabulous is that even the Egyptian was blessed for Joseph's sake. I want to walk so uprightly and honorably before the Lord that the Egyptians in my life are blessed with the same results because of my faithfulness in God's eyes.

What is not directly mentioned with any specific language has to be read between the lines, but I am speaking of Joseph's attitude and demeanor. It is pretty hard to find grace in your master's eyes or the Lord's eyes if you have a foul attitude. It does not say that Joseph was downcast or discouraged, taking anti-depressants. Joseph may have been grieving at various times about the loss of his family because this issue comes up later, but his day to day service and outlook on life had to be great or he could not have been this successful. One simply cannot be successful like Joseph and at the same time have a rotten attitude. God cannot use you or bless you to your fullest potential if you are denying his power and living in defeat. One has to claim victory in spite of the circumstances and be a part of the solution. We have to look upward to allow the resources of the Holy Spirit to fill us. Get vertical!

Joseph represents the ultimate paradigm of adversity by being a godly man who walks uprightly before the Lord. About the time one might resign themselves to the fact that they are a slave, but a successful one, Joseph perhaps sees light at the end of a tunnel, but only to learn it is a freight train approaching at high speed. Potiphar's wife falsely accused Joseph of attempted rape and Joseph is thrown into prison. When we face something like this, the devil whispers in our ear that it is vain to serve God; that no good deed goes unpunished; just look at where you are. This is why we look not to the things which are seen, but rather to the things which are not seen, for the things which are seen are temporal and circumstantial; the things which are not seen are of faith and they are eternal (2 Corinthians 4:18). The essence of our faith is summed up with these simple words: For with God nothing shall be impossible (Luke 1:37).

Just as Daniel was thrown into the den of lions, Joseph was thrown into prison. Both were godly men. Jesus, the perfect Lamb of God, was crucified. Yet, cream rises to the top and you can't keep a good man down, not one who walks with favor before the Lord. From prison Joseph answers the dreams of Pharaoh. This results in his promotion to second in command, only under Pharaoh himself. All the injustices that Joseph experienced and endured were elements of adversity, which God allowed into his life for a purpose, but without explanation. Joseph's faith and character were tried by fire. The fining pot is for silver and the furnace for gold; but the Lord trieth the hearts (Proverbs 17:3). Just as Job had no idea about the warfare that was taking place in the spiritual dimension, and was left with only his faith, so it was with Joseph. God told neither one what was occurring during the battle storm. God simply wants us to trust him. Only after both Job and Joseph successfully went through the firestorm did they realize that their faith produced a work of pure gold. Joseph was allowed to be thrown into a pit and be sold into slavery so that a godly man could interpret dreams and stand next to Pharaoh. Joseph, the dreamer, who was mocked as such, helped to save Egypt and the seed of Abraham, Isaac and Jacob from famine. Millions of people, including those of Joseph's family, would have been wiped out by this famine, but for the plan of God to use Joseph.

Most of us have never experienced anything like what Job or Joseph went through, but it is perfectly appropriate to do a reality check when we enter this kind of trail by fire. Examine yourself. Question your own motives and know that the heart is deceitful and desperately wicked above all things. Trust in God, not yourself. Ask God, even as David did, *Search me, O God, and know my heart; try me, and know my thoughts: And see if there be any wicked way in me, and lead me in the way everlasting* (Psalms 139:23-24).

Most of the calamities we face are the results of our own handiwork and failure. If you are walking perfectly before the Lord as Job and Joseph did, and you pray and ask God to show you whether you missed the boat or did something wrong or not, that much of an answer you will get, if only in terms of peace within your heart, which passes all understanding. Peace is priceless. God's act of withholding information and facts from you does not mean you did anything wrong; it only means you need to trust God. You want the whole plan and an explanation. You don't need that. What you want and what you need are two different things. Trust him. His grace is sufficient.

In reading and studying the word and from my own personal experience and from learning from those whom I know have walked closely with God, I can say the following with confidence: the Lord doesn't trick you or try and fool you with his will and purpose for your life. God is not in the business of misleading people. God is in the business of guiding people and saving them. If the Lord wants you to go to Nineveh or some other place he will make that clear. God doesn't expect us to guess about his plans for our lives. His word has promised that. *Trust in the Lord with all your heart, and lean not unto your own understanding. In all your ways acknowledge him and he shall direct your paths* (Proverbs 3:5-6).

No further explanation is also a type of answer. That may translate into the fact that God's doesn't think you need to see around the corner. That may in turn mean that you should simply trust in the Lord and wait patiently for him to guide you. Rest in the Lord. We can do that because God is reliable and trustworthy, and he is the best friend you will ever have. If God wants you to go to Nineveh and you disobeyed, you are going to know what the problem is. You might find yourself in a room without a view. If you want to go to Miami when God has something else planned down the road for you, then remember "no" is also an answer.

If you are not causing the problem, and you are walking uprightly before the Lord, the Holy Spirit will give you peace, assurance, and a spirit of rest so that you don't feel compelled to strain with achieving an outcome. Ask questions along the way. Are my ways pleasing in your sight, Lord? Am I walking in obedience to your word? Is there anything in my flesh that I am blinded to that is impeding me? These are honorable prayers of self-evaluation and openness and the Lord will see your broken spirit and hear your humble prayers and guide you.

If you know your heart is right and that you are willing to follow the leading of God in your life over your own preference, then just walk in faith and trust the Lord, and don't beat yourself up! I believe it is entirely possible to have joy if you focus upward and wait upon the Lord to renew your strength. It is entirely possible to practice the fruit of the Spirit while you are in adversity or jail, as was the case with the great apostle Paul. Joy in the midst of adversity is one of the fruits of the Spirit. We can have it! In order to have joy you have to be at peace within yourself. That also means you need to rest in the Lord. I think Joseph did exactly that and we can do it, too.

Watch and pray that ye enter not into temptation: the spirit is indeed willing, but the flesh is weak (Matthew 26:41). If there is anything you take away from this book let it be a greater understanding that we can't rely on our own goodness or trust our own flesh; we need Jesus. We need to trust and obey God and walk in the Spirit. In doing so, we also overcome adversity.

Oh, by the way, if you find yourself sinking out at sea, don't wave off the Coast Guard just because you have some romantic notion of what God's rescue plan should look like. God might send you an angel, but he could be dressed in ragged looking apparel and look like an unshaved homeless guy. Don't turn the hand of God away because the servant speaks in heavenly tongues and you don't like it. Keep your options open.

CHAPTER 6

WE DON'T REALLY KNOW WHAT WE BELIEVE!

It is amazing how many Christians have not been baptized. All of us should be baptized. It's not a recommendation like PMI because your credit score isn't as high as your mortgage lender would like it to be. It's a commandment!

Why do we need to do this? It is not wrong to ask questions sincerely, but our questions can sometimes be part of our problem, if we don't get the answer which pleases us. We question God far more than we need to. We find it hard to just trust and obey him. This human propensity seems to reflect our desire to want to know all the facts and see around corners with our headlights. That's never going to happen because God is trying to teach us to walk in faith and obedience.

We live in an age where democracy teaches us to question the government, and that is generally a good thing, because there should be constant evaluation, thoughtfulness and participation in how we govern ourselves. Government should be of the people, by the people, and for the people, and if it's not, we have a duty to change it. Voting in local and national elections is an honor and a civic responsibility.

Just don't confuse democracy with God's government or leadership. We don't get to vote on whether we approve of God's laws, and his plans are not subject to review committees. That's a really good thing because we would all be just like California legislators, who could not vote on a budget, because they are not of the same mind or spirit, and they cannot, for the life of California, agree on what to do. God's word is forever settled in heaven and his laws are well established and set firmly and no lower earthly court can overthrow his laws or surpass his wisdom. God's plans are higher than our plans, and if we don't see that, we are deluding ourselves. The proverbial issue of "just who is God anyway?" needs to get settled. I know a handful of people will be shocked, but it isn't you!

Having the political right to question local government causes blurred vision for some people. Young kids, who aren't old enough to vote and who are only beginning to learn how to discipline themselves and become responsible adults, drive BMW's with bumper stickers that read: Question Authority. The first time some of these kids get stopped for speeding they want to argue with the police and instruct them about their constitutional rights. A little bit of knowledge can be a dangerous thing. Kids grow up learning to question their parents, their school teachers, and others in authority. By the time young people reach adulthood many think it is perfectly O.K. to question God's authority.

I also want to acknowledge that there is a time, place and manner to do all things. If we question God's principles with humility and sincerity, and our questioning is because we want to understand righteousness and follow Christ and ensure that we walk in obedience, then we do so for the right reason. If we ask questions in that light, we are simply searching for truth, not challenging authority. There is a big difference between asking questions to understand truth and simply questioning the authority of the one who offers it.

God's character, integrity and sense of justice will never manifest vicissitude. Unlike earthly government, changing trends, culture and values, or the rule of earthly wealth and power, God's ways are pure, just, full of goodness and altogether enduring. This isn't like municipal government where next month it is time to rotate City Council members, and it's your turn to be Mayor or God, depending on what your delusion is. God doesn't change. He is the same, yesterday, today and forever! We need to better understand this through God's word. We need to become more comfortable with surrendering our will to God's will, and we need to learn to become better followers. Some of our adversity stems from the fact that we struggle with *following* because we want to lead and we haven't really settled that contentious issue of who rules and reigns in our lives. This takes us right back to square one. Who's the boss? Is it you or is it God? This issue needs resolution.

If you struggle with this issue I can offer a practical suggestion. Confess your weakness before the Lord and tell him how much you struggle with this. Just be honest about the whole issue. Surrender your Miranda rights to the Lord and offer him a full confession, but don't offer your confession as some conditional, polite, but insincere negotiation plan for compromise. Ask God to help you better understand how wonderful and great he is because that will help you want to follow him! Ask the Lord to remove the scales from your eyes so that you might get a glimpse of how truly wonderful he is. That's one of his names: *Wonderful*. Once you get a glimpse, there won't be any confusion about whether to *follow* him.

Let me illustrate this point.

Even in our earthly affairs we all know what it is like to have a rotten boss and how great it is to have a good boss. A good boss tends to have insight for the big picture in life, compassion and be willing to forgive you when you make mistakes, at least some mistakes. In my line of work, if you shot the wrong guy, or even the right guy, but for the wrong reason, that would be a problem, believe me! I had many good supervisors over the years whom I enjoyed working for; however, one in particular comes to mind. Let us, shall we say, call him Dennis. Dennis was probably the best supervisor I ever had for a lot of different reasons. He was fair, hardworking himself, competent, just, honest, thoughtful, considerate and generous. This guy was about as good a supervisor as you might find anywhere! It was a joy for me to work for him. These are the kind of people we all want to serve.

Now, if you thought it might be nice to work for a guy like Dennis, you are absolutely right, but imagine what Dennis could do for me if I shot and killed the wrong guy. Dennis wouldn't be able to do anything except say that it was sure nice knowing you, Mr. Malmin, while you had your act together. Now, imagine what it would be like to work for and serve someone who, is not only wonderful in every way but divine also, and willing to die in your place, in order to forgive an eternal death penalty for your sin, even if you shot and killed the wrong guy. Imagine a Savior who has your eternal interest at heart and who loves and understands you better than you understand yourself, and who wants to bless you and make you prosper in everything that you do (like Joseph in Egypt). This will start giving you a glimpse of Jesus and what an honor it is to serve him.

When it comes to obedience and service, some people get gun-shy. They are afraid to submit and they often spend more time questioning God and his word than just accepting his ways and commandments. If the answer doesn't suit our liking, we sometimes reject the answer as not being good enough for us. God does not have to prove himself to us anymore than he did with Job. This issue can turn into a contentious debate or disagreement over what we perceive to be truth, but God does not argue over these things. Therein lies a problem. You and God can't both be God at the same time. So far, I am speaking to those who claim to be Christians.

I touched on this in the previous chapter, but the issue is so important I want to re-emphasize it. You can't pick and choose what parts of God's laws, commandments and ways you want to accept and follow, like food items we select off a food menu at the cafeteria, and throw away the provisions of God you find disinteresting or which you are not fond of. You will never have an intimate and wonderful relationship if you are not committed to Christ. If your commitment and faithfulness is up for grabs, if something better comes along, you are not going to have a meaningful, deep relationship. If you are competing with God over who is going to be God, you aren't going to have much of a relationship with him.

Sometimes people practice what I like to call, a casual dating relationship with the Lord, where they share a glass of grape juice together on Easter or a movie during one of the Christmas holidays. Some might not even do that if their favorite NFL team was playing that day. All of these typologies, by any reasonable standard, represent shallow and superficial behaviors that don't define love at its deepest level.

If you are not a born-again disciple of Christ, if you are not sure if you are saved or not, or if you just feel self-sufficient, happy with your life, and unconcerned about sin and don't see your need for a Savior, then you need to ask God to reveal himself to you and show you *why* you need him. If you are honest about that God will respect your honesty and your request. You might not be ready for a relationship with God because you are still in a seeking, investigating mode and you may want to learn more about spiritual things. God will reveal himself to you if you search for him with all your heart. All of us started our journey somewhere along this road of life. Just don't let life pass you by! Today may be your last day. We rarely get prior warning about our last breath.

Once we understand that all of us have sinned and that sin leads to eternal death, and that Jesus is the cure, if we ask him to forgive us and come into our lives, then we start to realize why we need him. The Holy Spirit will show you the sin in your life that you don't even recognize. If you are seeking God to help you with all of this because you care about your eternal destiny and the life you have right now, God will meet you at your point of need and help you. This is why Jesus said that if you seek, you shall find; if you knock, it shall be opened unto you. The only nexus to this, which I can see, is simply sincerity on your part.

A big part of all of this is simply understanding that sin is terminal and that it will destroy your soul. Such death is not only something to be concerned about in the eternal life of the hereafter, but sin will mess you up [sic] bad, right here, right now, on planet earth, and it will destroy your life if you keep walking in it. Hard, foolish living can kill you sooner rather than later. Even good living, as we think of it, eventually leads to death because of the *fall* of man through the first sin of Adam and Eve and *curse* which ensued.

Scripture refers to the consequence of sin by referring to it as the *first death*, and the *second death*. The *first death* refers to our natural death on earth, which resulted from the *fall*. We grow up thinking it's normal to grow old and eventually die but that wasn't the plan. It's the progressive results of sin and the consequence of the *curse* which followed. We are all born in sin and that leads to the *first death*.

The *second death refers to eternity and damnation, and the lake of fire.* Those who die in Christ, truly knowing him, will also reign with him and live with him forever, and they will be spared the *second death* by virtue of their salvation in Christ, which is entirely based upon the forgiveness of sin through Christ's sacrifice on the cross.

Scripture warns us that the *second death* is the one we better be careful to avoid. Don't spend a lot of time worrying about how beautiful you are or other inconsequentially selfish things that will quickly end in the *first death*, in what will seem like the mere blink of an eye. Rather, be concerned about the *second death*, which is to say, be concerned about your eternal soul, and make sure you know where it's going. Live wisely.

The right now, right here, and in the moment, brings up another point. I follow Jesus not only for the security and peace of mind over my eternal salvation in the life hereafter, but also for the blessing, joy and honor of serving him right now. Jesus is the best friend you will ever have and when, or if, you ever surrender you heart completely to him, there will be a joy that you experience that words cannot fully describe or measure and nothing that earth has to offer can be compared to it. It's not that I don't ever have hard days or difficult things to deal with in life, because I certainly do, like everyone else, but the joy of walking with the Lord is so real to me, so profound, and life changing that all other suffering or hardship is not worth comparing to what I have in Christ. In this regard, neither life nor death has any control over me and I belong to Christ no matter what happens. When I saturate my spirit in his presence my joy is profound.

Out on the street some lost soul might wonder if I have been smoking crack because that's the only intense sensation they have known on earth by which to measure joy or pleasure. Jesus described it, as such, to the Israelites who lived in the desert: [and who knew fully what it meant to thirst] *he that believeth on me, as the scripture hath said, out of his belly [or deep within your inner being] shall flow rivers of living water* (John 7:38). To the woman from Jacob's well in Samaria Jesus said: *But whosoever drinketh of the water that I shall give him shall never thirst; but the water that I shall give him shall be in him a well of water springing up into everlasting life* (John 4:14). The apostle Paul describes this in his writing to the church, speaking to followers of Jesus, many of whom had never seen Jesus, whom having not seen, you love; and whom, though now, you see him not, yet believing, you rejoice with "joy unspeakable and full of glory" (I Peter 1:8). This sense of indescribable joy, over someone we can't see or physically touch like other people, comes from the Holy Spirit. As you develop your sensitivity to the Holy Spirit you can literally feel his presence and anointing in your life as you walk in the Spirit. It's wonderful! God's Holy Spirit makes Jesus come alive and real to those who seek Christ.

Once we get a glimpse of how wonderful Jesus is, and what he did for us, and the price he paid to die on the cross for us, we should come to an understanding that he is the most wonderful thing that could ever come into our lives. Jesus deserves our complete devotion. There could be nothing in our life worthy or great enough to repay him for his sacrifice or the love and blessings he bestows upon those who love him. The Lord desires more than a superficial relationship with each of us. God wants your whole heart, and not just a small, over crowded storage room in the basement of your heart.

If our relationship with Jesus is to be meaningful, and if we want it to develop into something profound, we can't simply have a casual on-again, off-again, "dating" relationship with him, where we aren't completely sure whether we will honor or obey him or accept his words, commandments and teachings. We can't have it our way and his way at the same time. He is either Lord of all, or Lord of nothing. He is either our Lord, or he is not. There is no halfway deal with Jesus and we need to understand this and accept it, and change our behavior so that he is Lord and Master of our lives, and of everything we have and everything we are.

There is a wonderful song I grew up with. The lyrics are: "Where he leads, I will follow." Some of us wouldn't follow the Lord to the corner store if the weather were a little inclement. This probably describes all of us at some point in our faith, but as we journey, our faith and commitment get stronger, and so does our willingness to stand up for the Lord, even when it costs us something. When your faith grows deeper it can reach the level of Shadrack, Meshack and Abednego, who were willing to be thrown into the fiery furnace because of both their love for God and their desire to walk in obedience and not compromise their faith.

God refers to us, his church, as his bride. God wants a perfect bride without spot or wrinkle. Our love for the Lord should be pure and our commitment well anchored. Our relationship with the Lord should not be up for grabs, because someone or some *thing* more appealing comes along. Our love should encompass our whole heart, energy and total being. The Great Commandment says: *love the Lord thy God with all thy heart, and with all thy soul, and with all thy mind, and with all thy strength* (Mark12:30).

If our desire is to become rock solid in our faith and commitment, wherein we produce fruit for the Kingdom, we should not be feeling indecisive or experiencing confusion over how deep we are willing to go in our commitment with Jesus. If you are sensing conflict or consternation about this, it most likely means you haven't surrendered all of your heart. I invite you to do so. I will go a step further. God is so good, longsuffering, patient, tenderhearted, just and forgiving. He will work with you even if you fail, but there is a caveat: you need to be honest. Tell him you are not yet fully committed and that you need his divine help in softening your heart and turning your life around. Honesty, humility and brokenness are keys to prayer that produce powerful results.

Do we, as Christians, know what the Lord requires of us? I believe most of us would have difficulty trying to answer this and we would get vague and philosophical. Well, you know, it depends on what you mean by that, and we would dance all over the place trying to answer this simple question with confidence. Most people would struggle with this because they are not sure of the answer. I am speaking in general terms here, not whether the Lord is calling you into medical school or Bible school. God wants us to love him with all our heart, and to love one another even as he loved us. Jesus wants us to pick up our cross daily and follow him, and deny our own interests so that we serve others. God wants our obedience in all things. God wants us to follow like we mean it. God wants us to know the rules because we know his word.

Consider this. We don't know well enough what God's word even says because we don't immerse ourselves in it, as we ought to. Even if the word of God is pointed out to us, many believers aren't sure if they completely believe or accept it as the inspired, divine, word of God. Is it the authoritative word of God? If you get right down to it, there are a lot of Christians who are not sure what they believe about the Bible or even about God. The Bible says: *Study to show thyself approved unto God, a good workman that needeth not to be ashamed, rightly dividing the word of truth* (2 Timothy 2:15). Too many are unable to discern what the truth is or how to evaluate it because we don't fully appreciate how the word plays into all of this. We don't know what we really believe.

We want to believe that God loves us, and he does. We want to believe that God cares about us and that maybe he even has a plan for our lives, and he does; but when we start getting down to specifics, sometimes we don't even know what we believe about the Bible or what it says, because we don't read it enough, or at all, nor do we ask God to give us a better understanding of what it says, or what it means. Our whole attitude and position is so tenuous, we are left hanging in the air, unsure of what the Bible says, or whether it is even completely reliable and true. If you want to better know and understand the heart of God, reading his word will help you. It will be very difficult to know with confidence whether you are doing the right things, or not, if you don't know what his word says. His word reflects core values of integrity, guidance and blessings in the form of promises. Don't you want to know what they are?

Some of us are also afraid of walking in obedience to the word of God because, quite frankly, we are not stupid, and we know deep down inside that obedience will cost us something. We don't know how far we want to go with this obedience stuff. We haven't firmly decided anything, let alone whether we want to obey God's spiritual laws. Besides, isn't God loving and forgiving; so, why should I obey him if he forgives me anyway? Can you see how manipulative this could get? Our corruptible behavior can effactually turn grace into "cheap grace."

How can I answer these hard questions, if I am not even sure about my own commitment? Will you decide to walk with Jesus, give him your heart and serve him or just admire him like many did because he healed people? Like the two thieves on the cross, we each need to make an important decision as to what we are going to do with Jesus. Are you going to accept Jesus and surrender your heart to him completely? How far are you going to follow Jesus? Is there an unconscious line drawn in the sand, which if crossed, reflects a cost and price too high for following Jesus? We don't really know what we believe. Does any of this describe you?

Back in 1992 a movie came out entitled "A Few Good Men." Actor Jack Nicholson plays the role of a tough Marine colonel who has command over Guantánomo Bay in Cuba. Actor Tom Cruise plays the role of a prosecuting military attorney in a court martial during a murder trial. During a pivotal scene in the movie, Cruise confronts Nicholson in a military courtroom with a taunting tit for tat cross-examination, which prompts the colonel on the witness stand to derisively ask, "You want answers?" Instantly, the contumelious prosecutor erupts back at the Colonel, "I WANT THE TRUTH!" The scene artistically produces in-your-face tension, so acute, that you can cut the air with a knife. Nicholson, who has the stature of a giant, puts on an extraordinary performance by defiantly thundering back a tremendous crescendo which rocks the entire courtroom: "YOU CAN'T HANDLE THE TRUTH!" The actor's line is said so well, and with such compelling force and facial body language, the whole movie is often remembered by this one line. Simply viewing the scene takes your breath away. (http://en.wikipedia.org/wiki/A_Few_Good_Men)

This scene and the truth of the statement make me think that much of our spiritual walk with the Lord could be summed up with this one line. We usually have good intentions but we are so duplicitous that we don't know what the truth really is, and we aren't all together sure we want to know. We're not even sure what we feel or believe because we can't even articulate it, let alone be committed to live it or be willing to die for it. Too many of us can't tell you whether or not the Bible is God's divine, authoritative word, or, whether we should follow *everything* Jesus says or not. We don't want to be disrespectful to our Lord, but the fact is, we don't really know what we believe! Our definitive view of biblical truth is so shaky half the time that we couldn't tell anyone what we really believe and have it be consistent with what we said last month.

The disciples all said they would die before they denied Jesus, yet all of them actually fled when it was time for Jesus to face the cross. Peter was known for denying Christ three times before the cock crowed three times, but the disciples all ran away and were afraid to stand up or have any affiliation with Jesus. We need to decide where we stand with Jesus.

Scripture speaks of rightly dividing the word of truth. Why is the word of such importance? Jesus is the truth and his words define it and reveal it for us. Jesus said: *I am the way, the truth, and the life: no man cometh unto the Father, but by me* (John 14:6). Jesus emphasized with authority that his words would never fade away, when he said: *heaven and earth shall pass away but my words shall not pass away* (Luke 21:33). The word of God stands alone on its own merit, and it represents the very essence and character of God himself. *In the beginning was the Word, and the Word was with God, and the Word was God* (John 1:1). The word represents God's blueprint for victorious living in Christ. Our own words will ultimately reflect what was in our heart all along, and they will represent life or death. *For by thy words thou shalt be justified, and by thy words thou shalt be condemned* (Matthew 12:37). I was only five years old when I intentionally and with careful deliberation, asked my father to pray with me as I invited Jesus into my heart. The record in heaven will have that moment recorded in The Book of Life, the words of my mouth, on that day and at that time, inviting Jesus into my heart.

We live in a world where precious few things are completely clear or defined. Half the time it is hard, if not impossible, to even know what the rules are because they change faster than present day technology. What represents state of the art standards today will be obsolete in six months. Social values change to accommodate special interests. Often, it is hard to know what people really mean because we are so collectively deceptive. I don't always tell people what I think because my thinking is vile and ugly and if I did, no one would ever speak to me again.

No often means not right now but maybe later.

Never usually means sometimes if the right conditions are present.

Wrong means it might be wrong, but if it feels right, it must be right.

Always means at least until the next election.

Sinful is often defined as merely an alternative life-style, considered viable and equal.

Earthly standards of accountability are so dismal, inconsistent, reversible, and changing that we literally learn to not pay too much attention to authority and challenge it whenever necessary if it conflicts with our personal interests. We learn to live the way we want to and we become satisfied with calling our own shots, rather than relying on anything the word of God might say. Since God is loving, forgiving and longsuffering, some might say, we have a lot of leeway to make our own choices, and besides, I don't really see God holding anyone accountable for anything. We have free choice! How can anyone really say what's right or wrong. This is so subjective and judgmental. People say that truth is relative, which means, I shouldn't have to pursue it because it's too complicated. I hear this all the time. This really becomes just an excuse to do what we prefer to do, our own thing.

In a world where nothing is ever what it seems to be, Jesus is real, sincere, and without guile. What Jesus has done for us is divine and eternal. He is the ultimate, sui generis, heavenly Father, with power to forgive sin. We need to come to grips with whether we are going to follow Jesus and serve him or not. We do not need to understand all mysteries. This is why we speak of our journey as "walking" with the Lord. We will never be able to put God in a test tube, or under a microscope, but reading, studying and opening our minds to his word, will come very close to accomplishing the same thing. The most important decision you will ever make will boil down to whether you embrace or reject Jesus. If you accept Jesus and believe in his teaching and his promises, then the next thing is to ask yourself if you are going to serve him, as your Lord and Savior.

Our faith, then, largely boils down to these two simple decisions: Are you going to accept the gift of Christ? If we decide to follow Jesus, we need to surrender our will and agenda to his words and commandments. We would do well to follow the Lord's blueprint for living and serving others just like we would by conscientiously following the manufacturer's service instructions for our new car.

If we decide to follow Jesus, and put our trust in him, based on what he did for us at the cross, then the only thing that makes any sense is to also accept his authority, and his holy word, but not by picking out verses from the Bible which we like and throwing others out the window. Jesus' words endure forever or they don't endure at all. You are either going to surrender your life to him in obedience and serve him or you're not. Just don't be fooled into thinking you can play whatever side of the fence you happen to like and be eternally safe while doing your own thing. If you are set on having it "your way," you probably have heaven mixed up with Burger King. So, you can feast at the Lord's Table, or, you can go to Burger King.

The reason I am being so forceful and explicit about this issue is because of the consequences that are involved. Jesus cautioned us that we could not serve two masters by playing both sides of the fence. Jesus warned us even further about who will go to heaven or hell when he said: *enter in at the strait gate: for wide is the gate, and broad is the way, that leads to destruction, and many there be which go in thereat: because strait is the gate, and narrow is the way, which leads unto life, and few there be that find it* (Matthew 7:13-14).

These are sobering words. This is why I emphasize that we should know what the words of Jesus say. Jesus said, referring to the narrow gate, *I am the way, the truth, and the life*. We are talking about our eternal souls here. Jesus rules your life, or, he is not your Lord. We better decide what we are going to do with Jesus and his words, because we will be judged by our own deeds and words and by how we responded to Christ's invitation for forgiveness. Jesus said, *if you love me, obey my commandments* (John 14:15). The truth of Jesus is straightforward and simple and it doesn't take higher learning; it takes repentance and a desire to obey and walk with Jesus.

If thou shalt confess with thy mouth the Lord Jesus, and shalt believe in thine heart that God hath raised him from the dead, thou shalt be saved. For with the heart man believeth unto righteousness; and with the mouth confession is made unto salvation (Romans 10:9-10).

I am so glad Jesus doesn't sugarcoat the truth and I love it that he says it like it is! Jesus plainly tells us what we need to do. Jesus commanded that we go into all the world and preach the gospel to every creature, baptizing them in the name of the Father, of the Son, and of the Holy Ghost (Mark 16:15/ Matthew 28:19). The apostle Peter said, in part, that we should repent, and be baptized, every one of us, in the name of Jesus Christ...(Acts 2:38). Baptism is a commandment! Why ask why? Do I have to? No, you get to! It's an honor, my friend!

Baptism is important because Jesus told us to do it and that makes it good enough in itself. I still appreciate, however, that one can have an honest heart and simply want to understand how this truth works and know more about it. When you get to heaven you can ask John the Baptist how it felt to baptize Jesus.

Baptism represents a statement of our faith, conviction and trust in Christ. It reflects our affiliation with Jesus and it intrinsically acknowledges Christ is our Savior. Obedience to baptism signifies to the world our submission to Christ, and it reflects that we asked Jesus to come into our hearts and forgive us, and make our hearts new, and that we are not just thinking about being identified with Christ as our personal Savior, but that we have sealed the deal, like one who signs a written covenant. In the same way I wear a wedding ring on my hand to announce to the world that I am committed to the one I love, and that I am not available to anyone else, so my profession of faith and my baptism tells all the world publicly that I belong to Jesus.

Baptism also has a powerful symbolism that we are buried in a grave of water to our old carnal nature of sin and death. When we rise out of the water it symbolically reflects our new nature in Christ, forgiven and washed in his blood. Many people I have seen being baptized, including my son, have been deeply moved to tears. The moment is holy and special beyond words to adequately describe it. Some people feel a powerful presence of the Holy Spirit descend upon them at the moment of baptism. I have seen more brothers and sisters in Christ weep at baptisms than I have at funerals. It is a holy and very personal moment of obedience to the words of our Savior. If Jesus himself submitted to baptism and it was good enough for our Master, it's good enough for you! Don't make me come after you. I'll throw you in the water myself!

Scripture states that *the earth is the Lord's and the fullness thereof; the world, and they that dwell therein* (Psalms 24:1). What do you give to a God that owns the heavens and the earth; surely, not another red tie or sweatshirt, right? What could you actually give Almighty God that would be of great value to him? That which you perhaps don't even realize you have at your disposal: the ability to make choices of obedience.

Obedience is far more important to the Father than we think. God's word says that to obey is better than asking for forgiveness through sacrifice (1 Samuel 15:22). Think about your own children. We teach them to obey so that they live. This is exactly what God does for us. If our children did not obey, the price would ultimately result in death. They would run out into the street, never seeing the approaching traffic, never being able to judge speed or distance, and they would be killed by the impact of kinetic energy. You will be killed by the impact of sin unless you follow and obey God's ways.

As our children reach the age of understanding and accountability, after they have been trained and nurtured in obedience, the time comes when obedience is no longer a matter of understanding the principle, but rather a matter of our will and choice. Would you rather have your fifteen-year-old smirk or mock you as they derisively say: "Oh, I'm sorry, please forgive me," or would you rather have them simply obey you?

The principle of obedience is tremendously important.

God is patient and longsuffering with us regarding most issues, but he doesn't entreat us with long-winded, eloquent or vituperative closing arguments about why he is right and we are wrong. God does not disrobe himself of his majestic dignity or grovel with us in order to cajole us into obeying him. God never defended himself to Job and he isn't going to do so with you or me. We have become so accustomed to having people plead with us that I think we actually have reached the point where we like it. It makes us feel important and empowered. Oh, please do what I say, but only if you feel like it and don't be mad with me for asking. We enjoy this delusional game.

My wife does this with our cat. He is the cutest thing you have ever seen and his little mug is to die for. I don't allow him on the kitchen counter because he doesn't belong up there where we handle food and he could get injured by jumping up on the stove area thinking it is no different than the sink counter. I don't want his paws burned by our hot glass top-heating stove surface. My wife understands this completely but she loves the cat so dearly that she does what mothers do: talk gently to their babies. My wife says:

Oh, Pooky, you really shouldn't be up on the counter top.
Daddy doesn't like that!
Oh, Pooky, you better get down before Daddy sees you.
Pooky so naughty, so naughty!
Daddy doesn't like that, Pooky.

The whole thing is so ridiculous you just have to laugh. I also have to give my wife a bad time, so I tell her: "You tell him, honey! Give him another tongue-lashing!"

And you wonder why some men think "no" means "yes"?

Pooky does! He knows that "so naughty" means "so cute."

God is not insecure about anything, let alone his position about what is right or wrong, or about what is best for your life. Nor is God threatened or insecure that you might not understand his good motivation. God doesn't play silly games. If you do not know the Lord, and you have not invited him into your life, he will not impose his way upon you or force his way into your heart. We really need to learn that it is a privilege for us to walk with Jesus. The Lord just lets consequences fall on us, as they should, with regard to our choices and our disobedience; and, he doesn't run around making backroom deals to vitiate justice or mitigate our punishment. God didn't bend the rules even for his own son.

But the blessings for obedience are just as real as the consequences we encounter for disobedience. One of the most vivid examples and lessons of obedience we can learn is found in the New Testament in the book of Luke. I like to call it the Simon Peter Principle. Now, the disciples that Jesus called to work with him in his ministry came from different walks of life. Matthew was a tax collector. You might prefer to think of him as an IRS Agent. Simon Peter was a fisherman.

This story begins with the background fact that there were two ships by the lake, one of which belonged to Simon, and that the fishermen were washing their nets. Typically, this would be something you do after you finish fishing. I am sadly reminded that there is a reason they call it "fishing" because we don't always catch fish when we go out otherwise we would call it "catching." My son, Daniel, and I have caught fish a few times and each time we did we had a lot of fun. However, the last four or five times we have gone out we have come back with nothing. Regardless of how good you are or how much experience you might have, the activity is still called "fishing" and often the best in the business "catch" nothing. Tide currents and the time of day can be important. Experience tells us that sometimes the fish just are not biting.

As this story unfolds Jesus tells Simon to launch out into the deep, and let down your nets for a "draught" (King James Version / Luke 5:4). I had to look this word up in the dictionary because I was unfamiliar with it and I knew other translations of the Bible, like the NIV, sometimes use the word catch, as in lowering your nets for a catch. Merriam-Webster's Collegiate Dictionary, tenth edition, copyright 2001 lists this word as being derivative of 15th century Britain and defines it as:

draught \'draft\, draughty \'draf-te\ chiefly Brit var of Draft, Drafty.

draughts \'draf(t)s\n pl but sing or pl in constr [ME draghtes, fr. pl. of draght draft, move in chess] (15c) Brit: checkers.

This dictionary also defines draft as the act of drawing a net; also the quantity of fish taken at one drawing. The word *draught*, from British fifteenth century, has a dual meaning. The other meaning has to do with checkers or chess, as in the checkerboard game for two. I find this little nuance interesting because of the dual meanings of the word draught found in the Kings James Version of the Bible.

I have no idea if Jesus meant this to have a double meaning or not and it doesn't change the principle in any way, so it doesn't matter. I just found it provocative that the one definition of this word could have anything to do with a game of chess or checkers, because Jesus' words to Simon Peter, if only in my mind, are an invitation of sorts, to a game of spiritual chess. The principle of faith works this way. I dare you to take a chance on God's offers. Malachi spoke of it with regard to how God will bless you if you are faithful with money. Jesus does fundamentally the same thing with Simon.

Consensus among preachers seems to be that Simon and the others were experienced fishermen. The inference, which can be drawn from this, is that these fishermen knew what they were doing because of their experience. I don't tell my wife how to boil water in the kitchen and she doesn't tell me how to handcuff bad guys. Herein the spiritual game of chess begins. Experienced fishermen know when the fish are biting and they know when it's "Miller time." Trust me on this! This is exactly how the principle of faith also works. God says exactly the same thing to his kids: Trust me, kids! Today the fish will be biting, even if you failed at it.

Simon is just like the rest of us. Even when we are trying to behave, it's hard to keep our mouth shut. I would have undoubtedly said something really stupid like, Lord, I've been doing police work for 28 years now and I know where the trunk is on my patrol car. You don't need to tell me where it is. Simon Peter knows not to go that far, but he still can't help himself because he feels compelled to say something very polite, which will point the facts out to the Lord, because, face it, we're not sure if God knows all the facts. Doesn't that make you laugh? Yet, Simon Peter also knows Jesus is unpredictable! That is exactly what we need to remind ourselves.

Simon answers the Lord by saying, *Master we have toiled all night long and have caught nothing.* The chess game could have stopped right here and nothing would have happened, but thankfully it did not, because Simon said, *nevertheless, at thy word I will let down the net. And when they had done this, they enclosed a great multitude of fishes: and their net brake. And they beckoned to their partners, which were in the other ship, that they should come and help them. And they came, and filled both ships, so that they began to sink. And when Simon Peter saw it, he fell down at Jesus' knees, saying: depart from me; for I am a sinful man, O Lord* (Luke 5:2-8).

I can so vividly see all of this happening in my mind that I can smell the fish and relate to even how Simon Peter felt and it makes me weep. Jesus could have told Simon during the dinner hour that your heavenly Father blesses those who obey him, and Peter would have politely nodded his head in respectful agreement, but he would have forgotten Jesus' words by the next day. I'm sure I would have, because it would have probably been another fact or piece of information that we pick up or get bombarded with in school, like another history date to remember. What Jesus did was create a life defining moment for Simon Peter and for you and me if we acknowledge it. This was an unforgettable moment for Simon to treasure till the day he took his last breath of air before entering paradise. It will be for me also!

We have no idea how badly we cheat ourselves by not obeying the Lord, nor do we have any concept of how much God wants to bless us when we do obey. The Simon Peter Principle is a beautiful paradigm. Once again, an old chorus comes to my mind, which sums up this principle so beautifully with the simple lyrics: "Trust and obey, for there's no other way, to be happy in Jesus, than to trust and obey."

Before we can receive these wonderful blessings on a regular basis, we have to make up our mind that we are going to serve the Lord with all our heart and obey him in all things. And before that, we need to actually become a member of the family. It's all about fundamental principles. You can't get to second base until you get to first base. Ask the Lord to come into your heart and cleanse you, and make you a new creature. Then make up your mind you are going to serve him all the days of your life and commit yourself to that goal. Don't let your walk with Jesus be up for grabs. This is important stuff. It's about life and death.

God sets before us a path and a way of life for each of us to choose that will produce either blessings or curses. The principles apply to everyone. The key, which opens the door to God's blessings, is obedience and the key, which opens the door to curses, results from disobedience. Again, remember that God is not a respecter of persons. While the promises in Deuteronomy were given by God, through Moses, to the children of Israel, the principles apply generally to everyone. *For he is not a Jew, which is one outwardly; neither is that of circumcision, which is outward in the flesh; But he is a Jew, which is one inwardly; and circumcision is that of the heart, in the spirit, and not in the letter; whose praise is not of men, but of God* (Romans 2:28-29). Other Bible versus speak of salvation in Jesus as being for both gentiles and Jews and anyone who calls upon the name of the Lord. Salvation is available for everybody, just like all the principles and teachings we find in the Bible. I stress this because it's the truth within the principle, which is forever enduring, and the truth becomes no less reliable or valid because it was given to some particular group of people who received it first. Electricity works in all continents just like photosynthesis and all other forms of science. Spiritual truth works exactly the same way and it endures forever. The word of the Lord endures forever (1 Peter 1:25).

Let's examine God's blessings and his curses to see how they work in context to obedience and disobedience.

> *If you fully obey the Lord your God and carefully follow all his commands I give you today, the Lord your God will set you high above all the nations on earth. All these blessings will come upon you and accompany you if you obey the Lord your God: You will be blessed in the city and blessed in the country, The fruit of your womb will be blessed, and the crops of your land and the young of your livestock--the calves of your herds and the lambs of your flocks. Your basket and your kneading trough will be blessed. You will be blessed when you come in and blessed when you go out.*
>
> *The Lord will grant that the enemies who rise up against you will be defeated before you. They will come at you from one direction but flee from you in seven. The Lord will send a blessing on your barns and on every thing you put your hand to. The Lord your God will bless you in the land he is giving you.*
>
> *The Lord will establish you as his holy people, as he promised on oath, if you keep the commands of the Lord your God and will walk in his ways.*
>
> *Then all the peoples on earth will see that you are called by the name of the Lord, and they will fear you. The Lord will grant you abundant prosperity--in the fruit of your womb, the young of your livestock and the crops of your ground— in the land he swore to your forefathers to give you.*
>
> *The Lord will open the heavens, the storehouse of his bounty, to send rain on your land in season and to bless all the work of your hands. You will lend to many nations but borrow from none. The Lord will make you the head, not the tail. If you pay attention to the commands of the Lord your*

God that I give you this day and carefully follow them, you will always be on top, never at the bottom. Do not turn aside from any of the commands I give you today, to the right or to the left, following other gods and serving them.

However, if you do not obey the Lord your God and do not carefully follow all his commands and decrees I am giving you today, all these curses will come upon you and overtake you:

You will be cursed in the city and cursed in the country, Your basket and your kneading trough will be cursed, The fruit of your womb will be cursed, and the crops of your land, and the calves of your herds and the lambs of your flocks. You will be cursed when you come in and cursed when you go out.

The Lord will send on you curses, confusion and rebuke in everything you put your hand to, until you are destroyed and come to sudden ruin because of the evil you have done in forsaking him. The Lord will plague you with diseases until he has destroyed you from the land you are entering to possess. The Lord will strike you with wasting disease, fever and inflammation, with scorching heat and drought, with blight and mildew, which will plague you until you perish. The sky over your head will be bronze, the ground beneath you iron. The Lord will turn the rain of your country into dust and powder; it will come down from the skies until you are destroyed.

The Lord will cause you to be defeated before your enemies. You will come at them from one direction but flee from them in seven, and you will become a thing of horror to all the Kingdoms on earth. Your carcasses will be food for all the birds of the air and the beasts of the earth, and there will be no one to frighten them away. The Lord will afflict you with the boils of Egypt and with tumors, festering sores and the itch, from which you cannot be cured. The Lord will afflict you with madness, blindness and confusion of mind. At midday you will grope about like a man in the dark. You will be unsuccessful in everything you do; day after day you will be oppressed and robbed with no one to rescue you.

You will be pledged to be married to a woman, but another will take her and ravish her. You will build a house but you will not live in it. You will plant a vineyard, but you will not even begin to enjoy its fruit. Your ox will be slaughtered be-

fore your eyes, but you will eat none of it. Your donkey will be forcibly taken from you and will not be returned. Your sheep will be given to your enemies, and no one will rescue them. Your sons and daughters will be given to another nation, and you will wear out your eyes watching for them day after day, powerless to lift a hand. A people that you do not know will eat what your land and labor produce, and you will have nothing but cruel oppression all your days. The sights you see will drive you mad. The Lord will afflict your knees and legs with painful boils that cannot be cured, spreading from the soles of your feet to the top of your head (Deuteronomy 28:1-35 NIV).

Another thirty-three verses continue in this vein through the end of Chapter 28 of Deuteronomy. The cost of disobedience is overwhelming. Oh, dear Jesus, help us to understand that our sin separates us from you. Lord, I pray if we already walk with you, help us to not take our sin lightly or the price you paid to redeem us from our iniquity.

Thou shalt also consider in thine heart, that, as a man chaseneth his son, so the Lord thy God chasteneth thee. Therefore thou shalt keep the commandments of the Lord thy God, to walk in his ways, and to fear him ((Deuteronomy 8:5-6).

And it shall come to pass, when all these things are come upon thee, the blessings and the curse, which I have set before thee, and thou shalt call them to mind among all the nations, whither the Lord thy God hath driven thee,

And shalt return unto the Lord thy God, and shalt obey his voice according to all that I command thee this day, thou and thy children, with all thine heart, and with all thy soul;

That then the Lord thy God will turn thy captivity, and have compassion upon thee, and will return and gather thee from all the nations, wither the Lord thy God hath scattered thee (Deuteronomy 30:1-3).

And the Lord thy God will circumcise thine heart, and the heart of thy seed, to love the Lord thy God with all thine heart, and with all thy soul, that thou mayest live (Deuteronomy 30:6).

Moses wrote: *I call on heaven and earth to record this day against you, that I have set before you life and death, blessing and cursing: therefore choose life, that both you and thy seed may live* (Deuteronomy 30:19).

Most of us with our sleek BlackBerry cell phones or iPhones probably think we have nothing in common with the children of Israel. After all, I know where I'm going because I have GPS in my car and my phone. We have a lot more in common than you might think. On a bad hair day, we are all capable of being ignorant, treacherous or obstinate and then either defensive about it, or proud of it! This is why sin is so beguiling. We see the foolishness of others, but not in ourselves. At least, that's how I am. My own stupidity has at times been embarrassing. I could have argued with the Lord as to whether there were any fish in the lake. Let me give a personal antidote.

My wife had been attending a small Home Group with fellow Christians for about a year or so and she kept telling me how wonderful the people in this group were. She kept inviting me to come and meet them and eventually I did. We had a wonderful potluck dinner and time of fellowship. On the next occasion, my first Home Group meeting, the group discussed that one of their members, who was going through chemotherapy needed a ride to the hospital the next day. When the question was posed as to who might be able to pick her up at the house and take her to the hospital for her chemo treatment, there was a long pause and it became quite evident to me that no one was jumping at the opportunity or volunteering, largely because everyone else had jobs to go to the first thing in the morning. I volunteered to go since I was recently retired and I could make the time to help out in this way.

We bantered back and forth about this a little bit because this lady had never met me before and didn't even know what I looked like. I told the group to just call her and tell her I am a retired cop, and I'll be there at 10 A.M. sharp to pick her up. I followed the directions up into the Santa Cruz Mountains and turned off the main road onto a smaller residential street nestled in the redwoods. It was beautiful up there in the Santa Cruz redwoods.

One of the things I pride myself in is being able to read a map and navigate myself to your house, because you called 911. After years of working the street, I took pride in being able to decipher which side of the street even number houses were on and which side the odd numbered houses would be on. Occasionally numbers could be tricky because one jurisdiction ended and another began, and if you didn't know that area well, it would throw you completely off. For example, you might be in the 4300 block of El Camino Real and the next address has a number in the 800's. You just left one city and entered into another. One thing is always true. If the even numbers are on the right hand side, the odd numbers will all be on the left hand side. God made it that way when he aligned the firmaments.

I don't even remember exactly how it happened and I became so embarrassed that I would rather not remember anyway, but I drove up slowly along the street checking out the numbers until I was a house or two away. I got out of my car and started walking up to the house. I knocked on the front door. Although the numbers on the house were not visible I knew from my training and experience that this was the right house, because I was an expert at this.

If the house to my left was number 26, the one before it 24, then the one to my right, which I stood in front of, had to be 28. I was puzzled why no one answered the door, and why Barbara wasn't ready.

Some guy came walking around the side of the house and inquired if he could help me. I informed him I was there to meet Barbara. What transpired next was unbelievable. The gentleman said, "Oh, that's Barbara's house over there," pointing to the next house over, toward my right. Without so much as batting an eyelash I answered, "No, it's not!" I guess I knew better. After all, I had a college education, more confidence than brains, and I had been a detective, so I had all those things going for me, which was nice, but I had the wrong house and I was willing to argue with this guy about it. He replied, "Yes, it is," at which time he informed me that the house I was standing in front of was his house. I'm surprised I didn't say, "No, it's not!" As I drove Barbara to the hospital for her chemo, I explained that I was not sunburned, just embarrassed by my own unbelievable stupidity and arrogance. It's a wonder I didn't argue with Barbara along the way about whether she had cancer.

I am superior, better educated, and I am endowed with greater intelligence, wisdom and insight, and I make far more money than those desert rats (Israelites). See how easy that was? That is exactly why I suggest we have more in common with the Israelites that we might think; at least I do.

The best thing that can be said about any of us is that we all possess gifts, talents, and untold potential locked up inside us. The worst thing about all of us, is that we are all born in sin, and we need a savior who can forgive us, and unlock our potential, and help us to become more than we can ever be on our own.

Two people cannot walk together in accord unless they agree. If you are not sure if you agree with this statement, why didn't the children of Israel follow Caleb and Joshua into the Promised Land? If you don't know what you believe, it is hard to walk in accord with Jesus and be of the same mind and Spirit.

I was assigned to the Detective Bureau where my primary duties were juvenile matters. Depending on the needs of the department, I worked other crimes, as well, and when we had a major case we all worked together. I shared an office with another Detective who was a Juvenile School Resource Officer. We had previously worked both patrol and traffic together and we both were POST certified radar instructors. We got along very well and we liked each other.

One day my partner told me about a federal prosecutor who had asked for our help with his son. My partner told me this United States Attorney was prosecuting big federal drug cases, sending people to prison for many years at a time on heavy-duty federal charges. The prosecutor and his wife didn't know how to handle their sixteen-year-old son who was fooling around with marijuana and they wanted one of us to talk to their kid and set him straight. This was a bazaar situation. I wanted nothing to do with it. I knew if I went over to their house the phone would ring in the Chief's office the next morning and I would probably hear about it. I could just imagine the Chief asking me, "Did you really say that?" I would have replied, "Oh, yes, and much more!"

My partner, being the good friend he was, agreed to talk to the family so I did not have to. The detective was trying to do the family a favor, but was uncomfortable doing this father's work for him simply because dad wasn't man enough to do it himself. My partner and I talked about this and we came to the conclusion that the husband and wife did not ostensibly share the same values over drugs. If two are not in accord over what they believe, it is pretty hard to walk in harmony, and this is what you get: a father who is insecure in having a heart to heart talk with his son, and a wife who does not necessarily support her husband's values. Maybe she thought a little marijuana wouldn't be so bad.

While my partner was talking with the kid in his room, the mother knocks on the door and interrupts their conversation to bring the boy a piece of chocolate cake. Without actually saying a word, the unspoken message said it all: here you go little sweetheart, have a piece of chocolate cake and you'll feel better, and Mommy will protect you. The whole thing was nauseating.

It was a good thing I wasn't there! I would have eaten the chocolate cake myself and then searched the mother to see if she had any weed on her person! Rest assured I would not have gotten a subsequent invitation to the Queen's Ball from that family!

It is pretty hard to be in accord or have harmony with Jesus, or, even your spouse, if you don't know what you believe, or there is disagreement over what you actually believe. How can you walk in obedience with Jesus if you don't agree with the Lord and you are unwilling to submit to his Lordship?

Sometimes, even when we know what we believe, we shoot ourselves in the foot because we violate common sense. We may think we are special. Gravity won't apply to me. I know how to drive on black ice. I'm a trained professional. I've learned my lesson; I can handle it. Let me give you a poignant example of this.

I was transporting a felon to the hospital for a medical appointment. He had already been convicted and was awaiting sentencing on serious felony drug charges that would take him back to prison for many years.

This inmate shared with me that he had been in prison most of his life for mostly property crimes, thefts and lots of drug arrests. He had struggled with drugs most of his life. His drug of choice was heroin. He told me that he eventually realized his life was going to hell in a hand basket because of drugs, and so he sought help and was able to overcome this horrible addiction and stay clean for six years while out of prison working in society and having a productive life. Overcoming this addiction was a big accomplishment.

His countenance fell and I could see the regret in his eyes. I asked him what happened. The prisoner told me he went back to visit an old girlfriend and they reconnected. He moved in with her and they began living together. The girlfriend happened to be an attorney who used heroin and the inmate fell back into addiction, developed problems with the law, and was now back on his way to prison for a very long time. What impressed me about this man was his honesty and how he spoke of his false pride, thinking he could move into the residence of this woman, sleep with her and not be drawn back into heroin. He said, "I thought I was strong and that I could help her."

Would to God that we would all understand that God has plans to give us a hope and a future and that his laws serve a purpose; his plans work; ours don't! There is a reason we need to follow God's laws and commandments and not pick and choose which ones we decide are O.K., while we throw others away.

Walking in obedience before the Lord is a personal decision. We don't have to know all things, understand all things, or be brilliant. We just need to humble ourselves before Jesus and obey his commandments and allow him to be Lord of our lives. Whether we live or whether we die boils down to our choice regarding obedience to Christ. We sometimes don't know what we really believe, but if we go no farther with that position, it maintains the status quo of failure. Doing absolutely nothing about our uncertainty is a choice itself. Try putting your trust in Jesus! He is trustworthy! The decision you make is important because it represents life and death.

Remember, you either accept the words and gospel of Jesus or you don't, because there is no halfway, almost eternal, investment deal with Jesus. In the same way a woman cannot be "a little pregnant," so it is with our salvation. You are either saved or you are not! There is no in-between. We don't hear enough fervent preaching about repentance and accountability. We want to believe that we can have our cake and eat it, too. Redefining the rules of surrender represents fallacious thinking on the part of the world: that you can do it your way and not surrender at all. Remember, narrow is the gate and few will find it. We want to tickle our ears only with the "make me feel good doctrine of blessings" that Jesus wants to give us, but we don't want to hear anything about surrendering our will or about repentance or accountability. We want eternal life and heaven but we want to do our own thing at the same time. Be careful. You can't be master of your own life and at the same time think Jesus is Master and Lord.

Jesus said that no man can serve two masters: for either he will hate the one, and love the other; or else he will hold to the one, and despise the other (Matthew 7:24). If you are not sure what you really believe, you better decide. This is important. It represents life and death. Jesus said: *Go into all the world and preach the gospel to every creature. He that believeth and is baptized shall be saved: but he that believeth not shall be damned* (Mark 16:15-16). That pretty much says it all right there.

Remember what God's word tells us in the most well known verse in all of the Bible, quoted all around the world: it tells us that *God so loved the world that he gave his only begotten Son, that whosoever believeth in him should not perish, but have everlasting life* (John 3:16).

For God sent not his Son into the world to condemn the world, but that the world through him might be saved (John 3:17).

He that believeth on him is not condemned: but he that believeth not is condemned already, because he hath not believed in the name of the only begotten Son of God (John 3:18).

Seek the Lord and ye shall live (Amos 5:6). Make up your mind today that you want to live. It simply starts with a decision on your part. You can choose not to believe or you can choose to believe. Choose to believe! By faith and conviction you can also choose to accept the Bible as the divine, authoritative, infallible word of God. The word of the Lord endureth forever (I Peter 1:25). What Jesus did for us on the cross was eternal, and his words will never pass away or fail us. Make up your mind to trust Jesus and take him at his word. If you see the eternal value of this, don't let lack of commitment become an issue that separates you from God. Don't let your decision to surrender your life to Christ become more complicated than it needs to be. With faith all things are possible with God.

The spiritual battle you face all boils down to a decision, just like everything else in your life. During your lifetime you will never have all the answers or proof that you wish for, so, there will be a component of faith involved in your decision, just like most everything else in life. It takes some degree of faith just to buy a vehicle these days. The manufacture, which makes your vehicle, might not exist tomorrow. We apply some element of faith, however, rudimentary, to almost every decision we make. Think about that for a moment. You wouldn't marry your spouse if you did not have some faith that the marriage would be good, nor would you ever put your money in a bank, nor would you ever fly on a commercial airline. Whether you realize it or not, you practice faith every time you turn the light switch on because you expect the science of electricity to work. Does it work all the time? No, occasionally there is a minor glitch and we go for an hour without television... these are hard times we live in! Are there any guarantees in life about anything? Actually there are. I'll give you two of my favorite ones. Jesus said: *I will never leave or forsake you.* He also said: *I will come again and receive you unto myself, that where I am, there you may be also* (hebrews 13:5/John 14:2-3). He's coming back!

CHAPTER 7

HOW DO I GET THERE FROM HERE?

In reading the New Testament, one of the many interesting things I see, was that Jesus offered personal invitations to individuals he encountered. The Lord's invitation for substance and intimacy was not only for the purpose of meeting people at their point of need for the normal things of life, but they were life defining, invitational moments that could change their lives for eternity. A casual encounter at Starbucks might get framed in the form of a simple question: What would you have of me? What's on your heart, or, what can I do for you? A blind man asked of Jesus that he might receive his sight (Mark 10:51).

On one such occasion two of his disciples, the "Sons of Thunder," asked Jesus if he would give them whatever they asked of him. In response Jesus asked them: What would you have of me? They answered: Grant unto us that we may sit, one on thy right hand, and the other on thy left hand, in glory. Jesus gives a pithy answer: *you don't know what you are asking for, but more importantly, you need to understand that whosoever of you will be the chiefest, shall be servant of all; for the Son of man came not to be ministered unto, but to minister, and to give his life a ransom for many* (Mark 10:37-45). The words of Jesus define his very mission on earth, and they should be the ultimate paradigm for us, defining our personal and organizational priorities for Kingdom business.

In better economic times corporate America has often sent its elite to opulent offsite meetings to devise mission statements that reflected the corporation's new and improved goals, values and marketing strategies. These meetings can last for two days with a dozen board members sitting at a conference table in Maui or New York City, haggling out the appropriate language. Just the travel expense alone for one of these offsite seminars has to be more than what some third world mayors earn during a four year term.

Jesus defined the most important mission mankind has ever known. His mission is often referred to around the world as "The Greatest Story Ever Told," because it represents the plan of eternal salvation offered by Christ, shedding his blood on the cross as he offered unto his heavenly Father his own life as a ransom for humanity's sin. In his mission statement Jesus not only defined his mission to the Sons of Thunder, but he explained what Kingdom ministry and servanthood were all about to his disciples and he said all of this with only a handful of words. These same words should define our mission: be servants; love people as I have loved you, feed my sheep! I love how profound the words of Jesus are, yet he makes it so simple that even a child can remember what we are suppose to do, and it's a short list: Love God, love our neighbor.

Christ is calling us to not only be servants, he is also calling us to pick up our cross and follow him. I don't see anything in Jesus' words, deeds or ministry where he calls his followers to ignore the poverty and despair all around us so that we can seek wealth, fame and riches. In fact, Jesus says just the opposite, urging us to build up treasures in heaven and he tells us and shows us how to do that.

Jesus led by example in everything he did. He didn't travel first class and then send his disciples on some old boat. Jesus traveled with his disciples in the same boat, and he had to catch a few minutes of shuteye in the back of the boat because he didn't have his own yacht or master bedroom. In fact, Jesus did not even have a decent room or hotel in which to be born. The Lamb of God came to us in meekness and humility and was born in a manger. Jesus even carried his own cross toward Calvary so that they could crucify him.

When we search for an answer to the question, "How do I get there from here?" we are typically seeking God's will and direction for our lives. That's a good thing, most of the time. Why would it ever *not* be a good thing? Because even when we have good intentions, invariably we will ask for the wrong things because we are looking for status, position and power, and it becomes easy for us to ask God to lead us into that ministry of prosperity wherein we start at the top, rather than the bottom, just like the Sons of Thunder did. Even after I read it, I catch myself ignoring what Jesus said: whosoever of you shall be chief, shall be servant of all. This is the principle of servanthood. Who seeks that?

Can't Christians be filthy rich and wildly successful? Yes, and examples of that in the Bible are given in the character developments of Abraham, Job, and Joseph. Jesus, interestingly enough, proffered a commentary about John the Baptist saying: *among them that are born of women, there hath not risen one greater than John the Baptist: notwithstanding he that is least in the Kingdom of heaven is greater than he* (Matthew 11:11). I find that to be a staggering statement considering Jesus is the Son of God and he could have said that there was none greater than himself. Such a statement would have been true and he certainly could have reminded us. Yet, this statement of Jesus is also reflective of and consistent with his august humility, servant-like spirit and meekness.

If Jesus asks you what he can do for you today, don't ask for something stupid like a new Corvette, a little nip and tuck job, or earthy riches. You might think about asking that your faith, courage and character be increased so that you too would be willing to give your life in service; but to start with, perhaps, ask him if you can serve others in some unassuming position as a foot washer where you know others do not want to go, and this will undoubtedly please the heavenly Father. When I was three years old I earnestly prayed for God to help me fly just like Superman. I stood on the front porch and jumped off it to the grass three feet below believing that any moment I would fly like a bird if I just kept increasing my faith, just a little bit more. I was certain that I was about to break through at any moment and I was ready to soar into the heavens like an eagle. I am so grateful that God answered my sincere prayer...

God said, "No."

I love the Sons of Thunder because they are so stupid; they are just like me! They ask this completely vacuous question of the Son of God: if Jesus would give them *whatever* they asked of him. No! Next question. I'll bet these two guys probably argued over who could drink the most wine without passing out and they probably asked Jesus to give the winner a cookie or some other prize. The Sons of Thunder! You gotta love these guys!

In contrast to some question the Lord might make a seemingly bold and confusing statement like "you must be born again" or maybe he would ask you for a drink of water. While speaking with the woman at the well, he might very well make what appears to be an outrageous statement such as, *if you had asked for water to drink I would have given you living water. Whoever shall drink of this water (from Jacob's well) shall thirst again, but whoever drinks of the water that I shall give him shall never thirst, but the water that I give him shall be in him a well of water, springing up into everlasting life* (John 4:10-14).

Jesus wants to engage us in dialogue and provoke our minds and hearts into thinking and asking meaningful questions about those things that are of importance to us. If we allow that door to be opened, it creates wonderful opportunities for profound, life changing things to happen in our lives.

Jesus not only cared about the big picture of eternal salvation and the forgiveness of sin, but he also cared about people and their individual needs and whether they had something to eat for lunch. Don't you just love to eat? Wouldn't you just love to have lunch with Jesus and ask him a bunch of silly questions? On my birthday can I fly just like Superman, Lord? Why do I have to be baptized? Is sprinkling or immersion better? How come the Pope is so important when we already have you, Lord? Will there ever come a day, Lord, in which I am able to put childish things away and become the man you want me to be? Are we almost there, Daddy, [Abba, Father]?

The invitation to talk about issues of the heart is an open-ended, unilateral offer that is always on the table. The Master doesn't bother you with things you have no interest in. Jesus won't even open the door without you inviting him in. If you are in a relationship with Jesus, it would be a good idea to establish an open door policy with him. Don't assume that because you view yourself as a child of God that such a policy automatically exits. Treat the subject like you would with anyone else that you deeply love. Tell the Lord your heart belongs to him. My house is your house. Make the invitation bilateral.

Intimacy doesn't occur by assumption. It becomes established by invitation, choice, behavior and mutual consent. Tell the Lord you have an open door policy and that he has free reign to speak to you and to search your heart and thoughts and motives at any time of the day or night, with or without a warrant, and that you value his direction and guidance in your life. This subject can be a book in itself, because the words and questions intrinsically implore us to cut to the chase and be honest about what is really in our heart. What is important to you? Where are you going? Where do you want to go? What are you passionate about? Implicit in asking such questions is that you are invited to open your heart and be honest about your dreams.

Maybe life has taken its toll on you and you no longer have dreams. If this reflects your struggle or grief in life, then your acknowledgement of the fact and your response is as honest, personal, and real as it gets. I admire your courage in acknowledging the situation. If you no longer have dreams and your hope has been destroyed, that would be the perfect thing to talk to Jesus about. Jesus is The Great Physician. Jesus is the Master of all good things and a healer when it comes to restoring relationships, which have been lost, damaged or broken. He knows how to cure the sick, heal the brokenhearted, and he can even raise the dead. He can restore your dreams! For I know the plans I have for you, declares the Lord, plans to give you a hope and a future (Jeremiah 29:11 NIV).

When you talk to Jesus, know that he loves you and wants you to feel free to be honest. You don't have to tell him how badly you feel about global warming, because he knows that is not what broke your heart or what weighs you down, and, he knows that you drive a gas guzzling SUV anyway. Talk to him about the good stuff, the real issues that are on your heart.

I shared earlier a little bit about my getting into police work and how earnestly I prayed about that, asking God to help me find the right career in which to serve him. It was my way of dedicating my life to Christ. Nevertheless, I had no interest in reading to the blind, as you will undoubtedly recall because I wanted to chase bad guys at Mach-3 with my hair on fire. This bears repetition only because of an important principle. In our pursuit of God's will for our lives, the Lord does not always make you go to some horrible place that you detest or, for that matter, do some horrible thing which you loath. It just seems that God has a wonderful way of using our existing talents and interests to produce fruit for the Kingdom of God, if you submit yourself to him. My contribution to the Kingdom of God was that I got to take people to jail. Glory to God; it doesn't get any better than that! Come over here you filthy animal! I'm taking you to jail. God knows how pathetic my humor is, and he loves me anyway. It's hard to believe, I know.

Now, the Lord, might lead you into something new and give you new interests and talents that you did not have before, but it would be, in my opinion, uncharacteristic of the Lord to throw away or discard your natural talents, training and experience. If you have a great voice, love to sing, and have

182

the ability to compose on top of that, why would you not put that to good use? You can use those talents for the glory of God no matter what profession you end up choosing. There is a place and a need for your talents whether you are singing in the Mormon Tabernacle Choir or you happen to be in the bush where there is no electricity and people don't have shoes. And, if you happen to be in the jungle like I was, your songs of praise are no less precious to the Lord because you don't have a Lexus in your driveway.

Getting started on our journey always seems like the hardest part. Few good, enduring things happen by chance. In fact, one might say, that nothing happens without a plan or a vision. It is sometimes quite interesting just how true this can turn out to be, but even lunch won't get served if no one has a vision or plan for making it happen. It is also possible for spontaneity and creativity to take place and every little jot or tittle in life doesn't require tedious planning. The plan can arise suddenly without a lot of labor and it can be spontaneous. It could even be a small plan, like some of mine, but the plan usually begins with a dream or a vision of what could be. The landscaping around my house falls into this category.

I had a section of front yard that had two trees and a fair amount of bare dirt and weeds. The two trees each posed their own issues. One tree was the saddest looking thing you ever laid your eyes on. The other tree dropped pinecones from one hundred and twenty five feet in the air. Some of these cones were not developed and were like large avocadoes, but hard as a rock. If one of these pinecones were to fall and hit someone on their head, it would literally be capable of killing the person. A smaller section of the front yard by the sidewalk had lawn on either side and also by the curbline adjacent to the street. The green grass just made the bare dirt and weeds stick out like a sore thumb. I used to joke that the dirt area looked like a place for drug addicts to smoke crack.

I removed both trees. I ordered a replacement tree from North Carolina in the form of a red leaf maple. They shipped it to me UPS in a small box that was 48 inches high and 4 inches square. The roots were in a small container of dirt that wasn't any larger than my coffee cup. It had a few baby leaves on it but it looked to me as though this "tree" would take a couple hundred years to actually become a tree. I followed the instructions for nurturing the so-called tree during the winter months and for planting in the spring. The tree is now growing like wild fire and beginning to look like a real, honest to goodness tree, not just some wanna be!

I purchased some Fescue sod to replace the weeds and cover the bare dirt in the front yard. I planted roses in the front yard where the yard was separated into two different elevation levels, delineated by an elegant brick partition. The large tree that dropped pinecones was replaced with a large water fountain on a circular brick foundation. I installed lights to illuminate the water fountain at night. I had a very large driveway that was big enough to accommodate six vehicles. I removed the broken and cracking cement driveway and replaced it with varied earth tone colored cobblestones that were laid down in a very attractive pattern. We gave the house a fresh coat of paint. The transformation was amazing and it turned our ordinary house into a small estate. I did a fair amount of the work myself digging the ground and laying pipes for the electrical wire that went to the water fountain. I planted each rose bush as though it was going to be located in a beautiful estate.

We got so many compliments from passing neighbors that mothers pushing baby strollers with their kids stopped to chat with me and tell me that their little children like to take walks so they could see the water fountain. Several people who were just driving by stopped in the middle of the street, rolled down their windows to tell us how beautiful the water fountain and landscape looked. I had a lot of fun doing this little project. The cobblestone driveway makes our house look beautiful and compliments the rest of the landscaping. It's amazing what just a fresh coat of paint can do. The point of this is that it all began with a modest vision or dream of what could be. The dream was implemented with a plan. Without a plan nothing really happens.

Martin Luther King had a dream. We are starting to see the fruits of that vision and of the work that is being accomplished in this area. God had a dream and a vision of creation, which included a plan for us to be sons and daughters of his family.

If you don't have a dream or a plan, ask God to give you one and he will guide you into a plan that will produce fruit for the Kingdom and bless you on top of it all! God is the great creator. His plans are higher than our plans. His creativity, goodness and beauty go beyond what we can even imagine. He has a plan for you even if you were unaware of it. Our vision is limited by our imagination and faith. We tend to see things in limited, fixed, small opportunities or possibilities. We do so because our life, strength and understanding is limited and measured. Our days (here on earth) are numbered and our resources are finite. As such, we view the world this way and, although we don't intentionally try to do so, we view God through our distorted vision. We fail to see or comprehend how great, magnificent, powerful and beautiful he truly is. The word of God tells us this quite clearly (1 Corinthians 2:9/1 Corinthians 13:12).

Our propensity to think small is something the enemy uses against us to tempt us and bring doubt into our minds on what God is capable or willing to do for us. Satan is a liar and a thief who wants to take your hopes and dreams in God and dash your faith into a meaningless exercise of fantasy and wishful thinking. When Jesus tells us that he has gone to prepare a place for us in heaven, Satan doesn't want you to even believe that, however, if you claim the word by faith and you insist on nurturing that mentality, then Satan will try and persuade you that the place that God is preparing for those who love him is just a small cluster of condos...and that they have water rationing up there.

When I think of implementing my dreams two examples immediately come to mind. There is short term planning, such as my wife and I have plans to have lunch tomorrow at The Crow's Nest in Santa Cruz. They have a killer salad bar and the view and ambiance is world class. After lunch we can take a stroll on Sea Cliff Drive and look at the ocean or perhaps the sunset.

Then there is strategic planning for life that may be five, ten or fifteen years down the road, all the way to one's eternal destiny. This is equally important. I don't want to sit on the couch the rest of my life watching "Dancing With The Stars" and look back and realize I never did anything constructive to help others. I don't want to ever look back in time and regret that I did not serve the Lord with more enthusiasm or feed his sheep.

The Lord gives us a glimpse of his plans and how he looks at both of these issues, long term and short term strategic planning. The neat thing is that all of his plans are strategic, creative and serendipitous. God's word will not return void; it always produces something creative, healing, forgiving, or life altering, and the gates of hell shall not prevail against his church. Consider the short-term needs we think of so often. Jesus said, *take no thought, saying, What shall we eat? or, What shall we drink? or, Wherewithal shall we be clothed? (For after all these things do the Gentiles seek) for your heavenly Father knoweth that ye have need of all these things. But seek ye first the Kingdom of God, and his righteousness; and all these things will be added unto you* (Matthew 6:31-33). In other words, live by faith! God is for you!

Creation wasn't an anomaly; it was a plan. God created mankind in his image so that we could have fellowship and communion together. Our free will and disobedience screwed it all up and brought sin and death into our lives. God had a plan. He sent his only son to pay the cost of what no one else could offer: an equitable price to cover the cost of our sin. God's holy word reveals another portion of his plan, which says that if we suffer with him we shall also reign with him (II Timothy 2:12). God says his Kingdom and government will get bigger and we are a part of his plans.

I recently saw a neat documentary on television about some of the science of how the universe came into existence and how it is growing. For years now, astronomers and scientists have detected that the universe is getting bigger and bigger. One scientist on the program explained that a "galaxy" is considered to consist of one hundred billion planets. Our galaxy is called the "Milky Way." The program went on to say that there are over one hundred billion galaxies and that if each star was represented by a grain of sand on earth, there would not be enough sand on planet earth to represent the number of planets in the universe, and the universe is growing in size. Pretty amazing stuff! (Title: The Universe; episode title: Alien Galaxies. Aired 7/31/2007 in San Jose, CA on Channel 62, HISTP, Comcast Cable T.V.)

Consider this a glimpse of God's plan, which we find in scripture. Isaiah the prophet writes about the coming of our Lord and Savior, Jesus: For unto us a child is born, unto us a son is given: and the government shall be upon his shoulder: and his name shall be called Wonderful, Counselor, The Mighty God, The everlasting Father, The Prince of Peace. Of the *increase* of his government and peace there shall be no end, upon the throne of David, and upon his Kingdom, to order it, and to establish it with judgment and with justice from henceforth even forever. The zeal of the Lord of hosts will perform this (Isaiah 9:6-7) [emphasis added].

In Jeremiah we read: *As the host of heaven cannot be numbered, neither the sand of the sea measured: so will I multiply the seed of David my servant, and the Levites that minister unto me* (Jeremiah 33:22). These are sneak previews of God's plans. God is not the god of the dead, but the God of the living. These words are staggering: "of the increase of his government and peace there shall be no end."

So, whether you plan ongoing to medical school, into public service, full time ministry, police work, or you just want to improve the landscape in front of your house, you need to start with a vision. A vision represents a dream of what the future could be. A vision needs to be cultivated into an actual plan or strategy otherwise nothing will happen. The Bible tells us that where there is no vision, the people perish (Proverbs 29:18). Sitting on the sidelines watching others play in the game does not get you into law school. Lacking vision, faith and courage will never open doors for you. You have to decide what is important to you and what you feel passionate about. If you are only twenty years old and you don't know what your dreams are all about, that may actually be a blessing. Seek the Lord and ask him to give you a vision, a plan, and a strategy for pursuing his perfect will in your life. That's the best plan of all! God will honor your sincere prayer. If you follow your own plan, there are considerations that come with that choice. You should carefully weigh your alternatives. The choice you make represents your future.

There are a couple of things I see which can complicate our plans and so I offer a caveat or cautionary note for you to consider. Having a plan is great unless it's not a good plan. Some things are impossible to plan for, and, sometimes the best laid plans in the world go awry. Moreover, it doesn't matter what the plan is, if it's not God's plan for you. This is where your faith and willingness to walk in God's ways and serve him become an all-important part of your decision making. If God and his perfect will for you are not all-important, then you pretty much will probably do whatever you feel like.

When you pray for guidance in this area you need to approach it sincerely with that phrase we repeat all the time in saying the Lord's prayer, *thy will be done*. The perfect mind-set is to remember that my plans are not always God's plans, and that God's plans are always better than our plans. Once that issue gets settled, then it becomes a matter of sincerely praying thy will be done. Please lead and guide me, Lord. He has promised to do so.

Sometimes we are driven by our passions and though we truly want to serve and be a blessing to others, we are blinded by our own ambition. In the world, ambition is generally thought of as something that is either mostly good, or something that you have to have a certain amount of it or you won't go anywhere. Ambition gets favorably dressed with propitious cloaks of acceptance and praise in our culture most of the time. We somehow come to a belief that having ambition and drive makes you a "mover and a shaker," and of course that is very complimentary language in American culture. It may not necessarily be very spiritual, and it may not be the thing that the Lord wants you to accentuate in your life and career.

There is a phrase in the Bible which says many are called but few are chosen. Jesus spoke about this and about humility. Jesus said those who would be first shall be last, and those who are last shall be first. That goes contrary to everything we are taught. You don't teach your son to be last or to put others in greater esteem over yourself, yet that is exactly what Jesus taught us, to be foot washers and servants of others, even as he submitted to death on the cross. We are taught and bombarded with messages that say you deserve to be rich and famous. We get this even in the church, at times, and there are some pastors that only preach the gospel of prosperity, but never the gospel of repentance, obedience or sacrifice. It's hard to not have any of this affect our thinking.

One of the dangers of following one's own plan is that our own natural ambitions and the tendencies of the flesh get in our way. I will offer myself to the Kingdom of God for the purpose of being Moses, Elijah or some other great apostle like Paul or maybe John the Baptist. It's quite a sacrifice you know! In truth it probably is, but I said that sarcastically, because none of us are saying let me be the least in the Kingdom or if we do, it's only because we are praying on the street corner for others to hear us. We don't pray that way in our closet.

My prayers all suck. Lord, I'll be the next Billy Graham if that will help your Kingdom out. There is a pretty good salary that comes with that position, right, Lord? As long as I am giving myself so completely to the Kingdom of heaven and service to mankind, can I have all the tricks that go with that position? You know, that little neat thing where Elijah called down fire from heaven? Oh, and can I be on the Oprah Winfry Show, Lord? You get my point. No one is standing in line to just be a foot washer. No one is standing in line to pick up their cross and follow Jesus, but that is exactly what Jesus is looking for: servants with hearts motivated by humility willing to do lowly jobs that are sometimes low on our list.

Bill Hybels has authored a book entitled <u>Too Busy Not To Pray-Slowing Down to be with God</u>. In one chapter Reverend Hybels talks about being sensitive to the leading of the Holy Spirit as God answers prayer and guides us. Hybels writes that one of his church elders with thirty years of service was frustrated and apparently venting over the fact that he had seen pastors come and go, and that everyone who had left felt a "leading" to leave the church and go elsewhere when the invitation involved more money, more benefits, a bigger staff and a larger house. No pastor has ever been led to a smaller church with a smaller salary and fewer benefits, the elder reportedly complained.

The reality of what this represents is both representative of human nature and ironically humorous in a pathological sort of way. The caveat for this, which Bill Hybels gives, is that he needs to be very careful and watch out if money, promises, perks and toys are enticingly offered to him. Hybels warns that prosperity has ruined more people than servanthood or adversity ever will. (Too Busy Not to Pray-Slowing Down to be with God. IVP Books, second edition 1998, p.163.)

What we often hear people say is that they feel God "leading" them to pastor a large, successful church and receive a huge salary increase. It is not a matter that God doesn't reward hard work or service because he does. It is the so-called "leading" that makes me laugh sometimes. God is gracious and wonderful but man is deceitful. No pastor ever said that all the perks and the salary were just too tempting; I had to take it. No pastor has ever admitted that their decision had nothing to do with the will of God, nor has anyone ever been heard to just simply admit the offer was what they always wanted. What gets marketed is God's divine will as the selling point, followed by a gracious acceptance speech, and the obligatory expression of humility and acknowledgment that "God is so good!" Well, of course he is good, but would God be any less "good" if he lead you to Darfur or reduced your salary? Come on now! Do I hear an "amen" anywhere?

Don't ask or volunteer to be famous or to become some hot shot like the two disciples. Be willing to be a dedicated humble servant that will go anywhere for little or no reward and be a foot washer. Don't seek wealth, power or notoriety. Seek justice for the widow and the orphan and be a foot washer who loves people and seeks no approval from man. If you truly believe you are up to doing this, God will test you to see if you really mean it. God never puts untested people in charge of his children. If your ways are pleasing in his sight, like Joseph in Egypt, God will reward you and you might be the next Billy Graham, Moses or John the Baptist. Oh, did I mention, John the Baptist was beheaded for the sake of the gospel? Be careful what you ask for; you might get it!

I am not against hard work, prosperity or recognition associated with Kingdom business. I am against the works of the flesh that beguile us into seeking notoriety, fame, wealth and worst of all, the praise of men because of our ambition.

In the context of Kingdom business, it almost does not matter what you do in terms of your profession; it's how you do it, and whether you do it as unto the Lord, or for yourself and your own gain.

God doesn't need you to win the lottery so that you can buy him a new church. God is not having a cash flow problem nor does he need a small loan from Bill Gates. Let me give a personal example of my own failure and blind ambition.

It's easy for me to say don't volunteer to be famous or become some hot shot, but that is exactly where my own blind ambition was leading me. One of the things I loved to do was work traffic and issue speeding and other traffic citations to people. When asked in court if I ever had a quota, I always answered truthfully, "No, your Honor; I get to write as many of these as I want!" I became a radar instructor and had a lot of fun teaching that class to other officers. Over the course of my career, I wrote well over ten thousand radar citations alone.

My love for radar and my understanding of how the science worked eventually led me to develop a dream which had tremendous potential for law enforcement, not only in a general sense which applied to traffic enforcement, but also in our fight against terrorism. Traffic radar works by transmitting a radio wave at a moving object. The radio wave (signal) bounces off the moving vehicle, and the signal returns back to the transmitting unit. The difference between the transmitted signal and the return signal is used to calculate speed. Laser technology is also used like this to calculate speed.

One of the most dangerous and irrevocable results of high speed vehicle pursuits that plague law enforcement in the United States, and all over the world for that matter, is the unintentional deaths of innocent bystanders who get killed when the police chase criminals.

My dream was that the science of radar and laser technology could be used to simply transmit a radio wave or laser beam at a vehicle and have it disable the car's electronic ignition system. This would render the electrical system inoperable and cause the vehicle to lose power and thereby terminate these high speed vehicle pursuits which occur all around the country and which result in untold millions of dollars in civil litigations and court trials. Simply engineering an electronic ignition system with a cut off switch or microchip that responded to law enforcement radar or laser beams could disable vehicles so that high-speed pursuits were virtually eliminated. New autos would all need to be phased in with this technology, but the science to make it and do is completely feasible.

This technology is just waiting to happen. I wanted to have a part in making this happen. I considered this idea a wonderful opportunity to help law enforcement save lives and avoid unnecessary deaths, and a wonderful opportunity to develop a new technology that could produce tons of money. I am sure a certain amount of notoriety would inevitably come with it, too.

I prayed that God would help me with this whole idea. I knew that if I had the right backing the efficacy of a successful prototype could produce millions of dollars. If the technology was patented and sold worldwide, the profits could be staggering. In my sincere prayer I told God that if he helped me and blessed this thing I would donate 95% of all my profits to the Kingdom of heaven for spreading the gospel and good news of Christ. I was very excited about the possibilities.

As time rolled on I seemed to go nowhere with this. I felt myself become frustrated. I continued to try and walk in faith and be tenacious and not just cave in to the first waves of adversity. The concept of how to proceed with this was in my thoughts constantly. I began to reach a point where I realized that for this to work I really needed God's help because it was certainly bigger than me and I did not want to get caught up in something that I became obsessed with, especially if it wasn't God's plan for me. How could it not be God's will to help people though, with all the good this would produce, right?

Sometimes we only see the so-called good side of our intentions and not a comprehensive analysis of our thinking or the outcome of the solution. A wonderful friend told me his church was struggling with finances, and that the church membership lacked funding to acquire their own church building. He told several people that if he won the lotto he would buy his fellow believers a new church building. While my friend undoubtedly meant well and perhaps even had a pure heart, I privately thought the idea was almost pathetic. Wouldn't my friend be better off trusting God rather than the lottery? Besides, I thought, the whole body of the church needed to be involved in such an effort and not just one wealthy donor. If everybody in this church just tithed there wouldn't even be an issue. The other thing in my mind was that God is not shorthanded or unable to provide for his own church. God doesn't need one of us to be a superstar so we can "buy" him a church as though he could not afford to buy his own lunch, or anything else for that matter, you know? God doesn't need the Lotto any more than he needed Abraham to father Ishmael because Abraham thought God needed help to fulfill his promise. Is there anything too hard for the Lord? (Genesis 18:14).

I thought that my good friend, without knowing it, would ultimately be tempted with the praise of men, and others would say that brother so and so "bought" this church for us. Of course they would mean he bought the building. Isn't he a wonderful Joe? God doesn't want us to be entertaining a false sense of pride that when things were tough we bailed God out of a jam. By the time men got done with it, the project would no longer be a building, but a church. So and so bought a church for us. No one would plan it that way but human flesh would turn it into that. Trust me. The whole lottery thing seemed like a bad idea to me.

Meanwhile, as I waited for the Lord's guiding on my vehicle pursuit technology, weeks went by without anything. I reminded the Lord that he said if a son asked his father for a fish, would you give him a serpent, or if your son asked for a piece of bread would you give him a rock? And, just for good measure, I reminded the Lord that he said seek and ye shall find, knock and it shall be opened unto you. I said I'm seeking, asking, knocking and requesting an answer to my prayers. After nearly getting angry about it because I hadn't heard anything, I told the Lord that I wanted a *response* even if the answer was not what I wanted to hear. That is a dangerous prayer! The following week the Lord spoke quietly to my spirit. It wasn't what I wanted to hear but the message was crystal clear. What I sensed the Lord saying to me was this: *Son, the same problem would result with the rewards of your vehicle pursuit technology as with the man who wanted to win the lottery so that he could buy my children a church.* You may recall I privately thought that idea was *pathetic.*

I caught myself thinking "No" like Peter did when the Lord told him you will deny me three times before the cock crows. I then wondered, would I do that? The answer was, yes, my son! I never saw the ambition deep in my own heart. I would have undoubtedly smiled with a false sense of pride at every donation I put in the offering plate at church. Wow, am I good or what? I'm so brilliant and unselfish. Look at all the good that is happening worldwide just because of me. I could really beat people over the head about tithing then! I would be so pleased with my own lovely self! It would have grieved the Lord and harmed me. It wasn't a good idea for me. The pain of realizing what my flesh is capable of doing stills stings, but I'm glad the Lord showed me. I dropped the whole idea. Hopefully, someone else will develop this and turn it into something productive that helps law enforcement as well as Homeland Security with our fight against terrorism. As for me, I simply need to learn more humility so that I become a more devoted servant and foot washer. Be careful with ambition.

Hybels' elder used the example that no one ever says I feel "led" to go to a smaller church and take a huge cut in pay. It's funny how that all works! I suspect you could do research on this and if you asked a thousand pastors across America if they knew of anyone who ever voluntarily did this the answer would be no. But like Elijah who lamented to the Lord that he was the only righteous one left who had not bowed to Baal, the Lord said there are seven thousand who had not bowed to Baal.

I found such a man who did exactly what no one else would normally do: leave a large prospering church and good salary and go to a small church and take a huge cut in pay. Pastor Paul Sheppard, who pastors Abundant Life Christian Fellowship in Mountain View, California, did just that and obeyed God, at great initial expense to himself and his family. His church is now growing like you can't believe and prospering because of his obedience, and God is doing mighty things with this church. God is looking for a few good men and women who can only be bought with the blood of Jesus!

I saw a video that Bill Hybels did based upon a book and principle he had written about entitled, "Just Walk Across The Room." Reverend Hybels speaks about his personal experiences witnessing to others about Christ and he speaks about how to reach out to others in a natural, friendly, compelling way. Bill Hybels has led scores of people to Christ. As he speaks about his efforts and techniques, he gets tears in his eyes, and his voice begins to crack with emotion. If we never led anyone to get on their knees in prayer to accept Christ, but we *just* loved them, that would be enough, explains Hybels. We would be fulfilling the Second Great Commandment. Our primary goal is to just love people, and be a witness that exudes the love and goodness of Christ. Hybels' words deeply touched my heart. Sometimes I forget that loving people is all important and that developing a cure for vehicle pursuits is no better than faith that can throw mountains into the sea, nor is it better if I bestow all my goods to feed the poor, and give my body to be burned, but have not charity; then it profits me nothing (I Corinthians 13:1-3). God tries our works with fire and if there is pride, ambition and glory in our own flesh, we need to surrender those things to the cross.

Success is a journey, not a destination. We don't have to be super stars, movie stars, or outwardly gorgeous people, just foot washers who love Jesus and reflect his inner beauty, character, goodness and compassion through our lives to a lost and dying world.

This brings me to another very important point about service to our Lord. Jesus doesn't need perfect people, just willing servants. Just look at the twelve disciples. Sometimes they are referred to as the "Dirty Dozen," after a popular movie.

Too many Christians (any number is too many) have a mind-set that when <u>circumstances</u> get better I'm going to do more for the Lord. I've been guilty of this. When my business gets on its feet I am going to start tithing. When the kids move out of the house I am going to get back in the choir and start singing again. When the house is paid off I'll think about serving in my church and doing more for the Kingdom of God. When all the planets are aligned with Venus and Mars and the weather is just right, I will start attending church regularly again, except on Super Bowl Sundays. If everything goes my way, I might start reading my Bible and serving the Lord. When my barns get bigger I am going to start giving above and beyond my tithing requirements, and start leaving my waitress a twelve percent tip!

When I worked in the jail for a few months, I constantly heard inmates telling me how they were going to serve society and help children when they got out of jail. It's not that there was anything wrong with the good intention, but the reality of it was few ever did anything about all their pontificating intentions. The road to hell is paved with good intentions. What most of these inmates ostensibly failed to understand or put into practice was that the road to repentance and the changing of their ways begins immediately, while they are still in jail. Be the best, most well behaved inmate on your pod, and stop stirring up trouble or being a part of it. Don't wait till you get out of prison. Start doing the right thing, right now! Just do what is within your power to do now, and don't wait for circumstances to become better farther down the road.

It doesn't really matter where you are in life on the ladder of success or accomplishments or how many times you failed in the past. It's not what you are going to do later on; it's what you are doing right now!

How do I get there from here? You start right where you are, especially if you are in a lion's den, a pit or shark infested waters. It's a journey my friend! The good news is that our whole life with Christ is just one day at a time. It's all how you decide to look at your circumstances. That lion which I may encounter in my journey today might eat me for dinner, but glory to God, I'll be the tastiest meal he ever had; and that lion will be speaking in tongues when he's done with me! You don't get extra points for worrying about tomorrow. Don't try and be someone you're not. Be yourself. Thank goodness we are not all alike. We are unique and we possess different skills, gifts, aptitudes, and strengths. Each of us will encounter opportunities that no other person will have. Only what you do for Christ will last.

If you come to the realization that you really did make a mistake, and careful, thoughtful consideration confirms you actually did blow it, ask for forgiveness, and get off the train which is heading in the wrong direction and correct your direction of travel when you can do so in a just and righteous way. Turn things around and get on the right track, heading in the right direction. Don't make a mistake more complicated than it really is and don't spend the rest of your life lamenting that you missed the boat. Oh, dear, I made a terrible mistake. I'll never be of any use to God or anyone else the rest of my life.

If you are going to feel sorry for yourself and eat worms over this, you might as well have a cold iced tea and some nacho chips to go with it. Live life richly and know that some of the best lessons we learn in life are the results of our own mistakes. Most of us make a ton of mistakes. Why should you be any different? Don't let fear of failure stop you from becoming a success. The most tragic thing any of us can do is simply sit on the sidelines and do nothing because something might go wrong along the way. Things are guaranteed to go wrong in life. Jesus acknowledged this and said: *in the world, you shall have tribulation: but be of good cheer, for I have overcome the world* (John 16:33).

Rest in the Lord and wait patiently for him (Psalms 37:7). *Delight thyself in the Lord and he will give thee the desires of thine heart* (Psalms 37:4). *Commit thy way unto the Lord; trust also in him; and he shall bring it to pass* (Psalms 37:5).

The just shall live by faith!

CHAPTER 8

LEARNING HOW TO PRAY FOR THE RIGHT THINGS

It is really hard to pray for world peace or hunger when you are hungry yourself and hurting because your soul is starving. It is next to impossible to be fully effective in ministry or achieve your full potential when you are hurting yourself, overwhelmed or in need of spiritual CPR. You need to examine yourself and measure your own health. This does not mean that if you have not peaked or reached your perfected state, then you should wait until you are at the top of your game before you serve others. It's not a matter of perfection or nothing at all. Look at the twelve disciples; the "Dirty Dozen." If we all waited until we were perspicacious, we would be waiting a long time and we would never serve anyone or accomplish anything. All of life is a synergistic balancing act of asking God for discernment, wisdom, direction, faith and courage, while applying common sense, good judgment and integrity to all of our affairs.

You don't have to be your own resource. That should be good news for all of us. Be committed to Christ. We clearly need the Lord but we also need wisdom, balance and sensitivity to the leading of the Holy Spirit. We fix our eyes on the goal, which is the cross of Christ, the author and finisher of our faith. We strive in our faith to perfect our works and bear fruit. But too often we struggle to help others, when we, ourselves, are ill, hurting, depressed, bitter, angry, sleep deprived, or otherwise out of sync with the Holy Spirit. These deficiencies constructively attenuate our good efforts and make us comparable to the blind leading the blind.

There is a point where, unless you are walking in the Spirit, your flesh will render you spiritually useless. We have to effectively manage our own lives and overcome some of our own deficiencies if we want to serve and bless others in a meaningful way. Without the help of God we won't accomplish that. The apostle Paul wrote: For if a man knows not how to rule his own house, how shall he take care of the church of God? (I Timothy 3:5). He that is slow to anger is better than the mighty; and he that ruleth his spirit than he that taketh a city (Proverbs 16:32).

Let me give you a couple of examples that generally apply to me and I think you'll see what I mean. When I get up in the morning, that event, in itself, is a form of dying to my flesh. I have to crawl to the coffee pot in much the same way as a soldier crawls on his belly to avoid overhead gunfire. It takes me a couple of hours to wake up. It's the only time in the day wherein anyone could actually accuse me of being laconic. I don't want to answer any questions or be engaged in any kind of problem solving or unnecessary talking. King Solomon with his wisdom understood this great mystery when he wrote: he that blesseth his friend with a loud voice, rising early in the morning, it shall be counted a curse to him (Proverbs 27:14). I find a deep solitude and holiness in drinking my cup of coffee while staring out into space, perhaps watching my sprinklers water the lawn.

Once I am awake I have pretty good endurance. I have frequently worked long 12-hour shifts at work. I can go without sleep for 24 hours or more, but you probably would not want me flying the commercial aircraft you intend to fly on. If I go for prolonged periods of time without eating, I initially get very grumpy. I sometimes refer to this phenomenon as being baptized in pickle juice because it depicts the foul mood and personality of irritability so well. Both my son and I get totally depleted if we go too long without food. We reach the point of not being able to think clearly.

Sleep deprivation does the same thing to the point that it can cause people to break people down completely and induce them to give up information or intelligence they are trying to hide from authorities. Sleep deprivation is an interrogation technique used by the military, the CIA, numerous foreign governments, and even to a lesser extent by some police, where interrogations last over twelve hours and suspects become exhausted. You would not want your personal doctor performing surgery on you if your doctor had not had adequate, restful sleep. My point is that even competent caregivers are, at times, quite fragile. We need to understand and appreciate our limitations and realize that there are times we might be in such a condition ourselves that we become be a liability to others and not a blessing.

Make sure you are healthy and of sound mind and spirit and that you know what you are doing before you reach out to touch someone. You might make things worse. The wrong words can produce death as much as the wrong actions. Be bold and full of faith, but be circumspect also and full of wisdom. Learn also how to take good care of yourself. That will allow you the energy and insight to minister more effectively to others when those opportunities arise. You can't help others very well if you are in need of CPR yourself.

One ubiquitous issue I see, which people struggle with when facing adversity, is that it is hard for people to just be blunt and completely honest about their real feelings, especially if those feelings involve anger. For a variety of reasons, including the misuse of anger, and ignorance about anger as an emotion, sometimes people come to the perception or belief that all anger is bad, possibly sinful, but certainly inappropriate and to be generally avoided whenever possible. You know what I am talking about. We can't even admit anger to ourselves sometimes.

Once upon a time, in a far, far away land where a meeting took place, one of my friends had a bad hair day and just about went into vapor lock because he did not want to discuss something at this meeting that had come up spontaneously for discussion at the table. He felt it was off the subject at hand since it wasn't on the agenda for that day. That was his subsequently stated position. I honestly thought he was about to get up and walk straight out of the meeting if we pursued the issue. It got extremely awkward and quiet and everyone felt very uncomfortable and no one was quite sure what to do. At least one person felt hurt by what had just happened.

About ten minutes elapsed during which time we walked on eggshells and skirted around other topics. Eventually, everyone's emotions quieted down a little. I came back to the issue and told the group I felt compelled to say a couple of things because I wanted to be honest with the people that I all loved in this room. I explained my position that we needed to be able to talk about and deal with matters or issues that were not always easy to talk about.

I confronted my friend, whom I love very much, and in front of the group told him with sincere tenderness that I was sorry if my words or the pursuit of the previous subject made him angry, and that my intention was not to do that. I told him I valued his opinions and his intellect and that I wanted to be close to him as a friend and be able to talk about anything, or at least be able to ask him questions about his beliefs and his thoughts on issues I struggled with. I told him I did not understand where all his anger came from, but I wanted to better understand what was coming from his heart. This broke the ice and turned everything around. The very first thing my friend said was that he had not been angry, only "frustrated" with discussing an issue which wasn't on the agenda. Guess what: life is full of real issues that are not on the agenda. What I found to be particularly interesting was that my friend could not even acknowledge that he had gotten pretty angry.

The meeting ended on a good note and we all affectionately said goodbye. This story is simply intended to give a real life example of conflict, which involved the denial of anger. This can and does happen in marriages all the time. It has happened in my marriage a couple of times. One of us might scream; I'm not angry! Well, of course you are not!

Refusing to even acknowledge anger, of course, effectually circumvents real life and our feelings, and it often attenuates any useful or redeeming value anger might serve.

Some issues or topics, however, are so inherently sensitive or emotionally explosive, that we need to be very tender, sensitive and respectful to each other when such issues are broached. Sometimes that has to be done at the right time when it is safe to do so. That may require a trained professional who can help foster that environment or then give the appropriate guidance and advice you may not be prepared to give.

No one wants to be sitting next to someone and because we innocently ask a question, the person next to us goes into vapor lock and starts drooling with rage and anger. We can diminish some of this exaggerated emotion if we honestly process some of our anger with God and ask for his help so that we have neither denied our feelings, nor lost our sense of balance in life over a simple question, which we were asked. Asking for God's help in processing our own rage will help us and prepare us to be more capable of calmly discussing hot topics with others. Doing this does not require that you abdicate your opinions or your integrity. Consider that not knowing what position to even take does not make you a "bad" guy either. Remember the Lord's invitation: Come now, let us reason together (Isaiah 1:18). [In this setting, apoplectic, vituperative railing or violence is not necessary in order to be heard]

Avoiding the truth and our real feelings about things rarely serves anyone well in the long run, although not forcing an issue is usually prudent, because timing is everything. It will not serve you well to tell Aunt Sally that her salad tasted like carpe and that you hate the taste of fish and she should have known that! You've got other issues which you need to talk about and the salad isn't the real issue. Being nasty in the name of being honest isn't the answer. There is also the issue of kindness.

There is also such a thing as legitimate, righteous anger and the Bible speaks of it scores of times. In our personal lives sometimes we just dance all over the joint, but never really identify those real issues that are deeply troubling to us. Anger often falls into this category. You've seen this before and know what I am talking about. It is easy to live in a state of denial. This happens in relationships all the time.

Sometimes we don't even want to know what the truth is. It's simple, yet painful: we can't handle the truth. There are certain roads we just don't want to go down and certain things we just don't want to talk about. As human endeavors and weaknesses play out in our lives, that may be the best course of action at times because we can't control what other people do, but we can take responsibility for our own actions. With your heavenly Father, not having the faith, courage or honesty to pursue truth is a unilateral choice. If you find yourself isolated from God, it won't be because he walked away. *Draw nigh unto God, and he will draw nigh unto you* (James 4:8).

Often, it is hard to be honest with others, but even harder to be honest with ourselves. Now, try being honest with God. Hello? Are you still with me? Learning how to be honest is paramount to overcoming adversity. What we might discover inside ourselves may be so ugly that we don't want to talk about it with others or even acknowledge it to ourselves, but facing these giants in our lives, and acknowledging our own limitations, become the first steps to overcoming adversity. If we don't even admit that we need help, how can we pray about it? If we are not truly honest with ourselves, how can we honestly pray about these things?

As I mention in a previous chapter, there are times where I come to the realization that the ugly truth is actually very simple: *I don't want to be like Jesus, nor do I want to do the right thing!* So, I pray, Lord, help me to *want* to do the right thing. It's a start. Lord, don't ever let me become too satisfied on this side. Lord, create in me a clean heart and give me the desire to serve you.

Whom do pastors talk with about their own extremely personal matters, such as sex? What would you do if you were a healthy Christian male pastor, but for various reasons you could not fulfill your sexual drives and needs even though you were married? Go see a good therapist, right? What if one spouse just could not, or would not, seek counseling? Do you throw the marriage away? What do you do when you begin having dreams about sexuality matters that reflect your physical and emotional needs, but which are also not conducive to you spirituality or the health of your marriage? What happens if abstinence leads to lust?

It is very possible to beat yourself up senselessly with something like this and feel guilty for having normal drives and libido and thinking if you were just holier or more spiritual none of these things would matter. These are really sensitive issues that real people struggle with. Three high profile people come to my mind that received national media attention when they struggled with their own flesh. I remember when I was in my thirties and I was going through a difficult time in my own marriage when one of these giants of the faith fell from grace. I remember lifting my voice up in prayer asking Jesus how I was supposed to make if this respected pillar of the faith couldn't. Even though the question was almost rhetorical, I felt the Lord telling me that the man who failed never asked for Christ's help, but instead sought his own solution.

What do you think a pastor should be told if he were experiencing these concerns in his marriage? Well, I hope you wouldn't rebuke him or scold him and tell him to stop worrying so much about sex and start caring more about the eternal side of his faith. I bring this up to make a point about prayer. There is nothing that we can't talk to God about if we are seeking his favor. I am convinced that a lot of people are more comfortable asking Oprah Winfrey or Doctor Phil what to do than they are in seeking help from the Lord for personal issues. Sexual matters are about as personal as anything can get. There have been plenty of churches split in half or destroyed because the pastor had an affair with someone from within the church. Obviously, bad choices were made in those circumstances. In every case you hear about, those involved were not willing to humble themselves before the Lord or others, to ask for help. Close friends could have offered practical advice, spiritual support, and in all cases professional counseling could have been sought.

What I find to be quite interesting is that God is no respecter of persons. More importantly, perhaps, is that we, collectively as Christians, need to practice what we preach to others. God doesn't say to anyone, well, since you are doing a fine job as the pastor of this church I will remove the challenge of your having to face any marital issues in your life or sexual temptations. God doesn't do that. The rain falls equally on everyone. We have to overcome adversity. Simply wishing that we would not have to face adversity will not eliminate temptation nor will it produce a resolution. Since we are all subject to the law of gravity, why would anyone think that we might not be subject to spiritual laws and principles or other life issues and temptations? We are all subject to trials and temptations. We can minimize some of these temptations by how well we control our thought patterns and prayer life, but we are not immune from life, or any part of it. If you preach to your congregation that they should hasten to the throne of God when troubles rise, then maybe you should do the same thing as the pastor or shepherd of your flock if your marriage is not what you want it to be or the issue of infidelity is starting to creep into your thoughts.

We can pray about all sorts of things and seek God's help in our business affairs, and we can tells others to trust him, and we can pray for world peace, but we have trouble telling the Lord that our sex lives are not very fulfilling or satisfying. Do we inquire of the Lord if there is something we can do about making that part of our lives more abundant and joyful? Hello! Is any of this familiar?

I think there are people out there in the real world who don't know what to do in some of these situations, and probably have no one they can confide in about what they are experiencing. What is even more tragic is that many feel that these are the last things in the world that they could ever pray about or talk to the Lord about.

If it's on your heart and it's important to you, it's worth talking about. I was in church a few Sundays ago and a wonderful sermon was given on the topic of prayer. I've never heard a pastor give such simple advise on this before, but he opined that if your heart is aching because of a lack of romance in your life, you should tell the Lord about it. The message was beautiful and it goes to the heart of what I am talking about. Your situation isn't limited by the particulars of any one person, group, gender or age and, and it might be reflective of someone who has been married for twenty years and their marriage has lost its romance. Romance and sex should not be some dirty little thing that you can't pray about.

When was the last time you had the courage to acknowledge to yourself that you were angry with God Almighty? Did you tell him how you felt? It's not an easy thing to do and it might remind you that God could strike you dead if he wanted to. I find that it is hard for me to even know what I feel at times. Where did that issue come from, you might ask yourself? Sometimes I just need time to analyze my thoughts and feelings. Sometimes we can feel disturbed and uncomfortable about something that happened in the course of our day, but never have the opportunity to explore it, let alone understand it. Appropriating the dimension of prayer to our lives takes these things to a whole new level that some may be unfamiliar with. Try it. You'll like it.

What you talk to God about should include real things and issues that are on your heart, even things which you have confusion about and don't understand. Prayer should include honest dialogue about your feelings, I believe. Don't limit prayer to only the big things. It's the little things that kill us or drive us crazy! Talk to Jesus like he is your friend. That's what friends do. If your marriage is failing, for example, and your heart is broken, you need to pray about those matters with the one who loves you, your heavenly Father. God's word repeatedly asks this question throughout the Bible: Is there anything too difficult for God? These words are there for our benefit to provoke both thought on the subject and conversation.

God knows all about your weaknesses, sins, failures, and your dreams and he loves you and wants to forgive you and offer you a hope and a future and an abundant life. Talk to him about what's on your heart. It doesn't have to be about world peace. As important as that might be, world peace is probably not what broke your heart, especially if the absence of peace is happening on the other side of your world. As serious and real as that may be, it tends to become impersonal unless you are directly being affected by it.

If the number one thing that weighs on your heart is peace in your world because your world faces inner city violence and the homicide rate in your city is out of control, that's a different story! If you live in Palestine or the Gaza Strip, then world peace literally means life or death for you and your family. That also is a reality few can fully fathom.

When it comes to meaningful conversation and prayer, the Lord surely is less concerned about the inconsequential in the same way you probably are. We don't derive pleasure talking with others about things which we have absolutely no interest in. We fall asleep during such conversations. So, why would we want to do have a meaningless conversation with the Lord? Sharing our thoughts in the form of prayer becomes less a matter of how big or small we deem an issue to be, and more a matter of whether the issue is one of importance to us. Is it something that we care about? If it's something that is important, or that we care about, then it's probably not inconsequential.

I am sure that the Lord understands and appreciates our thinking and our feelings over our issues in much the same way we do when we show love and understanding to our children. The Lord cares about those things which we perceive as real issues, and about those things which are important to us, for whatever the reason might be. We're not limited to approaching the throne of God by the size of our issue. We're limited by our lack of faith and courage and by our fears. I believe the Lord wants us to be honest with ourselves and with him about what's going on in our lives, and it doesn't have to be limited to big stuff. I firmly believe the Lord cares not only about the big stuff, but the little things, too. In fact, I think the Lord understands the little things far better than we do, and he fully appreciates how they impact us even when we fail to see or understand it.

This is the essence of what prayer should be all about: those things which we care about and have questions about; those things that are troubling to us, and those things which bring us joy but sometimes uncertainty or confusion. Let's talk about things that are of *interest* and *importance* to us and let's not get hung up about size. The Lord reigns over big and small and his love for you is profound. The Lord is waiting to have a conversation with you...or maybe lunch.

There are some things (behaviors) we are instructed to <u>not</u> do, and so it is unnecessary to pray about whether we should do those things or not. We already know the answer. You don't have to pray about whether you should love your neighbor. Jesus already told us to not only love our neighbor but our enemies as well, and that we should pray for those who despitefully use us. It is a waste of time to pray about whether your neighbor might be an exception to this rule because they are hard to live with people. You've been talking to the Sons of Thunder, haven't you?

New Testament scripture teaches in Paul's writings that whatsoever things are true, honest, just, pure, lovely, and are of a good report, to think on these things. You don't have to pray about whether you should do these things. Practice the fruits of the Spirit. Bless and curse not. Forgive one another. It's not God's will for you to murder your wife. God wants you to love your wife, not slap her, or kill her. You don't have to pray about doing the right thing. Just do it! Don't pray about whether you should tithe or not, just do it. Don't pray about whether you should be baptized; it's a commandment. Just do it! You don't need to pray about whether you should have faith in God or whether you should trust the Lord. You don't have to even pray about whether you should start reading the Bible, because it will help you in your spiritual growth; just do it!

If an issue or behavior goes against Holy Scripture, that is to say, the inspired, infallible word of God, don't waste your breath praying for God to change his word, his mind or his nature. Jesus is the same yesterday, today and forever! Save your breath to blow on the soup. Jesus said heaven and earth will pass away but my words will never pass away. The word of the Lord endureth forever!

Praying quid pro quo

There are exceptions to just about everything in life and this may be one of those things that could fall into that category. There are righteous examples of this in the Bible where a covenant was made with God out of a pure heart. The birth of Samuel and Samson come to mind. Notwithstanding legitimate example(s) where service was, or, is offered to God, our human tendencies make us susceptible to quid pro quo praying that will naturally lead to the pursuit of our own will, success and prosperity. Undetectable, unconscious sin will flourish in the human heart and eventually raise its ugly head when you least expect it. This is part of what makes sin so deadly; we don't see it or recognize it in ourselves. We need to be extremely careful with quid pro quo as a methodology.

I argue this because quid pro quo by its very intrinsic nature will eventually lead to bargaining or bartering. You scratch my back and I'll scratch yours. You support my election and I'll campaign for you. It fosters compromise and when it comes to God's nature and character and issues regarding right or wrong, God doesn't compromise. He hates sin and sin does not come without a price. The Bible tells us that the wages of sin is death. If God did not spare even his own son when it came to paying the cost of our sin, why would God allow you to get away with it?

On top of all of this, sin is beguiling and, at times, looks good because it can be disguised to appear even as an angel of light. So when there is sin in our hearts we frequently don't even recognize it, let alone clearly see it for what it is worth. Quid pro quo will lead down a road wherein we think we might be able to successfully manipulate God. You might think oh, I would never do that. Yes, you would and most of us would justify it by arguing that it was for a worthy cause! Do you ever catch yourself foolishly thinking this way? Yeah, dude, my plans are far from being perfect; they're almost illegal, but they are going to produce something really good! You need to stop smoking crack!

For these reasons, I would be really careful and respectfully cautious with this type of praying because there can be inherent pitfalls that we are blinded to with quid pro quo prayer. I spoke earlier of ambition and the weakness of the flesh. Lord, if you make me filthy rich I'll tithe fifteen percent! Well, hoopty doo! A lot of people tip their food server eighteen percent and some people tip twenty or more percent. You think God is going to fall off his stool because you offer him fifteen percent? I am being sarcastic, of course, in order to make the point. Here is what I believe to be a more circumspect, efficacious, approach if we are talking about integrity and trust in God: offer your entire life in service to Jesus without strings attached for little or no reward because he is worthy of everything you have! He is the King of kings and nothing we possess or offer him, including an entire life of service, is too good for him, or more than he deserves!

When you give, give in secret as unto your heavenly Father and not out of an expectation for some kind of immediate reward. This will turn into greed and manipulation before the sun sets. God, if I give ten dollars above and beyond what you expect of me can I have a blessing of one hundred dollars? Say...by this Friday would be just fine, thank you very much! That is not only quid pro quo, it's deceitful. We would be investing in the stock market based on insider tips, and all over riches! Do the right thing for the right reasons without an expectation of being repaid in this lifetime and God will bless you anyway. Let God decide what kind of reward or blessing to give you and let it be serendipitous.

Then there is the issue of Jesus telling us to take no thought for your life, food, raiment or what you shall eat because your heavenly Father knows you have need of these things before you even ask (Matthew 6:31). To clear up any potential confusion about this, please note that Jesus' words are an invitation to trust God for our needs and be preoccupied with Kingdom business and not worry about our own welfare. Live in faith and trust your heavenly Father. That doesn't mean you cannot pray about these things.

If your children are facing death and starvation, you should be praying about their needs. Will my stewardship please God if I don't care properly for my own family needs? You can't and won't save the world if you can't properly manage and care for your own family. Jesus said, *he who is faithful with that which is least [little things] is faithful also in much: and he that is unjust in the least is unjust also in much* (Luke 16:10).

Jesus prayed when he was in the Garden of Gethsemane about his own crucifixion because his soul anguished over what he was about to face. He endured the cross and despised the shame out of love for you and me. This is the greatest story humanity has ever known, that the Son of God would leave his home in glory to come down and be mocked and spit upon and nailed to a cross just to shed his precious blood so that you and I could be forgiven, if we ask for it. This is as big as it gets. Yet, Jesus cared about the children and said suffer them to come unto me. When the crowds had followed him all day and listened to his teaching he told his disciples to feed them, knowing there wasn't enough food present for five thousand people. Jesus cared about whether people had lunch or not. If you revisit or examine the story you will see Jesus fed them. If Jesus cared about whether people had lunch or not, he cares about other matters that are personal to you.

As long as we are talking about recipe tactics, which help or impede us with prayer, here is another common but very important behavioral practice that will make or break you. Don't sabotage your good prayers by honestly seeking God's will, direction or blessings for your life, but then turn around and embrace defeat by saturating your mind with thoughts of failure. The enemy wants to rob you of any battles you are winning.

What's in your heart automatically gets tested anyway for content and sincerity. If you say that you trust Jesus and will obey him no matter what the cost, believe me, you will be tested on this. It's a spiritual principle because we are to worship and serve God in spirit and in truth, and God deals in truth, justice, sincerity and faith. If we mean what we say, God wants to know it. If you talk trash like a used car salesman, God will politely point that out to you. The proof is in the pudding. Satan wants to know if you mean it, too.

If we say that we trust God with our lives and his will for our lives, but then we turn right around and profess defeat and failure, we have essentially reversed all the lovely words we spoke, as if to say, just kidding, I really didn't mean any of it; I can't really trust God with my life. It sabotages everything we professed with our mouth. Words are important. By your words you will be justified and by your words you will be condemned (Matthew 12:37). Embracing defeat and proclaiming it with your mouth is tantamount to telling God, you are not powerful enough or great enough to sustain your promises. It effectually sabotages your prayers. Don't do it.

The enemy whispers in your ear and offers you a way out by retractions and admissions that God can't really be trusted. It is a spiritual war of words and thoughts. Your answers are recorded in heaven. *For there is nothing cov-*

ered that shall not be revealed; neither hid, that shall not be known. Therefore whatsoever ye have spoken in darkness shall be heard in light, and that which ye have spoken in the ear in the closets shall be proclaimed upon the house-tops (Luke 12:2-4).

Tell God you are struggling with having faith, confess it, and ask him to help you with your doubts and unbelief. Thank him for his goodness and ask him to give you additional strength to overcome the enemy. Lift up your head and praise him for he is mighty and powerful to save to the uttermost ends of the earth and there is nothing too difficult for God.

We tend to dislike trials and testing because they don't feel good but they bring about good. They establish what is real and true from what is worldly, superficial, unreliable, fraudulent and corruptible. This is a spiritual principle. God allows the world and heavens to be shaken so that which cannot be shaken may remain. What remains after the storm is well grafted in the vine (Revelation 6:13/hebrews 12:26-27). What remains is righteous fruit. This is the essence of our faith.

This is spiritual warfare. There is a war of thoughts, ideas and words that you will be tempted with from your friends, co-workers and even family. We end up listening to everything those around us tell us even if it's contrary to God's word. Stop entertaining the negative, specious words of the enemy when God is in the midst of delivering you out of bondage. It is entirely possible to claim and embrace defeat from the jaws of victory by giving in to all the death and negativity we are bombarded with. Don't do it.

The enemy tempted Jesus in the wilderness after forty days of fasting when Jesus was weak and hungry. Jesus could have quit right there but he didn't, and the most notable thing he did, beside not giving up, was that he quoted the word of God back to Satan when he was tested and tempted with taking an easy way out. The word of God is powerful and sharper than any two-edged sword. It will never fail because Jesus promised that it would not. Claim God's words of encouragement and the many promises he gives us. Know what the word says! Read it! Scripture tells us to resist the devil and he will flee from you. God's word has power and authority. Use it to claim victory.

Part of becoming a victor is having an overcoming attitude and mind-set. You not only have to pursue victory but you have to claim it, and then hold onto it and preserve it. We see this all the time in professional sports. Championship games have momentums that change back and forth during the game. If you want to be a champion, you have to think like a champion and have a warrior-like attitude. The first sign of adversity does not have to dictate your defeat, unless of course, you allow it. Satan wants us to abdicate and abandon ship simply because there are showers in the forecast and the horizon is slightly overcast. Turn it around. Start singing about "showers of blessings." There is a song with this title we learned in Sunday School.

We need to rebuke the enemy and remind him that the Lord is with us and that the fight has not yet even begun! Talk back to the enemy and let him know you are in this for the long haul and that Jesus is your shield, your rock, and your defender! Make Satan uncomfortable for once in your life. Remind him that when God is done with him, he is going back into the pit where he belongs! You need to think and expect victory and not be stunned when you get in the end zone. You need to think and act like you have been there before and that you will be there again. Don't be shocked because God answered one of your prayers. Act like you expect it to happen on a regular basis.

Encourage yourself in the Lord, for he is good! God has promised to guide you and lead you. Remind yourself of what God's word says. If we, who are evil, know how to give good gifts to our children, how much more will our heavenly Father give the Holy Spirit to those who ask him (Luke 11:13).

Remember, God is a good God and he doesn't lead his children down a dark alley then push them off a cliff or give them cyanide laced Kool-Aid like Jim Jones did. God is not in the business of tricking people; God is in the business of redeeming people and giving us a hope and a future. You might be two footsteps away from opening the door to victory, but Satan will tempt you with words. Lucifer will whisper to you that things won't go well at this new job and you should return to your old one. No one is going to accept you. These people are all against you, the enemy will say. That is when you should reply: that might be true; we'll just have to see, won't we? But one thing I know, you foul thing of darkness: if God be for us, who can be against us? Warfare is largely a game of words and thoughts. Don't allow yourself to entertain all the what-if's that can possibly go wrong in life. Satan will have you up all night listening to his nonsense. Victory comes with courageous faith. Remind the enemy that there nothing too difficult for God! Tell the enemy that if God's grace and provision were good enough for Moses and Abraham, it's good enough for you. Tell the devil that if he keeps whispering doubt and defeat into your ear you are prepared to stay up all night long and ask God to increase your faith and courage. That alone will make him, for the moment, want to leave.

You can be a hundred yards from the finish line or one phone call away from success and you can give up and abandon ship because you have listened to every negative report Satan has offered you and you can allow your mind to think God isn't going to really help me. Satan wants to make you forget about Joseph in Egypt and how he was thrown into a pit and sold into slavery before God raised him up. During the storm God blessed everything that Joseph put his hand to both in the field and in the house. Remember? The enemy does not want you to know the facts found in the word of God, nor does he want you to rely on God's word or his promises. Think positively and claim victory, but do it not because of head knowledge or because of your own wisdom or strength, but because you trust in the Lord.

When I am having a nervous breakdown about my foolish issues, Jesus seems to still care about helping me with these things, not because my foolish issues are worth entertaining, but because he loves me in spite of my foolishness and he wants to help me and enable me to stop fretting and refocus on Kingdom issues that are more important.

Earlier I talked about being honest in praying about things which are issues from the heart and that these matters don't have to be limited to big things. I want to share an example of something that I struggled with which was about as low on the scale of eternal matters of importance as anything could probably get in life.

Like the plant that sprung up and provided shade for Jonah, sometimes little things become more valuable to us at a given moment of our selfishness, than our concern or love for the souls of dying men and women.

This is going to be a little embarrassing but I want to tell you how the squirrels in my backyard robbed me of my joy, peace and victory. Actually, I allowed these things to happen. The squirrels did not steal anything; I forfeited my peace of mind and victory through my own small thinking and by not taking dominion and control over my anger. I gave in to the anger and allowed it to fester. Here is how it all happened. This is a good example of inappropriate anger.

My wife and I bought this lovely home and the Lord played a very real and wonderful role in helping us acquire it. It was nothing short of the Lord making the deal happen. In December we will be celebrating our tenth year in this wonderful home.

For all of the last eight years I have struggled with trying to have a nice lawn in our backyard. The yard is distinctive in that it has tall shade trees that reach forty or more feet into the air on three sides of the lawn in the shape of a horseshoe. These small, yet tall shrubs and trees afford beautiful greenery and privacy, too. The challenge I encountered was that one side of the lawn got plenty of sunshine and one side got almost none. The side with sun flourished just like those do who love the Son (pun intended). The side with all shade never got enough sun and the lawn was always anemic, like some poor guy who was seriously going bald.

As I previously wrote in an earlier chapter, the absence of knowledge is a killer. You don't have to intentionally do anything wrong, but not following the principles of success will produce failure regardless of whether we are talking about spiritual matters or gardening. The rain falls on the just and the unjust alike. In my case in wasn't so much the rain as the squirrels.

I did not know very much about what I was doing and, of course, we who fall into that category never realize that we don't know what we are doing. I mean how hard is it to plant a little grass? I went to college. This is not rocket science. So, I planted grass. According to my faith, the seeds germinated and baby grass began growing. All of this requires water, of course. Well, I watered the lawn until there were fish swimming in it because more is better, right? Winter came and the shade turned to nightfall. The side that was in the shade went from very little sun light to virtually no sunlight. When spring arrived the weather got a little warmer and planting new seed again produced visible results.

I thought, like the scripture says, that some seed falls into bad soil and some seed is choked out by weeds and the scorching sun, so I figured I'd give it more water! My seed germinated and began producing baby grass. I was so thrilled that I wanted to name each blade of grass. I let the grass grow too tall and then I mowed the lawn, thereby cutting it too short. After doing this in the summer when the weather is hot, it caused the grass to go into shock. I learned after talking to people at the Orchard Supply Hardware store that experts tell you to not cut the grass more than a third of its height or it will overwhelm the grass and send it into shock. Well, that represented two or three years of labor that went down the drain tubes right there.

While on a road trip taking women to state prison, I talked to another deputy about my lawn not doing very well. My coworker told me that I was watering the lawn way too much and that was why the side in the shade had salmon trying to swim up stream.

After two more years of planting seed every year to fill in the dead spots and thin bald spots, I again managed to get baby grass growing in the shade. I eventually learned to trim the side of the bushes and in between the trees on the shaded side so that some sun could get through to the lawn even in the winter months. This made an enormous difference because all living things have to have a certain amount of sun or they won't grow no matter what you do. This is very representative of our spiritual lives, by the way. If you don't get enough of the Son in your life daily, you will be anemic no matter how many books you read about positive thinking.

In spite of the knowledge I was acquiring, the squirrels would dig holes all over the shaded area of my lawn and dig up freshly planted baby grass, yanking it out by the roots. There were holes all over the yard but never where the grass was real thick and healthy. This went on all year long but it really got bad in the summer. The first few times this happened, I tried to overlook it like one does when a baby cries too loudly while you are having lunch in a restaurant. It is important to have a little compassion. It doesn't come across well if you walk over to the table and tell these people, please make your baby shut up! I'm trying to have lunch here, you know? Being full of compassion I tried to approach the squirrels this way and be forgiving with them at first. Then I tried to talk with them. Oh, little sweethearts, each of you is just so cute Daddy can hardly stand it. Would you please not dig holes all over Daddy's nice lawn? Thank you, precious!

None of my insincere tactics worked and I began to think ill of the little squirrels. It frustrated me to no end that they dug holes only in the soft soil on the shaded, overwatered side where the lawn was struggling to live. The fact that they left the thick grass on the sunny side alone manifested just how base their character was because they preyed on the weak grass like criminals who prey on the elderly! It made me realize these guys were evil!

Like criminals that rob banks, I realized these guys needed to go into custody. I purchased squirrel cages and over the months trapped those little demons by the dozens. At first I would put the caged squirrel in the trunk of my car and drive to a rural area by a lake and let them go. I told each squirrel as I released them that they were on double secret probation with search and seizure and that they could be captured at any time of the day or night, with or without a warrant, and that any future violation would be treated under the "Three Strikes Law" of California!

Word on the street got out to the squirrels and they attacked my lawn like there was no tomorrow. After four or five years of planting and replanting grass seed every spring only to have it torn up by squirrels during the summer, I began talking to the squirrels in much the same ways as Balaam did with his donkey (Numbers 22:23-31). One day I caught myself swearing like a sailor at the top of my lungs to the squirrels. It's like when you catch yourself snoring in church; it is a little embarrassing. As I evaluated my behavior, I was not ashamed that I had done this, only worried that someone like my neighbors might have heard me. I mean, maybe one would call the police and report that there was a mad man swearing at the squirrels in his backyard. The police might have taken me in for a mental health evaluation. I could just visualize the San Jose Police Chief calling the Sheriff in San Mateo County telling him, I have one of your deputies down here in my station, some sick puppy named Malmin. Miserable, wretched squirrels!

I tried to tone it down a little and measure my vituperative words to the squirrels like a water faucet by turning the volume down a bit, but that didn't work either. I tried to get spiritual about it, but all that did was remind me that everything I owned and possessed belonged to the Lord, and that I was only a steward, that the house and the lawn belonged to the Lord, just like every breath I took. I didn't have a problem with the Lord being the Master of my house, just not the lawn. I indignantly pointed out under my breath one day to the Lord, look what they are doing to *your* lawn! I felt like someone who was going through rehab but didn't really want to be in the program. There were good days and there were bad days.

Singer Amy Winehouse won a Grammy award in 2008 for a song entitled "Rehab" which has a catchy little tune. You can get it on the Internet or buy it from Apple's iTunes. The song depicts me and my foolish bondage to a tee. I get the impression Amy wrote and sung this song based on her struggles with drugs, but I love the song because it reflects my pathology and me perfectly. In an absurd sort of way, I almost feel like soul mates with Amy based on my anger addiction, you know? Stinking squirrels! I might as well be doing heroin.

I completely lost the victory, the battle, the war and my joy. After reading again about how God blessed Joseph and that the Lord made all that he did to prosper in his hand, both "in the house and in the field" I got more angry (Genesis 39:2-5). How come you are not doing that for me? One afternoon while I was having another nervous breakdown over the squirrels, I directed my anger toward the Lord. As though he was standing right there, I said it so vociferously the neighbors could have heard me:

You're not doing me any favors, you know!
You could be helping me with this, but you are not!
They're *your* squirrels!
Why don't you talk to them and forbid them from
coming into *my* yard?"

I walked into the house and felt like Peter must have felt after he denied Jesus before the cock crowed. I felt guilty and ashamed of myself, not only for being angry about the squirrels, but much more so for talking to the Lord like he was my enemy. I apologized to the Lord and prayed:

Forgive me, Lord, for being unfair to you about this.
You did not cause any of this, and you are not my enemy,
yet, I talked to you as though you were.
This is my problem and I have a terrible attitude.
Please, forgive me!

I wept as I prayed those words.

I also quietly thought: I don't deserve it but I wish you would help me with this problem.

Like a toothache that slowly goes away or a headache you don't realize has gone away, so it was with the squirrels. I realized approximately eighteen months later that I had not seen any squirrels on the lawn for a long time. At first I simply thought it was interesting. Then I thought that it was actually odd because it had been such a long time since I had even seen a squirrel on the lawn. I had seen them running along the fence and the cable wires that ran from the backyard to the utility pole in front of the house so I knew they were still out there. I wondered why they had decided to leave the lawn alone. Well, for whatever reason, it was wonderful, so why question it. I am not sure at that time I even remembered how angry I had gotten about the squirrels or the fact that, after doing so, I had asked or wished for the Lord's help with that matter.

A few weeks later I had an argument with my wife about something and I felt angry and discouraged. The next few days I paced around the house bumping into things and talking out loud again as I prayed, "Jesus, help me; help me, Lord." A couple of days later the Lord spoke to my spirit and softly whispered: *if I could help you with the squirrels, I can help you with this, too*. It caught me off guard. I was dumbfounded. I had to digest what was said and contemplate the whole issue of the squirrels again. No one else knew what was going on in my thoughts regarding any of this, but just then my son, Daniel, out of the thin blue air walked into the kitchen and asked me, "Dad, where are all the squirrels you used to have?"

I stared speechlessly at Daniel for a second as though the cat just got my tongue.

"I saw Oscar's cat chasing one of them up a tree the other day," Daniel volunteered.

"You mean the gray cat that is in the backyard all the time?" I asked.

Daniel replied, "Yeah, that's Oscar and Steve's cat, Cheech."

I realized the neighbors' cat that we were both talking about had been in our backyard all the time, probably every day for the last eighteen months or more. It also validated that I was not the only one who realized the squirrels were gone. I realized that the Lord had agreed to help me because I asked for help and because he cared about me in spite of the fact that I had been a bonehead! The Lord honored my desire to be honest with him. He not only helped me but he forgave me. The Lord closed the mouths of the cats when the prophet Daniel was thrown into the lion's den and he sent a cat named Cheech to conduct routine patrol in my backyard and chase those squirrels up trees. My squirrel problem is gone. What is far more important than the squirrels being gone is that I repented, and my rotten attitude is gone, at least on that subject. I suspect that this was what the Lord really cared about far more than the squirrels. Now, I wonder what my next issue is going to be.

My frustration and anger over this problem with the squirrels was ridiculous and I know the Lord did not want me having a meltdown over something this trivial, especially when there are so many more important things in the Kingdom worth fighting over. If I had to lose sleep at night, why could it not have been for something more worthwhile? People are dying of starvation and I'm having an apoplectic fit of anger because my lawn isn't perfect! Yet, I suppose it was my frail attempt at trying to be honest with the Lord, both to acknowledge my lawn-anger problem and repent of my foul attitude that made a difference in all of this. The squirrels were intrinsically an inconsequential issue of my petty, selfish thinking and anger but they, nevertheless, served as a vehicle for ultimately addressing and identifying the more important issue of my overall attitude. All of this, including my desire to examine my own ugliness and immaturity, resulted through the medium of what we call conversation.

Sometimes people simply refer to this as *prayer*. If it is important to you, pray about it. If it robs you of your peace, pray about it. If it cheats you out of sleeping well at night, pray about it. If it's worth getting angry over, then pray about it. If it will potentially cheat you out of being the person you know the Lord would want you to be, pray about it. We all have issues. Some of our issues are childish and selfish. Most of them are associated with our surfeiting and desires, and not about the welfare of others, but this is reason enough to pray about them. As the Lord helps us to mature, he shows us how unconsciously selfish we often are. For this very reason, as I begin to grow and slowly mature, I pray a little more about others, and less about my lawn. But none of that would happen if I didn't pray at all. Did you love your child less when they were two years old? What does childhood have to do with any of this? It's simple: I am childish even now but the Lord still loves me and nurtures me and forgives me. He doesn't have pertinacious parameters that say when you grow up, son, then I'll talk to you. He speaks to me now, even though sometimes I'm a jerk. Will you stop being selfish or childish when you graduate from college? I doubt it. Look at it this way: prayer is an indispensible tool that connects you with the Father. The Father doesn't stop loving us because we are immature. He loves us in spite of our immaturity and our childish ways. If the Lord would help a bonehead like me, he'll help you, too!

Our prayers don't need to be eloquent or deeply mature. They just need to reflect what is really in our heart, even if it's ugly, or, especially if it's ugly. That's when we really need to pray, and, in my case, seek forgiveness. The hardest thing in life seems to be growing up and facing our own ugliness. From the time I was two years old I have always thought that it's *all about me!* Half the time I still think this way; I'm just too embarrassed to admit it. Your Father in heaven wants to be engaged with you even if you are still immature, and he loves you no less if you are. Jesus tried to convey this important message, and he emphasized that your Father in heaven hears your prayers, and that men ought to always pray, and faint not (Luke 18:1-7). The only qualifying caveats that I find in scripture are that we need to worship in spirit and in truth (John 4:24), which I believe is another way of saying, we need to approach God with sincerity and be honest. Our prayers should not be filled with arrogance and pride but rather with sincerity, honesty and humility (Luke 18:10-14).

All I know is that once I was lost, and now I am found. The Lord cares not only about your eternal destiny but also about whether you have enough food for lunch tomorrow. He cares about your broken heart, your marriage, your unemployment, your pending foreclosure, the fight you had with your son, your failing business and finances, your children, and your children's children. He cares about your future! He cares about you! God wants to be in relationship with you! Is there anything too difficult for the Lord?

CHAPTER 9

UNDERSTANDING FEAR AND CHOOSING TO OVERCOME IT

Fear is a ubiquitously powerful emotion that can effectively serve as a deterrent to success. In failure analysis, fear is pervasively present as a precursor to human endeavors. The Bible is full of such examples. Fear may very well represent the most powerful human emotion we experience, manifesting itself with a capacity to impair and distort sound judgment and efficacious critical thinking, and at the same time simultaneously induce a behavior known as *fight or fight syndrome,* which can trigger an instinctual survival reaction that evokes either panic or aggression.

Fear is not easy to qualitatively define or quantitatively measure because it's subjective by its very nature, so scientific terms are largely inadequate to fully describe how it works, in my opinion. The revered DSM (Diagnostic and Statistical Manuel of Mental Disorders) has a lot of esoteric diagnostic terms and labels for the manifestations of various behaviors including schizophrenia and a host of other disorders, and it offers many insightful tips for professionals to help them diagnose mental illness. While the DSM may provide many interesting diagnostic classifications it does not offer common cures, solutions, homeopathic remedies or practical advice to lay people, nor does it recognize the existence of the spirit world.

Fear simply defies homologous design, definition, application, and our full understanding of how it impacts others with any measure of specificity. Fear defies accurate predictability of how it will most likely impact individuals with devastating results, but not others, and the DSM doesn't explain it either. Fear is a truly a fascinating phenomenon.

In spite of all these elusive and sometimes ephemeral qualities, fear is socially well understood and accepted as a powerful human emotion. We can't precisely define how it will work scientifically in all cases, but everyone knows exactly how it works in principle. We simply have difficulty articulating it. Yet, if you ask a child why he cried, you will understand completely if he tells you, "The dog barked at me." What he most likely means is that the dog's aggressive behavior, manifested in the form of barking, frightened him. If you questioned the boy further, you might elicit other facts such as the dog advanced toward him, and maybe showed its teeth, by perniciously snarling or snipping at him. If you discover that the dog actually bit him or ripped his pant leg, you'll understand even better. The boy may not fear barking per se, as much as dog attacks, or threatening dogs.

Few of us probably understand the phenomenon of fear better than Satan. He is superbly accomplished at marketing it and at giving it away, free of charge. Despite fear's elusive, compositional qualities that are difficult to define, or its predictability factors, there is no emotion more powerful and destructive than fear which Satan can so effectively use as a weapon against us.

Fear is a powerful tool that blurs reality, destroys self confidence, courage, perseverance, and our faith in God. Horrific fear destroys all rationality and induces thoughts and feeling that all hope is gone, and that any viable option or recourse you may have considered is useless and impossible. In its most nefarious form, such thinking not only offers hopelessness and despair but it can promote acute depression that leads to suicidal behavior.

Fear can have such a driving force and impact on people in the stock market that it inhibits and restrains their normal trading choices, and that apprehension alone can effectively make people afraid to buy or sell stock for fear of losing money. Fear can indirectly make the stock market go down. For every action there is a reaction. If the perception is that things are likely to get better, faith will drive the stock market up.

Fear is such a powerful emotion that it tends to make people believe that perception is reality in spite of strong, factual evidence to the contrary. Fear can be based on real circumstances, facts and measureable data, but often fear becomes so blinding that facts get exaggerated and distorted. A perception of facts based on fear can become extremely misleading if fear is not carefully assessed, accurately processed and put into realistic perspective. For example, if someone only feels the pejorative emotion and power of fear to the exclusion of being able to see actual facts or consider other viable options, the result can lead to a false conclusion and produce catastrophic failure which may be irreversible. Cops have been known to shoot and kill unarmed, innocent people because they thought the person they shot was reaching for a gun. Such horrific tragedies can happen under circumstances, which are inherently dangerous, and potentially life threatening to begin with, and where there are usually high levels of stress and fear. The impact of fear on our decision-making is huge and it warrants our understanding of how this impacts our spiritual life and the choices we make.

The economic fears of 2008 were not imaginary. Some of the factors contributing to this staggering economic financial collapse included: pervasive financial greed, systemic corporate banking investment failures, fraud, a lack of financial integrity, and an absence of governmental regulation and control over investment schemes. Massive numbers of subprime loans failed, which probably should not have been funded to begin with in many cases. All of these economic conditions lead to a domino effect, producing unheard of numbers of home foreclosures, lost property taxes, lost revenues, reduced consumer spending, failed business ventures, and massive unemployment. In a market based on capitalism, free trade, good faith, and available credit, we can't inconsequentially bend rules and violate sound principles of financial management, stewardship and integrity and not expect something to go terribly wrong. The United States economic woes of 2008 will go down in history as the worst economic time since the Great Depression. Our passion for profit and prosperity far exceeded our integrity and our wisdom when it came to sound principles of financial management.

The biggest banks and auto manufacturers in the United States began failing in 2008 and conventional bank loans and the availability of new credit, for a period of time, came to a screeching halt. The Federal government recently handed out billions of dollars to various companies in tax dollar loans as a gesture of CPR to these dying corporations. The CEO's of these companies received millions of dollars in bonuses, despite their lack of acumen and failed leadership. Traditionally healthy business growth, as we have known it in the past has come, at least temporarily, to a standstill. Almost every business you hear of has been faced with cut backs or reductions of some kind, including layoffs. Major chain stores have gone out of business. The stock markets have been devastated with horrific losses. Individuals and corporate investment profits have been decimated. World trade has been impacted. Consumer spending has dropped, largely out of economic fears, putting some companies out of business. Thousands and thousands of people have lost their jobs. Real estate sales and property values have dropped dramatically while foreclosures have gone up through the roof. This chain reaction ultimately has turned into a global financial crisis. We're not completely out of the woods yet, but we will eventually get out of this mess. As of a couple of days ago, the stock market jumped upward over two hundred points just over the good news that Wells Fargo Bank had measurably good profits for the first quarter of 2009. The fact that any bank had good news to report after last year is a beautiful thing. Things are going to gradually get better economically.

This entire economic crisis, with as many contributing factors as there are, and as complicated as it may be because of the shear number of deceitful players in the game, could be described with these few words: there was an absence of integrity and good stewardship at every level where failure occurred and an absence of safeguards at some levels. The few safeguards that did exist were ignored and disregarded.

Everyone has heard the proverb that there is nothing new under the sun (Ecclesiastes 1:9). Nothing in my view could be more true, even today. Although there are new tools, toys, green technologies and never ending varieties of Viagra medicines being developed to enhance your sexual pleasure, the world is staggering from economic recession, greed, social injustice, corporate fiduciary malfeasance, and governmental corruption. If we emphasized and promoted ethics, integrity, responsibility and social justice half as much as broadcasting networks remind us that our television signals are going to change from analog signals to digital signals, we would be doing a good deed and we wouldn't even have to label it as being a *religious* thing. It's too bad the *second coming* does not get this kind of notoriety.

The world is no different today than when Jesus chased the money handlers out of the temple with a whip and overthrew their tables. The issue of righteous stewardship was an issue in the days of Jesus and it has been an issue for all of us in 2008. Although we have laptops, colored graphs, WiFi and cell phones today, men's heart have not changed. The greedy condition of the human heart has not changed. We still need new hearts. The whole world needs Jesus.

There are some valuable lessons that can be learned out of the economic tragedies of 2008. Here are a few to be considered.

First, and foremost, when it comes to big things which include your destiny, your future, your soul, your peace of mind, your wealth, your security and well-being, put your trust in the Lord, and not in mammon. If you have lost everything because you trusted others or because you controlled your own empire, this would be the perfect time to surrender what little you have left to the Lord of Hosts, because he can turn things around and make you prosper again, give you new hope, and he is the master at repairing and restoring that which was lost, broken and destroyed. The Lord can restore your hopes and dreams and give you a future that is sure. He will never leave or forsake you and he will lead you and guide you if only you ask him. If you walk with the Lord, adversity will not go away, but the Lord will help you overcome it, and fill your heart with joy while others are gnashing their teeth.

If you put your trust in others or rely on your own wisdom there will always be the possibility of future catastrophic failure. Without God, your worst nightmares could happen again. If you learn to put your trust in the Lord, your heart will never succumb from fear because the Lord will never fail you. He will go through the storm with you, empower you, and give you peace of mind in spite of the storm. Always remember that if you walk faithfully and circumspectly before the Lord with obedience and faithfulness, the Lord can circumvent the storm. He can rebuke the storm and make the wind cease, or he can guide you right through the epicenter of the worst storm hell can throw at you and you will not be harmed because his hand of protection is around you. All things are possible with God. You do not have to allow fear to rule in your life.

The second lesson we can learn is to never allow yourself to think that disaster cannot knock on your door because you have large barns filled with many good things. Be careful in your thinking to not allow wealth, prosperity and things to define who you are. Adjust and refocus your mind-set so that you surrender unto the Lord everything you have, your wisdom, your pride, every talent, possession, and remind yourself that everything you have belongs to the Lord, and you are his steward. Love the Lord your God with all your mind, with all your strength, and with all your heart and with all your soul. Then take comfort in knowing the Lord is your source, your provider, your comforter, your healer, and your strength. The Lord is your Rock, if your foundation is built on him.

The Psalmist wrote: *God is our refuge and strength, a very present help in trouble. Therefore will not we fear, though the earth be removed, and though the mountains be carried into the midst of the sea. The Lord of hosts is with us; the God of Jacob is our refuge* (Psalms 46:1-2,7). Jesus described end times saying there would be distress and perplexity among the nations and men's hearts failing them for fear and for looking after those things which are coming on the earth: for the powers of heaven shall be shaken. And when these things begin to come to pass, then look up, and lift up your heads, for your redemption draweth nigh (Luke 21:25-27). The whole world is being shaken up. The Bible speaks of the earth and the heavens being shaken, so that which cannot be shaken may remain (hebrews 12:26-27). Solid principles of faith in God and righteous stewardship will never be shaken or diminished by scientific assay, the bright light of integrity, accountability, strong, gusty winds or economic tsunamis.

A third lesson is never allow your past failures or losses to define who you are today, regardless of whether it was your fault or someone else's. God looks at us through his eyes with mercy, love, and forgiveness and sees the potential within each of us for what we can be as his sons and daughters. Don't allow economic failure, famine, unemployment, or fear to limit your vision of what your future can be. Guilt can motivate us to change our behavior but often we just beat ourselves up with it and God isn't in the business of beating people. He is in the business of saving people! The past is far less important than the future. Choose to walk with God. Surrender your life to him. Start practicing good stewardship now and don't fool yourself into thinking you will be motivated to do so when economic times get better. Do it now!

A fourth caveat or lesson to take from all of this is that earthly governments, run by imperfect people, will never suddenly become righteous without the blood of Jesus. Green technologies, which we in fact need, will not turn the world into a new Garden of Eden, where sin no longer thrives, and everyone will suddenly have more economic prosperity and blessings than they can bear. Satan isn't going to unexpectedly change his character and start helping people with employment, food, clothing, shelter and medicine, and he certainly isn't going to urge you to start following Jesus. Satan is going to spend eternity in hell and he wants to take you with him if he can. Don't fool yourself into thinking that sin and prosperity coexist in harmony and that we will all suddenly love each other without Christ's help and forgiveness.

The world is in a tenuous state of instability and it's not going to get any better; it will ultimately lead to Armageddon. The scriptures clearly foretell this event and the United States isn't going to stop it by pleading with rouge nations to stop developing nuclear weapons. We might as well tell them they can't have electricity because we're not sure they will use it responsibly. If we look at the conflict in the Mideast, the terrorism that is proliferating, and the countries that are developing nuclear weapons who profess a hatred for and a desire to destroy Israel, Armageddon is not that far away. Please don't misunderstand where my heart is coming from. I am not suggesting that we roll over, abdicate, or abandon ship. We, along with our neighbors, need to fight against terrorism but no political agenda is going to stop biblical prophecy from occurring.

Finally, understand that things will get better for those who put their faith in God. Things will not get better for those who put their trust in the wisdom of mankind. I am excited about the future, only because I know Jesus as my savior and because I feel his presence and Holy Spirit in my life. I have victory and joy in my life because of Jesus and his sustaining power, not because of anything else on earth. If not for the cross and work that Jesus did to redeem us, there would be plenty to be fearful about. If we walk with Christ beside us we don't have to be fearful. Always remember that!

Everything earthly produced through manufacturing, everything in the service industry field, and everything created from the information technology (IT) field is conceived and designed with only one thing in mind: profit, which ultimately translates into *money*. We spend most of our waking moments in life learning and preparing to work, then actually working most of our lives to earn money so we can have a home, food to eat, clothes to wear, a toy for our children and maybe a vacation and a little fun along the way. We hope to still have something to leave for our children or grandchildren.

For better or for worse, your life is directly impacted by money. It almost seems sometimes that life is "all" about money. We tell our own small children that this isn't true, but we go through life as though it were true. The pursuit of making a living is not wrong. A laborer is worthy of their wages. Neither money, nor the labor devoted to making a living, is intrinsically right or wrong. Jesus acknowledged this when he said your heavenly Father knows that you have need of these things.

The problem is simply that we ferociously cling to everything we possess. The first thing a two-year-old learns to say with utter passion, when they are around other children is "mine." As we get older and more sophisticated our toys become more expensive, but nothing really changes. Collectively, we have a hard time parting with money or giving much of it away in order to stop world famine, hunger, disease or poverty. Precious few are willing to part with their wealth or give their lives so that others may live. The Bible says that the love of money is the root of all evil (I Timothy 6:10). That is a pretty powerful and staggering thought and yet it is very important to be clear that the scripture does not say or imply that money itself is evil. Money is like a powerful tool or form of energy. It can be used for good or evil. Like fire, you can use it to warm your house, or burn it to the ground with explosive force.

What does fear have to do with anything? More than you might think. If we were not so afraid and we actually trusted Jesus, we would be more willing to part with our wealth and possessions and we would be more willing to take risks and chances in life to help others. We wouldn't simply entertain a notion that Christ might help us; we would expect his help and provision and have faith that he would provide it for us. Without thoughtfully realizing all the precursors which influence our choice, we embrace the fear that Jesus won't walk with us and protect us, rather than embrace the faith that he will. We take all sorts of risks in life to get ahead but not to help others. The world is engaged in a relentless pursuit of success. Let's explore this for a moment. Success and failure in life are often intertwined with parallel opportunities and choices that are influenced by either fear or courage. The issue of whether faith or fear will reign is a battle, but pragmatically speaking it's more of a choice. This battle over choice, choosing to practice faith and courage and overcome fear, has widespread application to both spiritual and earthly matters. It impacts not only the quality of our own lives, but it also impacts others by virtue of the fruit we produce or fail to produce for the Kingdom of God. This warfare, which we all face and the ensuing results of whether we overcome and prevail, impacts people all around the world, many of which are suffering in great need.

If we look with honesty and ask ourselves, what would it take to make the world a better place, two simple things immediately come to mind that most of us could hopefully agree on and neither one involves shoving religion down anyone's throat: the sharing of global resources and common standards of morality. In other words, taking care of each other on a global level like a good, loving family takes care of each of its members. We don't always agree on what is moral or immoral, to be sure, but laws against murder rape and theft are all based on common values of morality. Jesus spoke about morality and a lot about money. One such parable of morality was the one of the "good Samaritan" who helped the man lying on the side of the roadway that had been robbed and beaten. Helping the man who was robbed and beaten was not based on whether he belonged to the right organizations or not. We don't have to fix anyone or make them join our church, let alone coerce them into signing a document that says they accept Jesus. We just need to love people and help those around us. Jesus does the saving.

As Christians, we are connected to one another and with the world through our love for Christ. We are commanded to love our neighbors as ourselves. Picking up our crosses and following Jesus in service to the world around us is the heart and soul of our faith. It is impossible to do any of this if we don't share our resources.

If we desperately cling to everything we posses, as though we own it, we are already greatly confused. We are stewards of everything we possess, including every breath of air we breathe. It all belongs to God. When you die, you won't take any of it with you. As John Ortberg writes and preaches, "It all goes back into the box." (When the Game Is Over, It all Goes Back in the Box, Zondervan Publishers, 2007).

What the world suffers from is less a matter of available scientific knowledge, or a lack of good intentions, and more a matter of selfishness and indifference. Preserving our resources and our own good way of life to the exclusions of others goes contrary to giving our lives away in service to others. A lack of knowledge may be a killer, especially when it comes to disease or our understanding of how to cure cancer, Parkinson's disease, Alzheimer's, AIDS and the like, but the real problem is in our heart. The problem is we don't want to share our lunch money with someone else. If someone has to go hungry, it might as well be the other guy. This going to the cross business costs us too much. There are people dying by the thousands because they lack sleeping nets to protect themselves from mosquito bites that carry Malaria. Children are dying of malnutrition, starvation and disease but none of these problems are the result of mankind not understanding the cause of hunger, Malaria, or, the science of how to make inexpensive sleeping nets that protect people from mosquitoes.

Through the Internet, knowledge is instantly available to everyone. It is not an absence of knowledge, nor a matter that electricity doesn't work in certain continents, nor some silly theological debate over Pre-Tribulation or Post Tribulation that kills mankind. It's our selfish and sinful nature and our collective failure to practice what we preach and simply do the right thing! Often it isn't even an issue of confusion over what is right or wrong, although sometimes that happens, too. By and large it boils down to just doing what we know, believe or suspect to be the morally right thing. If we only did just what we thought was "probably" the right thing in Jesus' eyes we would be doing more than we are now. Like the popular Nike commercials say, just do it!

Herein lies the problem. Doing the right thing and succeeding at anything that is worthy is rarely easy and it often requires faith and courage. The "right thing" always seems to include good stewardship and stewardship is not limited to money. What obstructs faith, courage and good stewardship? More often than not fear does. Fear alone holds many back. Even if you think you know what the "right thing" is and you are committed in principle to following that ideology, the actual "doing" is the killer. And, why might that be? We count the cost of doing the right thing or of helping others and decide it's too high. Aren't you glad Jesus did not do that? We are afraid of all the many obstacles we perceive we will face or, actually encounter.

The consequence of our inaction is so horrible that it is uncomfortable to even speak of these things, so we usually don't. We make excuses for why we don't. We often just turn and look the other way because no one wants to look directly into the eyes of dying people who desperately need help. By turning our horizontal gaze away, we effectually close our eyes to these problems. Turning the other way is less painful than looking directly at the terminally ill, while feeling incompetent to change their circumstances. Instead of inquiring in the affirmative, *show me what I can do*, Lord, we proclaim to ourselves what we *cannot* do, and thereby conclude, I can't save all of them, and so we end up saving no one. We conclude the cost is too high. We conclude that my little bit won't help that much in the long run. I gave CPR to a baby who died and it felt like my own child died, but I also gave CPR to those who lived. The little bit of air I gave some made a difference. Which dying person should I have not bothered with? Your loose coffee change could save lives.

We are afraid of not succeeding, that the outcome won't be efficacious and that there won't be enough in it for me. We are afraid of the dangers inherently present with giving ourselves away and trusting God. We are afraid of the cross. We are afraid Jesus won't be there to help us when these dangers arise; after all, he was sleeping when the boat was about to sink during the perfect storm. We are afraid Jesus will be sleeping while we are perishing. We are terrified of death, and afraid that Jesus won't be in town, if we fall into harm's way. We are afraid that we will die just like Lazarus, when troubles rise, and we take no comfort in knowing Jesus can raise us from the dead because we are so terrified of death itself. We lack Kingdom vision for tomorrow because we are worrying about whether God will still feed the birds today. Oh, dear Jesus, help us overcome our fears, and increase our faith and courage!

Imagine with me, just for fun, what your faith, behavior and life in Christ would look like if you never had to overcome the obstacle of fear. That would give you a big advantage. Consider what your life potentially might look like if you had absolutely no fear.

We would all become giants in the faith because nothing would seem impossible to us. No battle or threat would intimidate us. We would all be successful because we would never run away in defeat from any present day Goliath or challenge in life. We would all be successful warriors. If we applied any of this imagination to Israel they would not have wandered in the desert for forty years unnecessarily because of their fear and subsequent disobedience. They would have thrown a huge celebration party at just having an opportunity to follow Joshua and Caleb into the Promised Land.

We would never face the fear of financial death or collapse. Satan would not be able to work us over into exhaustion with torment over all the things that might go wrong. We could always tithe and give abundantly to the works of God all over the world, because we would never fear that our own resources would run out. It would be like knowing Jesus and actually trusting him. Imagine that! Money would be viewed only as an object used for trading or paying for goods and services, and not as any means of security, power or wealth or source of influence. Money would stop being sacrosanct as we would stop viewing it as a tool of power, security or prestige. We would place no distorted emphasis on money because it would be thought of like asking for another glass of water in a world where there is no shortage of fresh, clean water. If you needed more, you never had to worry that God would not provide it when you needed it, or say to you, not today buddy; I'm going to test your faith first! And if there were a test of faith, you would never worry that you might fail the test.

Wouldn't it be great if we could just stop doubting and being fearful whether we could trust God or whether he would always meet our needs? We could even stop worrying about whether our faith was good enough or strong enough if we had no fear.

We would never have a fear of failure because we would always know that, first of all, the battle belongs to the Lord, and that it is not all about us anyway, and that even if we did make an honest mistake, God is for us, so who can be against us? We would know that any error we made could and would be forgiven. No endeavor, project or assignment would result in any kind of fear. Just give that assignment to Mikey; he's fearless and always successful! No amount of pressure could ever make you fearful if you did not have to deal with this obstacle.

No disease or life threatening condition or accident would make you worry or fearful because death itself would not be enough to raise your blood pressure. Satan could attack you from every angle, but you would not have fear from any of his tormenting arguments. Death itself would not bother you in the least because you would simply have no fear of it, just like you don't fear walking from your dining room into your living room. Death would represent nothing more than changing locations. In the absence of fear, there would be no anxiety about where our next location would be as we walked through the curtain of death. You would always know with an abiding conviction that the Lord is on your side and that he is with you at all times and no amount of crisis, circumstances or argumentative spin could make you succumb to fear. One triumph after another would develop faith like no one has ever seen before, because no amount of fear could ever weaken you or set you back.

Everyone would admire you because you would be just like Jesus, fearless, sleeping in the back of the boat while the storm rages. That might cause some problems. Such success might even start leading to other problems for you, such as the absence of humility. You might even start thinking success came from your power.

Put bluntly, you would have a very unfair advantage over everybody else and your faith in God and your commitment to walk in his ways would never get fully tested. You would effectively escape all quality control analysis by not going through the entire testing process and crucible. The fining pot is for silver, and the furnace for gold; but the Lord trieth the hearts (Proverbs 17:3). God allows trials and tests to come our way but remember: God hath not given us the spirit of fear; but of power, and of love, and of a sound mind (2 Timothy 1:7). This also means the Lord is not the author of confusion!

Stress is a fascinating subject but not necessarily synonymous with fear. Understanding how some of this works can be helpful. We don't have to be experts on this subject. We just need to have some basic knowledge and understanding and practice reasonable wisdom in how we deal with our fears. Fear does not have to rule our lives. Part of knowing how to handle fear involves learning how to better understand how fear impacts most of us.

I want to emphasize I don't know everything there is to know about fear or even how it works because I am not a psychiatrist, a doctor or a social scientist, and I am not terribly interested in the precise molecular chemistry of how this works, anyway. Moreover, I am far less concerned about what the world says about fear than I am in what Jesus says about it. I am interested in some of the physiological and practical applications of fear because I want to recognize it and overcome it in my daily life, especially with important decisions I need to make. Applying this knowledge to my spiritual life is even more important to me, because my goal it to trust and follow God and not allow fear to rule me, or be the deciding factor in my decision making. I am just a regular guy, probably like you, and not some giant who has never experienced fear. Learning how to practice the right kind of faith and courage enables us to overcome fear and that is exactly what I want for my own life.

We live such frenetic lives in such a chaotic world that half of us are on the verge of having a nervous breakdown on any given day of the week. Stress and fear are sometimes thought of as being "bad" things. To draw this conclusion would not only be a gross over simplification of the subject, but it would also reflect a misrepresentation of the truth under many circumstances. As we learn that everything in life is not all black and white, so it is with fear. Some forms of mild stress and fear are actually good, just like some kinds of bacteria in your mouth are actually good, so thank God that you don't live in a world where nothing exciting or interesting ever happens. Thank God for roller coasters and amusement parks and certain kinds of bacteria. (Ask your dentist if you have questions about good bacteria.) Remember, God is, himself, adventurous and very exciting, and he can take your breath away without taking your life away.

I view fear as an elevated form of stress. The perception of danger, for example, helps facilitate one's mind-set to be in a condition of high alert. Such a state of mind does not have to reflect fear or panic necessarily. For example, one might simply recognize the possibilities and dangers that are present but control your thinking and emotions so that you can make a reasonable and sound decision. For example, say I am in uniform working the street and I confront a bank robber. If the bad guy refuses to obey my police commands to put both hands high in the air, and he starts reaching for his waistband and pulls out a gun and starts lifting his gun toward me, I am going to shoot him.

A mind-set that accurately perceives dangers doesn't necessarily eliminate fear, but with training it can minimize it and control it to a degree in which I can still function and have control over my own behavior. You don't allow your mind to run wild with all the possibilities of what could happen, nor do you try to assume what the eventualities will actually be. At this stage you simply do not know what the outcome is going to be. You are going to find out, very soon, but we are still a few nano seconds away from crossing that bridge. You simply don't know how everything is going

223

to unfold until it happens. We have to deal with it one step at a time. All of life is this way, one day at a time, except you can have Jesus with you if you choose. Success in either police work or your spiritual life requires discipline and practice.

I made hundreds of dangerous felony arrests at gunpoint with this state of mind but never had to shoot anyone. While rolling in the dirt with a twenty-one-year old suspect under the influence of cocaine, I felt him reaching for and trying to pull my gun out of my holster. Another officer was with me and all three of us were rolling on loose gravel on the sloped shoulder of a roadway. This kid was like a slippery pig and neither my partner nor I could manage to get an effective control hold on the suspect. Neither my partner nor I could afford to take our hands off the suspect to reach for our radios to call for more help. The minute I thought I was starting to get a grip on the suspect's wrist or hand, he would slip free and start trying to grab my gun again.

This produced an intense surge of fear because I realized this was not simply a wrestling match anymore; the suspect's actions had elevated this conflict into a life and death struggle. I had to overcome the fear. The fear actually produced an additional surge of adrenaline. We got the kid handcuffed and no one got hurt. This kid will never know how close he came to an escalation of force on my part. Two more seconds of struggling and groping to take my gun away and I was prepared to hit this kid in the head with a steel flashlight, something I would not have normally considered doing, except that my life was literally in danger and the life of my fellow officer. We could have both been killed if this kid got my gun and shot us. Hitting the kid on the head with a flashlight might have possibly killed him, but it would have been less deadly than shooting him, something we could have legally done, and that's what I was trying to prevent. I didn't want to kill him.

Fear can alert you to danger so that you can prepare yourself for a life and death encounter. It can help you to preserve your life and defend it. Stress and fear can make you ready for battle! It can give you a big boost of energy all of a sudden, in an instant, right when you need it. The adrenaline rush that comes with fear is addictive and exciting. Cops love it. In law enforcement you wouldn't want to walk into some situations without any fear because it would put you at a disadvantage.

The ideal state of mind, if you will, is to not be oblivious to circumstances or threats around you, but be in a relaxed state of awareness and alertness, which allows you to perceive, measure and assess threats and then be prepared to take appropriate action. Our spiritual faith can serve us well and be analogous to this principle if we develop it.

You might be thinking that we are not all wired the same way and that you hate conflict, danger, violence and other forms of crisis. You are absolutely correct, as we are not all mentally or emotionally wired the same. I used to joke with my wife and tell her I deplored violence, but she just laughed at me!

We are all different, otherwise no one would want to be a librarian, no one would read to the blind, and no one would sing high "C" notes. We would all be members of Delta Force wearing fatigues singing "C-130 rolling down the strip," as we jumped out of a perfectly good aircraft with camouflage war paint on our faces.

During my police career, I woke up every day hoping I would face Jack the Ripper, have to chase him, and eventually go *mano a mano* with him to the death before subduing him and taking him to jail. My wife understood just how misguided and sick I was and so she would ask me in the morning, "Honey, is anyone going to jail today?" My answer would vary a little depending on whether she asked that precise question or not. If she did not ask "the" question then I would spontaneously blurt it out on my own: "Glory to God, somebody is going to jail today!" It represented a statement of faith on my part that there would be giants and battles to face and that justice and good would prevail over evil.

If my wife did ask "the" question (as to whether anyone was going to jail) I would reply tongue and cheek, "One can only hope, sweetheart, one can only hope...but I pray to God they resist arrest so I can use only that amount of force which is necessary to overcome resistance, so I can take them to jail." This became way too long-winded and technically legalistic and it stopped sounding funny, so eventually I truncated the saying down to, "I hope they resist arrest so that I can kick their butt and then take them to jail!"

Excessive use of force is a very serious subject and because there are horrible abuses, which unfortunately take place, I almost hesitate to share the private thoughts of joking between my wife and I, but I do so anyway, because I don't condone excessive force of any kind, and I have never done anything like this to feel guilty about in my career. Moreover, I joke about almost everything including subjects that are of a serious nature. Part of the reason cops do this is because the nature of the stress we deal with is so overwhelming, humor is a wonderful, and healthy way to dissipate some of that tension, so that we don't all end up with ulcers or in some psychiatrist's office drooling on ourselves. I can also tell you that I have never been accused of anything worse than being rude and officious in my career, so, please don't read anything sinister into my humor about wanting to kick butt, and then take crooks to jail.

For me, it was never a matter of wanting to kill anyone; nor did I. On the other hand, I got injured a number of times arresting bad guys, but none of my injuries was life threatening, thank the Lord! Like a good football game in which you can hardly wait for the game to begin, so it was for me, working the street each day. I wanted most days to be the most exhilarating day of my life. I wanted that day to offer the adventure of a lifetime. There were also some days you hoped nothing happened, and of course, those would be the days you had to chase some Philistine through alleys, backyards and over fences.

Let's be clear about this. Anyone who truly wants to face conflict, danger, violence and fight with people all the time has serious pathological issues. In this regard, I am not joking.

I worked for several police agencies over my 28-year career. Each agency had to follow state and federal screening protocols for hiring people that carry guns. They sort of want to know that you won't shoot the little old lady in the crosswalk because you thought she looked suspicious wearing a heavy coat in warm weather or because she waved her cane at you when you yelled at her to hurry up. They put you through a tough background investigation, a polygraph exam and a psychological screening process that goes for hours on end with written questions about whether you have stomachaches, dark stools, or whether you are afraid of the dark or hear voices at night. This is followed by an in-depth interview with a psychiatrist. By the time you get to the psychiatrist you are so happy to be talking with a human being instead of answering scantron questions with a number 2 pencil that you no longer care what anyone thinks.

I remember one doctor asking me why would I want to be a police officer. I actually started laughing in this interview and I said, "Well, I was hoping you were going to tell me that because it seems to me that anyone who really wants to do this job has to be a little crazy himself." The doctor politely smiled and perhaps agreed.

The cumulative effect of stress on the human body is a killer. It's mostly what does cops in after long careers of daily stress for years on end.

What are some of the physiological symptoms of acute fear? I have seen grown men urinate on themselves at the time of their arrest when guns are pointed at them and they have no where else to go. Others do worse. The physiological symptoms that fear can produce are quite amazing and debilitating. I have seen professional people like medical doctors have difficulty speaking, answering questions or providing basic information at the scene of a crisis out on the street. This is foreign to them since the stress they normally encounter is in a controlled environment or other setting. All of a sudden their whole world is out of control and they can hardly speak or think clearly. No one is completely immune from this, not even cops.

In police firearms training the decision to shoot sometimes involves threat assessments of shoot or don't shoot, and the training becomes very intense and real. Cops learn to cope with and manage stress, but they are not immune from it as I mentioned. One of the things in firearms training that range masters talk about is a concept designed to give officers an understanding of what they may experience in an actual gun battle.

We are told that at the moment of life and death, where good guys come face to face with bad guys, gun battles have sometimes ensued at a close distance of ten feet or less where both parties exchange multiple gunshots at each other and both miss all their shots. How can that happen you say? The stress is so profound that it affects one's hearing, vision, the ability to process information accurately or maybe even at all, and it elevates your heart rate, pulse and breathing to the point that sweat runs off your forehead and people can't speak normally or at all. Sometimes people shake so hard they can't hold their gun sufficiently so as to properly aim. Often, people say it throws everything into slow motion. Sometimes, a shooter's ability to process information efficiently is so impaired by the stress of the event that the person cannot remember certain details until days afterward.

Some officers suffer with nightmares after a shooting incident and they are never really the same again. Like veterans returning from war, one such police action or overseas conflict can leave physical, emotional, and mental health scars for years or sometimes for life. To say that stress or fear can be debilitating at times would almost be an understatement!

When suspects are finally confronted with the moment of truth (arrest) their choices are limited. You can fight with the police, submit to arrest or flee. It's called *fight or flight syndrome*. It's inherently dangerous for all involved because fear and emotion and pure panic can take over and lead people to do things they would normally not do. None of the criminal behaviors associated with fear at this level have anything to do with rational thinking, but they do involve choices.

Young men without much life experience are extremely dangerous and they lack the street sage of an older convict. Young kids barely out of their teens are sometimes willing to shoot and kill a cop over nothing rather than go to jail. Likewise, some older convicts decide in advance they will not go back to prison again and they are prepared to kill, if necessary, rather than let someone arrest them. Fear can be a dangerous thing if it is not controlled.

We cling to life so desperately that a real and present danger of dying can make people lose self-control and make them become hysterical. Drowning people often fall into this category and they will cling to and fight with their rescuer to the point that both drown. Drowning people are dangerous.

I had such an occasion as a young boy myself. I was twelve and my friend was fifteen years old. We witnessed a kid in the middle of a lake going down and screaming for help. We had to swim as fast as we possibly could just to reach him in time. It must have been a hundred yards or maybe more. I was an excellent swimmer. Yet, all I know is that I was absolutely exhausted from just swimming to reach him and that is when the real fight began. The drowning victim was totally gripped by fear and he was completely hysterical and gasping for air and trying to clutch and grab onto my friend who was trying to position himself behind the victim. The victim's eyes were wildly darting from one side to another and he looked like he had no idea who we were or even what we were trying to do. This poor kid should have known who we were because we were all part of a small church group, but he did not recognize us. He was hysterical in every sense of the word. The victim grabbed my friend in a life and death panic attack and both went down under the water. It terrified me because I realized then that this wasn't only a rescue, it was turning into a life and death fight for all of us.

When both came back up to the surface my friend had to forcefully break away from the drowning victim to get air himself and not get pulled down under again. I took my turn with the victim and struggled with him too, but I wouldn't let him lock onto me or pull me under the water because I could see how dangerous this was becoming. The victim was wildly flailing his arms trying to grab both of us. When a drowning person tries to pull you down under with them, everything changes. The victim clutches and grabs at you or anything they can get their hands on, hysterically trying to climb, as it were, out of the water.

My friend finally slugged the victim as hard as he could in the jaw and it almost knocked him out. It stunned the victim and knocked him senseless for a brief second or two. This enabled us to get the victim's arms under control and get behind the victim's head so that we could tow him from behind, and, at the same time, keep his head and mouth above the water. The rescuer's arm went under and around the victim's chin and neck so that we could pull him backwards. As long as we kept his head above water and talked to him, he managed to do better and stopped fighting with us. There were a few moments of complete terror while saving this kid. If there had not been two of us to restrain this drowning kid, I don't know if everyone would have made it.

Take this example of the drowning kid and apply it to your life spiritually. Intense fear is often so gripping and terrifying that it cripples your ability at times to process information or think clearly. You can't hear, see, think or process information accurately. You could lose control of your bodily functions but not even be aware of it. Fear can make you completely forget who Jesus is and, of course, that is exactly what Satan wants, a sense of total panic so that we engage in <u>flight</u> syndrome and not fight syndrome. If we fight, and call upon the name of Jesus, the Lord will empower us and we might just decide to fight back and not abandon ship. Satan loves to see people run in fear. The very mention of the name of Jesus and he knows he has a fighter on his hands.

We can't completely eliminate encounters with fear because they are part of real life, but you can prepare yourself for them in much the same way as police officers do. Develop a mind-set that no matter what happens you are going to fight and not give up. Visualize yourself overcoming. Prepare yourself mentally and spiritually for battle. Develop your faith and war tactics and knowledge of what the word of God says as you would with any other kind of practical training. Learn to confront fear. Fear turns into a war of thoughts and words.

One of the things I strive for is to never allow fear to be a deciding factor in my decision making process when it comes to anything I know the Lord would want me to do, or that is otherwise desirable and righteous. Don't be automatically dissuaded from pursuing good things, for example, because you lack strength in yourself or because you might fail, or the journey might be tough, or because others might laugh at or criticize you. Don't run from a good challenge if you should be involved in it simply because your resources are limited. Think of what you can be when you are willing to do the right thing, and it's God's will for you to do it. The angel of the Lord came to Gideon and said: The Lord is with thee, thou mighty man of valor (Judges 6:12).

When God is on our side and telling us to do something, we need to view ourselves in that light. Gideon was the least of all his family and not some so-called mighty warrior. When God authorizes a covert operation and he asks you to lead a group of commandos, you need to look at yourself differently. You should not view yourself as the failure you were last year or the skinny kid who didn't make the football team in high school or college. When you walk in obedience to the commission the Lord has given you that changes everything. I want to overcome my fears and insecurities so that the angel of the Lord addresses me as, "thou mighty man of valor."

Acknowledging fear and addressing it with the help of the Lord makes you more battle worthy for the next event. I absolutely believe that the worst thing you can do is deny fear, make believe it's not there when it is, and never confront it or never learn to overcome it. Believe in your heart that fear can be overcome just like any other adversary. Are you a man or a mouse? Make up your mind that you are not going to hide under the bed the next time you feel fear, unless it involves a pretty waitress.

All levels of fear don't involve life and death, such as the drowning boy, thank goodness. Some days the battles are much smaller and the consequences less onerous. Sometimes we have to just laugh at ourselves because our fears are so childish that they become amusing. Allow me to share such a personal anecdote. I was six years old and I had just learned how to whistle. This was not just any whistle but rather a manly "wolf" whistle, you know, the ones boys give to pretty little girls. This unique whistle, as we all know, has a distinct message all its own, which affectionately says: Hey there! You good looking thing!

Well, I was sitting in a restaurant with my dad ordering breakfast. Our waitress came and took our order. I noticed she was drop dead gorgeous so, as she walked away, I whistled at her. I just learned how to do this and I needed to practice. It never entered my mind that my father was not only a man of the cloth, but one about as godly as Elijah, and that whistling at grown women in his presence might be a little embarrassing for him. What would he say if the waitress asked, "What have you been teaching this kid, Reverend Malmin?"

Well, I whistled at our waitress as she walked away because I certainly did not have the guts to do it while she stood there taking our order. To my surprise the waitress stopped dead in her tracks, just a few feet away, spun around like a ballerina and asked me with a big smile on her face, "Are you the cute little boy that just whistled at me?" Then she started walking toward me! I was absolutely terrified! I felt my heart pounding suddenly and realized it was getting hard to breath. I was afraid this woman might walk up to me and kiss me on the lips or perhaps snatch me right out of my seat and make me marry her in the kitchen or something. I wasn't old enough for any of this. I was sure my father couldn't stop it or help me either. I felt a sense of overwhelming fear!

Without any deliberation or hesitation I lied through my teeth like I had practiced this all week. I answered the waitress with complete boldness, "Oh, NO! That was my Daddy!" Jesus could have been sitting there with us and I still would have lied. I didn't even feel remorse about lying. It didn't even matter that my father was a minister; I threw my dad down like a sack of potatoes! That's how scared I was. The fear was amazingly real and though the story is amusing, the incident made me feel threatened.

Had the waitress questioned me any further, I was quite prepared to continue lying and I would have sworn an oath on a stack of Bibles. I looked at my father and he was absolutely dumbfounded and speechless. The look on his face seemed to say, what did I do to deserve this honor? The look on my face was, well, what did you expect, dude? She was walking right toward me like she might kiss me, or worse! Everyone in the restaurant laughed, except me. I've been in therapy ever since!

That is how fear works. If the stakes are high enough, we are all capable of having a meltdown. That is exactly what happened when Peter denied Jesus three time before the cock crowed. The other disciples all fled, too.

Why is fear such a big deal? It can completely distort your view about reality. Even if your assessment of the facts is pretty accurate, fear can distort your view of what Jesus can do. Fear tends to blind us of our options, but it is completely possible to overcome it. Fear can paralyze you from taking the appropriate action if you allow it to. There is no other emotion so gripping that renders people incapable of thinking or doing the right thing. I believe there is no other emotion as powerful as fear to render people helpless or defeat them from the pursuit of either earthly or spiritual goals in life.

The good news of Jesus is that he has overcome the world. After overcoming life and death on behalf of humanity, Jesus rose from the dead. Soon thereafter Jesus appeared unto his disciples and said, "Be not afraid" (Matthew 28:10). Jesus said, "All power is given unto me in heaven and in earth" (Matthew 28:18). This power was given to Jesus by God the Father after the work Jesus accomplished on the cross. The work of the cross is profound and it changes everything for all eternity. If Jesus has all power, over all things, then that includes life and death, and he certainly has power to conquer and dispel our whimsical fear. All we have to do is ask.

The Bible has hundreds of scriptures wherein the message spoken by God, angels, prophets and Jesus himself, over and over again, begins with these wonderful words: Fear not! Study the word of God. Scripture tells us that perfect love casts out fear (I John 4:18). As our faith and walk with Jesus deepens and matures, our confidence and trust in Jesus also increases, and we have fewer meltdowns because we begin to actually accept and believe the words of Jesus. Our faith and trust in him begins to replace fear. Perfect love casts out fear.

It isn't our goodness or greatness that gets us through hard times, but rather the Lord's provision, mercy, love and forgiveness. The Lord of hosts is mighty to save and heal to the uttermost, and there is nothing too difficult for the Lord. The key is simply to be honest and to confess our fears and weaknesses and ask God to walk with us and empower us so that we can overcome. Jesus said, *My grace is sufficient for thee; for my strength is made perfect in weakness* (2 Corinthians 12:9).

Why don't you try leaning on him and trusting him. He will never leave or forsake you.

CHAPTER 10

THE JUST SHALL LIVE BY FAITH; IT'S SHOW TIME!

Nothing good or worthy is ever easy!

Nothing will ever happen if you sit on the sidelines and watch everyone else playing the game. Get in the game! You will never know what might have been, if you never try.

If you always play it safe, even a good outcome will be boring. Nothing exciting ever happened without some risk. You will never achieve your full potential if you play it safe or hide under the bed. John Ortberg writes about this principle in his very successful book entitled, If You Want To Walk On Water, You've Got to Get Out of the Boat (Zondervan publishing, 2001).

Who wants to sit through 12 innings of baseball if the score is zero to zero and no one even tries to steal a base? We might as well go play a game of checkers or sit in our backyard and watch the grass grow.

Success never happens without hard work and without overcoming adversity along the way. There are a thousand people who will criticize you and speak all manner of evil against you for simply having vision. Another thousand people will tell you that logistically it can't be done, no one has ever done that before, and that you, of all people, lack the talent to do it anyway. What are friends for, anyway, right? They are unexpected little blessings of adversity to make you sink or swim.

We all face giants. Life is hard for everyone, not just ourselves. We want to think someone else has it easy, and then we list forty eighty reasons why. Invariably, we will be wrong on most counts. Even those who seem to have everything also have heartaches, personal failures and profound losses along the way. No one is immune from the conditions or hardships of life. Why do I even mention this little tidbit of truth? We all tend to do this, including me, but we need to stop comparing ourselves to everyone else. What everybody else does, doesn't matter. It's what we do that matters. Only what we do for Christ will last and none of us will be judged by the accomplishments of our neighbor. It largely doesn't matter what everybody else thinks. It's what the Lord thinks of our efforts and our works.

Often, people around us, sometimes that we work with or know well, will encourage us to sit on the sidelines, tell us that we are crazy for having any vision or faith, and that our best efforts will produce only failure, embarrassment and regret.

You'll see what I am talking about. Nothing good necessarily comes easy. Once we see the adversity or cost of what we thought was righteousness, we wonder if we should have even bothered taking the risk. We start questioning ourselves, even if we know better. Once your attitude starts downward, like a vehicle on a slight downgrade, no further gas or force is needed and, just like negative thinking, our vehicle starts to build momentum from its own weight. Somebody close to you will want to persuade you that faith and courage are dangerous roads to be avoided. Play it safe instead they will say. Here is a real life example of how I encountered this very issue.

Our detective bureau had worked a big narcotics case for about two years. It involved a bar on a major thoroughfare in the Bay Area where drugs were being sold and the owner of the bar was using the establishment as a cover to facilitate his drug trade business. A large raid was planned. Representatives from the State of California Department of Labor and ABC (Alcohol Beverage Control) were asked to participate and help us with shutting the business down and taking the alcohol license away from this business owner. It was a major investigation. Large quantities of drugs were coming out of this bar. The night of the raid undercover agents scored another good drug buy inside this bar. Arrest warrants and search warrants were going to be executed. The SWAT team was going to execute the arrest warrants.

Late in the afternoon, only hours away from executing these warrants, the operation team leader asked me if I would help them with interviewing the main suspect, the owner of the bar. The reason I was being asked was that I spoke conversational Spanish well enough to be able to ask simple questions and conduct simple interviews.

I had the impression that fellow officers who worked with me on the street always thought that my Spanish speaking abilities were far greater than they actually were. It wasn't that my Spanish was either a matter of being very good or very bad. The issue for me was that there was a difference between explaining a speeding citation to someone and a big narcotics case where a business would be shut down and their business license taken away. In this case, someone could potentially end up in prison for several years, based on my less than perfect Spanish speaking abilities.

I was both flattered and cautiously perplexed that I would be asked to do such a critical task when there were at least six other officers who spoke Spanish as their native language, who were obviously a hundred times more qualified than I was. We had at least five agencies involved in this operation. I asked the team leader, "Out of all these officers you can't find anyone else beside me to interrogate the number one bad guy?"

"That's right," he said, at which time he started naming people who I would have thought of who were out of town, sick, off duty and otherwise unavailable. It was amazing because normally this just would not have been a problem.

I reminded the team leader that I was not as fluent as these other officers and that I felt they would all do a better job than I could if they were available. I did not want to risk the operation because my Spanish was not flawless and I told the team leader that as long as he understood my limitations, I would be willing to help. I told him that I would go out of my way to be careful and thorough and do my best, but that I could not guarantee perfection or that questions would not be raised in court later on down the road as to how precise and accurate my Spanish was.

The leader said he understood my limitations and concerns but said he thought I would do just fine, and he reminded me that all anyone can ever do is just their best anyway. The job was mine and he thanked me in advance.

The SWAT team hit the joint and made numerous arrests and more dope was found inside the bar. The bar owner was brought to the station so that I could interrogate him. I had representatives from the Labor Department and ABC with me. Neither one of them could order two tacos without screwing up the order. I asked one of our Lieutenants to join me and witness the interview process so that I could have both moral support and another witness who spoke at least some Spanish.

I had the suspect brought into this little interrogation room and we all sat around this small table. ABC and Labor Department personnel were going to conduct a civil investigation to parallel our criminal investigation. They had questions of their own which they wanted me to ask of the suspect. I introduced myself to the suspect and made a little small talk. I tried to be warm and friendly. I told him I was a "gringo" and that my Spanish sucked. He laughed at my self-depreciating humor and said my Spanish was fine.

I explained to the suspect that I wanted to ask some questions of him, but only if he wanted to talk with me. I was very deliberate and careful to explain his Miranda rights to him so that he understood his legal rights completely. Only then did I begin to ask him questions. I pointed out again that my Spanish was not perfect and that I might not pronounce some words correctly or that at times he might not understand me. I asked him at this point if he understood my Spanish and he replied, "Yes, your Spanish is perfect. I understand everything."

I told the suspect that I wanted to be fair with him. I suggested that if either one of us said anything that the other did not understand we would stop and tell each other that. I emphasized how important it was that we both clearly understood each other. The suspect agreed to inform me if I said anything that he did not understand. This laborious effort to lay ground rules was going very well.

The suspect waived his Miranda rights and the interview process and interrogation began. We reached a critical junction in the interview about an hour and a half into the interrogation. The suspect initially told me that he did not realize drugs were being sold in his bar. Overcoming this statement and proving that it was false would be huge because essentially the whole case hung on this fact, especially if we wanted to close the business down and revoke both his alcohol and business license.

I told the suspect that I did not want to be disrespectful to him, but that I did not believe him and that the facts of the case were strong enough so that even a twelve-year-old child would not reasonably believe his story.

"Drugs are being sold right under your nose," I told him, "and you want to tell me that you did not know what was happening in your own bar? Come on, man!"

The suspect sighed and exclaimed, "Well, I did know, of course, but this is a dangerous business and it could threaten my whole family for admitting these things."

I praised the suspect for his courage in telling the truth and I told him I respected him for that. This one seemingly little admission broke the case wide open and we obtained a full, detailed confession, not only on the drugs, but about employees who were being paid wages under the table without taxes being withheld, and about other workers' compensation insurance fraud issues. And, remember, this guy told me that he understood my Spanish perfectly. The case looked like a rock solid, slam-dunk victory!

As do all felony cases, this one also had to go to court. Until a guilty plea is made, or the defendant is found guilty by a trier of fact, no one in law enforcement prematurely celebrates or dances in the end zone. This case got scheduled for a Preliminary hearing. A Pre-Lim, as we often call them (short for preliminary hearing), is a hearing in front of a superior court judge, and not a trial.

The sole purpose of the hearing is to determine whether there is enough evidence for the case to go to trial based on evidence presented in the hearing. That evidence must persuade a judge that there is both probable cause to believe that the defendant committed the alleged felonies, and that he is probably guilty of the alleged crime(s). If the judge feels that there is enough evidence to take the case to trial the defendant is "Held to Answer" and the case is sent to superior court for trial.

Very few felonies get resolved without going to at least a Preliminary hearing because the defendants have absolutely nothing to lose. The defendant doesn't have to prove anything. The burden of proof is on the prosecution to prove each element of the crime occurred.

One of our robbery homicide detectives made a point of telling me how crazy I had been for interviewing this suspect in such a big case, and he told me, in so many words, that I was absolutely stupid for helping out with this case. He volunteered this to me, not because I asked, but because all of us who were involved with the case had been subpoenaed for court and I guess he wanted me to know how he felt, especially if my efforts ended up losing the case. I didn't ask for his two cents, but he gave it to me apparently for my own edification. I was a junior detective with far less experience than he had, so I listened to his words.

The dick (short for detective) told me that the defense attorneys were going to rip me apart on the witness stand and that I would never want to go to court again after they finished with me. It made me wonder how he knew the

Defense consisted of multiple attorneys since we had not yet gone to court. My supportive fellow detective and teammate reminded me about the Dream Team that represented O.J. Simpson in that famous murder case from southern California a couple of years earlier. My colleague suggested to me even how it was going to happen. Johnnie Cochran and his Dream Team would have a linguist from Harvard University persuade either a judge or jury or both, that I could not order two tacos correctly without violating the defendant's rights, and that I had not only misunderstood everything the defendant had told me, but that the defendant, although polite and agreeable, had no idea what I said at any time during the interview.

Any of this sound familiar to you? It should! This is exactly how Satan whispers in our ear or how he uses the words of others to try and bring fear into our thoughts about how we are going to utterly fail and fall flat on our face. The enemy whispered in my ear that I was not a very good speaker. These professionals are going to laugh you right out of court and you will end up looking like a total fool. You are not a linguist, let alone an eloquent speaker or smooth talker! That, you may remember, was what Moses said to God, that he couldn't speak very well (Exodus 4:10).

As the days got closer to our court appearance my heart was failing me for fear. I would-ah, could-ah, should-ah but I didn't do what I knew I could've. I could have prayed about this and encouraged myself in the Lord but, of course, I didn't. I listened to the voice of defeat and then I entertained it. I nurtured it. I empowered the words of defeat instead of choosing to walk in faith and have courage. Often I find the Lord looks out for me even when I am too blind to see his mighty hand moving.

Out of total fear and panic I called the Deputy District Attorney who was assigned to handle our case. I don't even remember who this woman was, but she ended up being like an angel that completely encouraged me and helped put my feet back on solid ground. I told her how afraid I was that some Dream Team would bring some hot shot from Harvard into court and make me look like the idiot my fellow detective partner suggested I was. What I told her must have made her mad because she preached, quite without intending to, a short but powerful sermon to me over the telephone.

She reminded me that I only offered to help because I had been asked to do so. She pointed out that I volunteered to the team leader that I was not a Harvard linguist or world class translator, and she reminded me that no one has to be either. She told me that all of life is imperfect and that we only need people to do their very best and that I was available and willing to help when no one else was able or willing to step up to the plate at that moment in time.

The D.A. said to me, "Detective Malmin, it's my job to not let anyone maliciously rip you apart or humiliate you on the witness stand for doing a good job."

The D.A. went on to say that she would not allow anyone to do that to me. She said it with such force and conviction that I believed it. She then said,

"It's my job to protect you!" Those were the most comforting words anyone had ever spoken to me in police work.

Like other fellow officers, I was often the one on point, working the streets, answering 911 calls everyday, never fully seeing the peril that we were exposing ourselves to. This profession, which I was honored to be a part of, represented the *thin blue line* but I had never had anyone stand up for me in such a committed way. This was impressive. I always thought of it as my job to protect everyone else. It was like another professional telling me, for the first time in my career, that they cared about me and that my life mattered. The words of this D.A. stuck in my mind: "It's my job to protect you!" Wow! If you think about it, that is how the Lord looks at our trials. It is his job to protect us. You just walk in faith and leave the big stuff to God. It's his providence and pleasure to look out for us and protect us from the evil one. This whole thing was so encouraging to me it completely reversed my whole mind-set and my confidence and faith returned. I stood in front of the mirror and told myself, Yu da man, dude! It sounded pretty good, so I said it again! That's right! I'm talkin' to you, dude! Finally, I said: you got till sunset to get out of Dodge! I could hardly wait to go to court!

I went to court and the judge wanted to know how I learned Spanish. I explained how I lived in Brazil, South America, for several years and first learned Portuguese. I also began to learn Spanish, having had contact with lots of Spanish speaking people in South America. Back in California, as a police officer, I learned to speak Spanish while working the streets for many years. Working the street I arrested hundreds of drunk drivers who spoke Spanish. This experience help improve my Spanish speaking abilities. I told the judge that in the current case before him I had been able to communicate effectively with the suspect also. I testified as to how thoroughly I covered Miranda with the suspect and that the suspect volunteered that he understood my Spanish perfectly. The defendant sat at the table with his attorney and never disagreed with anything I said. The judge held the defendant to answer, and the case never even went to trial. The defendant pled guilty.

If we focus only on the possibility of failure we would never try anything. If we worry too much about looking foolish, we would never do anything. If we entertain the sophistry of Satan, we would regret everything.

Don't worry about looking foolish.

Just take each day one at a time with the state of mind that it's not all about you, it's about Kingdom business. Whatever it is that you do, do it with your whole heart as unto the Lord, and not unto men. If your heart is in the right place, you will be able to survive even if others mock you or speak ill about you, especially if you are mistreated for Christ's sake. This takes all of the glory out of being an MVP hero because you don't do any of it for your own profit or gain. You do it as unto the Lord. Having the mind of the Lord takes some of the fear of failure out of the equation. You can also let go of the attitude that you have to accomplish something special in your own strength, and be some sort of superstar. Part of overcoming fear and being willing to take risk is being able to live with what you do because you do it for the Lord. When our hearts are full of love and righteousness toward God, we somehow are less concerned about whether we look good or whether we look foolish. Just remind yourself this isn't a bathing suit contest. This is Kingdom business!

Without faith it is impossible to please God. Why is that, do you think? *For he that cometh to God must believe that he is, and that he is a rewarder of them that diligently seek him* (hebrews 11:6). The profession of our faith makes it clear, and forever establishes, and reminds us, that the victory belongs to the Lord and it eliminates any confusion that we might have had anything to do with saving ourselves. Our faith appropriately acknowledges, describes, and gives credit to the one who is the author of our faith, the one we put our trust in: his name is Wonderful, Counselor, The Mighty God, The Everlasting Father, The Prince of Peace.... (Isaiah 9:6).

Dr. Reverend Lockridge, a minister of the gospel, was best known for a six-minute description of Jesus Christ, entitled "That's My King!" If you download the video or audio version of this from the Internet it will bless you.

> My Bible says my King is a seven way king
> He is the King of the Jews, that's a racial King
> He's the King of Israel, that's a National King;
> He's the King of righteousness
> He's the King of the Ages
> He's the King of heaven
> He's the King of Glory
> He's the King of Kings and
> He's the Lord of Lords......that's my King!
> WELL....I wonder do you know him?
> David said, the heavens declare the glory of God
> and the firmaments show his handiwork.
> My King is a sovereign King, no means of measure can define
> his limitlessness,
> No farseeing telescope can bring into visibility
> the coastline of his shore and supply;
> No barrier can hinder him from pouring out his blessings,
> He's enduringly strong,
> He's entirely sincere,
> He's eternally steadfast,
> He's immortally graceful,
> He's imperially powerful,
> He's impartially merciful.
> Do you know him?
> He's the greatest phenomenon that has ever crossed the horizon of this world,

He's God's Son,
He's a sinner's savior,
He's the centerpiece of civilization,
He stands in the solitude of himself
He's august and he's unique
He's unparalleled
He's unprecedented
He is the loftiest idea in literature
He is the highest personality in philosophy
He is the supreme problem in higher criticism
He's the fundamental doctrine of true theology
He is the cordial, the necessity for spiritual religion
He's the miracle of the age
His deity is!
He is the superlative of everything good that you choose to
call him
He's the only one qualified to be an all-sufficient Savior!
I wonder if you know him today?
He supplies strength for the weak
He's available for the tempted and the tried
He sympathizes and he saves
He strengthens and sustains
He's God and he guides
He heals the sick
He cleansed the lepers
He forgives sinners
He discharges debtors
He delivers the captive
He defends the feeble
He blesses the young
He serves the unfortunate
He regards the aged
He rewards the diligent and
He beautifies the meek
I wonder if you know him?
WELL, this is my King!
He is the King
He is the key to knowledge
He is the well-spring of wisdom
He is the doorway of deliverance
He is the pathway of peace
He's the roadway of righteousness
He's the highway of holiness
He's the gateway of glory

Do you know him?
WELL, his office is manifold
Hs promise is sure
His life is matchless
His goodness is limitless
His mercy is everlasting
His love never changes
His word is enough
His grace is sufficient
His reign is righteous and his yoke is easy
And his burden is light
I wish I could describe him to you but he's...yeah...
He's indescribable!
Yes, he is! he's God!
He's indescribable, yes, he's indescribable!
He's incomprehensible
He's invincible
He's irresistible
WELL, you can't get him out of your mind,
You can't get him off of your hand,
You can't outlive him, and you can't live without him.
WELL, the Pharisees couldn't stand him but they found out
they couldn't stop him
Pilot couldn't find any fault in him
The witnesses couldn't get their testimonies to agree
Herod couldn't kill him
Death couldn't handle him and the grave couldn't hold him!
Yeahhhh!!!!!!
That's my King! That's my King!
And thine is the Kingdom
And the Power and the glory forever, and ever, and
ever.........

(There are several versions of this text by Dr. Lockridge which he gave around the country over the years)
[Dr. Shadrach Meshack (S.M.) Lockridge (March 7, 1913-April 4, 2000)] (http://en.wikipedia.org/wiki/S._M._Lockridge)

Our spiritual relationship and walk with God is built on the principle of faith. For all the wonderful reasons Dr. Lockridge just described, we follow, trust, obey and serve Jesus. We do this walking in faith and obedience to God's word.

Jesus is simply wonderful and divine. We love Jesus because he first loved us. We love Jesus because he is real and powerful and we feel a witness to the truth within our own spirit. We furthermore have faith in Christ because we have experienced the touch of his Holy Spirit and healing power in our lives. Jesus still answers prayer and we feel his guiding power, forgiveness, healing and presence in our daily personal lives. The word of God says, *the just shall live by faith* (Galatians 3:11).

Everyday is a new day of unpredictable events, challenges, blessings and obstacles.

As a young man, one of the most stirring sermons I ever heard was given by Charles Crabtree, some thirty five years ago at a military religious retreat in Germany, when I was in the Army. Reverend Crabtree, who pastored Bethel Church, in San Jose, California, at the time, was the retreat's guest speaker.

Reverend Crabtree preached a simple but powerful message that our Christian life, among other things, doesn't have to be as complicated as we often make it. He reminded all of us that if we love the Lord, we should not be "baptized in pickle juice," and I have forevermore adopted that delightful saying. Our faith should not be up for grabs, based on circumstances, and a host of changing conditions, least of all whether things go just our way or not. Half the battle in our spiritual journey is simply making up our mind to follow Jesus. Once you do that you simply follow and serve Jesus the best you can with all your might and strength all the days of your life. As simple as that theology might sound, the Holy Spirit anointed the message and the truth of that message still speaks to me today. I don't remember what the title of his message was that night, but the theme of it could just as easily have been exactly what we are talking about here: the just shall live by faith.

We walk by faith. We walk in obedience to God's word. We trust God because he has promised to lead and guide us. Our faith produces a commitment to Christ. As we walk in faith and trust the Lord we become more battle worthy, more confident, and bolder because we learn through real life experience and crises that God is good and that he can be trusted. Answered prayers become less and less surprising because we begin to understand that God has promised to open doors and do impossible things. We simply have to learn to walk with faith in the Spirit and submit to Christ.

How does our faith grow and get stronger? One way this happens is by hearing "the word" and what better way of exposing yourself to "the word" of God than by reading it. The word produces faith (Romans 10:17). Why is "the word" so important? Well, in the beginning was the Word, and the Word was with God, and the Word was God (John 1:1). Jesus said heaven and earth will pass away but my words shall not pass away (Matthew 24:35).

Every answered prayer makes you stronger because you realize you can actually trust God, the word of God, and all of God's promises. The Lord will not abandon those who put their faith in him, nor will he forsake those who seek him. Prayer increases your closeness to God and helps you increase your sensitivity to God's Spirit and his guidance in your life. Just walking with Jesus and developing life experience and ongoing communication with him strengthens our faith.

As our relationship with Christ deepens and we become more mature, we also develop a greater understanding and appreciation that while the feelings of God's presence and closeness are wonderful beyond words, we are not ruled by feelings alone. The lack of feelings, ironically, may serve through hard times to also promote a deep level of trust in our relationship with the Lord, because the relationship is not based solely on giddy feelings, but on deep substance and faith that has been tried by fire.

In the early days of my father's spiritual birth, growth and development, he had an intense, euphoric sense of God's Holy Spirit being with him. He felt God's presence and anointing in his prayer life and that intensified and increased his faith. Like a baby that drinks milk from his mother, so it was with my father. It almost seemed like he was on a spiritual I.V. of Holy Spirit milk that was making him become bigger, stronger, and healthier by the day. Nevertheless, just as in real life, one can't live your whole life on baby milk. The day will come when you have to grow up a little and start taking in other foods besides milk. This is exactly what happened to my father and I am very grateful that he shared this very personal experience with me, because it has been a tremendous blessing to me over the years.

My father was walking in the fullness of the Spirit and feeling the presence of the Holy Spirit upon him in a powerful way. One day Dad said he felt that holy anointing lifting away and it felt just like Jesus was leaving him. My father cried out in earnest to God and asked, "Why are you leaving me, Lord?" The Lord answered him and said: *I am not leaving you, but I want you to walk in faith now.*

The just shall live by faith, not by feelings or circumstances!

This is a form of graduation. We're off baby milk and starting to take in other solid foods and eventually meat. Our security and sense of well-being is not limited to sensory perception. The just shall live by faith! This always reminds me that it is not how I <u>feel</u> that is determinant of my faith, but rather what I <u>know</u> that is all enduring. What I know is that the word of the Lord endureth forever (I Peter 1:25).

When you got married you may recall you were so "stupid-in-love" with your spouse, that some of your friends teased you about being in another world, lost in love and oblivious to anyone else. It is possible to experience some of that with Christ. New Christians are often this way. They want to tell everyone about their new love. They can't stop talking about Jesus. We should not allow that childlike love and affection to ever die. In fact, Jesus admonished us, that except we become converted, and become as little children, we won't enter into the Kingdom of heaven (Matthew 18:3).

Our childlike faith and love needs to be nurtured so that it doesn't die. Yet, as our level of love and maturity grows, that too should lead to a deeper symbiosis. There is a great comfort in knowing that your spouse understands you even if you are having a difficult day and life is not all smiles. Life also consists of hardships, failures along the way, and some discouraging times, to say nothing about anger and disappointments over injustice we face. How wonderful it is to know that your spouse still understands with complete assurance, that there is love inside your heart for him/her, and that even if you completely failed an hour ago, your love is still rock solid and committed. That knowledge is not based only on how we feel at any given moment during good times, but also on what we know at the deepest level of the heart. The same holds true for our spiritual faith.

Ergo, *the just shall live by faith* is the perfect commitment that defines our attitude and walk with the Lord and it depicts well-grounded followers of Jesus. This phrase reflects a biblical principle. God wants us to live by faith! This is not simply a catchy, but otherwise vacuous phrase that we asked some marketing company to come up with, like a cute jingle for a T.V. commercial during the Super Bowl half-time show. It is part of God's divine word: *the just shall live by faith* (Galations 3:11). This principle should reflect part of our mission statement because it is founded on the Rock of Ages. Storms, tempest, rain, sleet or snow have nothing to do with how we *feel* in our faith commitment. Our faith is based on what we know!

Feelings are simply another wonderful form of serendipity, like whipped cream on top of your favorite peaches. Regardless of whether you have whipped cream or not, think of the peaches as the substantive portion and essence of a heavenly crafted dessert, simply delicious and irresistibly sufficient to please the discriminating palate of any king. Oh, taste and see, that the Lord is good! Any whipped cream you receive, just like euphoric feelings, is just an extra portion of goodness, but it never reflects the whole. Don't measure a great heavenly dish by the presence or absence of a topping. Discipline your thought patterns so that you do not measure God's goodness or direction in your life to be conditional on your feelings. Feelings are often wonderful, but sometimes misleading and frequently they have nothing to do with facts or long-range reality, especially in Kingdom business.

When your light shines, genuine love, joy, kindness and the other fruits of the Spirit are noticed by the world. Cream rises to the top! That spiritual barometer, which measures the fruit of the Spirit in our lives, is often visible to others through our joy. If we want to be really good witnesses for Christ with our lives, and attract others to our Savior like bees to honey, the two things which, for better or for worse, will saliently stand out in our lives and be noticed by others, is the presence or absence of our love for others and our joy.

If you are baptized in pickle juice and unhappy most of the time, no one will want to be around you and your testimony wouldn't mean much. If, on the other hand, you are filled with joy and you simply love people, in spite of their flaws, you will attract others to your lifestyle and your relationship with the Lord. More importantly, you will be fulfilling the Second Great Commandment. That alone will please our heavenly Father and it will produce fruit! The word will not return void!

When you are experiencing adversity, remember the Lord is no less good or wonderful because you are having a hard day. I am learning that pain and suffering are producing growth and development in my own life. Theodore Roosevelt said, "True greatness comes when you're tested." If not for the blessing of adversity in my own life, I would certainly not always remember the goodness of the Lord, his longsuffering patience, mercy, answers to my prayers, and his guiding hand. Far worse than that, if everything went my way I would end up as the Captain of my own ship, inclined to and driven by my own wisdom, and deeply lost in darkness. Oh, give thanks to the Lord, for he is good, for his mercy endureth forever (1 Chronicles 16:34).

The fact that God is gracious, trustworthy, good, full of love, mercy, forgiveness, and his character holy and eternal, and his promises forever enduring, and unshakeable, is the very reason the apostle Paul writes, *Rejoice in the Lord always: and again, I say rejoice* (Philippians 4:4). Why would anyone write something like this? Because Paul knew the goodness of the Lord, and the fullness of his Holy Sprit, and he was persuaded that neither death nor life could separate us from God's love. This was why Paul sang songs and hymns of praise at the midnight hour while in jail. Circumstances don't rule. Jesus rules! The apostle Paul reminds me of a jet fighter pilot with a guidance system locked on Jesus. The circumstances and adversity of life don't define Paul *because* he is locked in. His eyes are on Jesus and his emotions are under control, and his thinking is sound and clear, because he is locked in on Jesus. Whether we live, or whether we die, we belong to Christ. It's a win-win situation.

Adversity has a wonderful way of drawing us toward the Lord, keeping us on course and it reminds us of our own frailty and of our need for a wonderful Savior. We have plenty to praise God about. Stay rooted in the word and locked on course with Jesus.

If we saturate ourselves in the word of the Lord, meditate upon his ways and precepts, walk in faith and obedience, and wait patiently upon the Lord, we will not be overcome by adversity; rather we will be more than conquerors! And, let us not be weary in well doing: for in due season we shall reap, if we faint not (Galatians 6:9).

EPILOGUE

Our faith is a day-by-day journey of overcoming adversity as we surrender our so-called rights and pick up our cross and follow Jesus. *He that overcometh shall inherit all things; and I will be his God, and he shall be my son* (Rev. 21:7).

If we read God's word and hide it in our hearts, we will have a foundation for victory. The principles that I have discussed in this book are not mine. These are biblical principles, precursors to success, found in God's word. Collectively they could all be summarized by the words of King Solomon: *Trust in the Lord will all your heart and lean not unto your own understanding. In all your ways acknowledge him, and he shall direct your paths* (Proverbs 3:5-6).

If any of the principles recited in this book encouraged you or helped you, let me know. Send me an email at mbmalmin@comcast.net
May God richly bless you!